# WORKSHOPS
## You Can Build

David and Jeanie Stiles

Illustrated by David Stiles

FIREFLY BOOKS

# A FIREFLY BOOK

Published by Firefly Books Ltd. 2005

First printing

Publisher Cataloging-in-Publication Data  (U.S.)
Stiles, David.
    Workshops you can build / David & Jeanie Stiles ; illustrated by David Stiles.
[224] p. : col. ill., photos. ;   cm.
Includes bibliographical references and index.
Summary: Plans, ideas and suggestions on how to design and build a workshop.
ISBN 1-55407-028-7
ISBN 1-55407-029-5  (pbk.)
1. Workshops.    2. Workshops—Design and construction.
I. Stiles, Jeanie.    II. Title.
684.08 22    TT152.S75    2005

Library and Archives Canada Cataloguing in Publication
Stiles, David R.
    Workshops you can build / by David & Jeanie Stiles ; illustrator, David Stiles.
Includes bibliographical references and index.
ISBN 1-55407-028-7 (bound).--ISBN 1-55407-029-5 (pbk.)
1. Workshops—Design and construction—Amateurs' manuals.
2. Homeoffices—Design and construction—Amateurs' manuals.
I. Stiles, Jeanie, 1944- II.
Title.
TT152.S735 2005     643'.58     C2005-900400-2

Published in the United States by
Firefly Books (U.S.) Inc.
P.O. Box 1338, Ellicott Station
Buffalo, New York 14205

Published in Canada by
Firefly Books Ltd.
66 Leek Crescent
Richmond Hill, Ontario L4B 1H1

Cover and text design by Tinge Design Studio

Photography by Simon Jutras and David and Jeanie Stiles unless otherwise noted.

Printed in Canada

To Ann and John

# ACKNOWLEDGMENTS

Many thanks to our friends, both old and new, who opened up their workshops and studios, and allowed us to photograph and interview them. A special thanks to Redjeb Jordania for his valuable suggestions in regard to the boathouse workshop and to Simon Jutras for his artistic eye and excellent photography skills. We would also like to thank Lionel Koffler and Michael Worek of Firefly Books for their continued support and enthusiasm for our projects.

# CONTENTS

# INTRODUCTION

As we sit writing this book, at a desk in a cozy corner, sheltered from 35 miles per hour winds and 6 inches of snow outside our window, we are once again reminded of the many advantages of having a workspace in our home. For us, carpentry, designing, illustrating and writing are all done in and around our home. David's workshop is only a few steps from the house and our design studio is in a converted guest room. Working at home, something that used to be a novelty, is now commonplace. The advantages and practical aspects of working at home are obvious – no commuting, keeping your own hours, anything you want in the kitchen, fresh roasted coffee beans and the personal freedom to be your own boss.

This book is written for anyone who wants a space in or next to his or her house, for business or for a hobby. It contains workshop designs and ideas for carpenters, mechanics, ceramists, artists, gardeners, designers, writers and professional business people.

Once the decision to work from home has been made, the question of where to put the new workspace arises. Simple solutions include converting a spare guest room into an office, finding usable attic space, dividing a large room into two smaller ones, using a corner of a large room or foyer, or remodeling a basement or garage. Other more extensive and costly solutions might be to build an addition onto your house or even build a workspace that is separate from the main house. In this book we will discuss the pros and cons of all these possibilities and help you to find a solution that is perfect for your specific situation.

Readers will find more useful building information in our other books and on our website which are listed in the "Further Reading" section at the end of the book.

# CHAPTER ONE

# WHY AND WHERE TO BUILD

With the ever-increasing trend towards home offices, many people are working out of their houses rather than commuting to work. Some city apartments have a small room that formerly served as a maid's room and today is often used for a new baby's bedroom. Once the baby has outgrown it, the room can be converted into a small workspace. David's first design studio was in one of these 8' x 10' spaces. It is a perfect size for a drafting or computer table, shelves and storage cabinets, with room for drawing tubes, stored in upright containers in a built-in corner unit. The advantage of being able to close the door – keeping out the noise of busy household activities and voices of small children – is obvious.

## Corner Workspace

If you are not lucky enough to have a separate room for a workspace, it can be quite a challenge to convert existing space. As the ubiquitous computer takes over so many areas of our life, more and more of our living space becomes covered with unattractive office machines. What starts out as a tiny office niche can quickly grow into an unruly workspace.

One way of dealing with this is to convert an existing space into a mini workspace. For instance, what used to be a foyer can, with a little imagination, be turned into an office space to house a computer, printer, answering machine, scanner and fax machine. By using rollout drawers, strategically placed shelves and corner units made out of a beautifully finished wood, an attractive central hub can be created even in a small apartment.

In our situation, we found that we were constantly running from one end of the apartment to the other, wasting much valuable time that otherwise could be used to write and do design work. With one of us writing from a computer in the bedroom while the other was designing from a closed off room at the opposite end of the apartment, the obvious solution was to create a communication hub halfway between, in the foyer. This space was already being used to answer the phone and open the mail but was cluttered and disorganized and didn't have a proper desk. Much work was relegated to the floor and stacked in unrecognizable and messy piles. This area had nothing more than a large comfortable club chair and a low counter with storage underneath. Our goal was to convert this space into a home office, while not appearing too much like an office space, since it was within view of the living room. Our solution was to build an L-shaped desk in the corner of the foyer (see Fig. 1.1). Detailed building instructions for this desk are on pages 135–137.

Fig. 1.1

# Basements

Converting a basement or attic into a workspace can often be a simpler solution than building an addition or separate structure. Advantages include the fact that unless you are making structural changes, you may not need a building permit. Also, since your electrical, heating and plumbing are nearby, it will be easier to tap into them.

Creating a workspace in your attic or basement may be as simple as building some shelves and a table, or it may involve building partition walls, installing new flooring, adding electric circuits and heating ducts or even adding new windows and doors.

Before committing your plans to paper, take into consideration how much of the work you are capable of doing yourself and how much will have to be hired out to professionals. Keep your budget in mind and try to get a rough idea of how much your building materials will cost. Talk to friends who have done similar projects and learn from their successes (and mistakes). Research magazines and cut out articles that relate to your project and then put your ideas on paper.

Begin by taking careful measurements of walls and floors. Don't forget to measure heights of ceilings, door clearances and locations of electric circuits. Also consider how you will be using the workspace and if there is enough room to get equipment and material into the house. Making detailed plans will not only help you, but will also help any professionals that you hire to understand exactly what you want. Draw your plans as described on pages 23–27, using a scale of ¼" equals 1' for the plan (overhead) view and ½" equals 1' for the elevations (side views).

In most houses built after 1960 there is considerable room in the basement which can easily be converted into useable space. Many homeowners already have a cluttered and unattractive workbench in a corner somewhere that is rarely used. The first place to look for workshop space is the basement. It is easy to get too, already has heat, light and water and requires no structural change to the house itself.

Lack of sufficient natural light can limit the usefulness of a basement for the home office worker and for authors and artists. For them, it is preferable to construct a workshop in an upstairs room or in a separate building. If, however, the basement is your only choice, it is important to spend the time and money necessary to add plenty of light and paint the walls and ceilings a light color to add the illusion of space. One artist we met used a basement that was built on sloping ground to her advantage, installing glass doors on the ground level side, allowing plenty of ambient light to enter. She covered the remaining walls with wallboard, a perfect surface for tacking up art work in progress. She also painted the basement floor white, using Drylock, an oil base masonry waterproofing paint, which helps keep out moisture. For potters, the moist, humid air of a basement can actually work to their advantage, helping to keep the clay moist.

Here are some things to consider before you begin building a workshop in your basement:

○ Plan your basement workspace so that it is far away from the furnace and shielded by a soundproof partition. Remember that the air intakes on the furnace must be kept clean and free of dust and dirt and that a forced air furnace usually circulates air from the basement, so don't box the furnace into too tiny a space. To build a partition in a basement you need to use masonry screws to attach the base plate of the partition to the floor (see Fig. 1.2), and common 3½" nails to attach the top plate to the overhead floor joists (see pages 59–63 on building partitions).

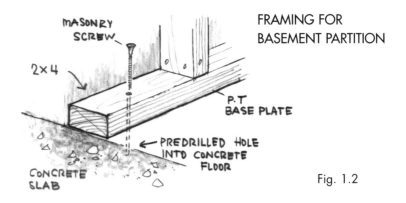

FRAMING FOR BASEMENT PARTITION

Fig. 1.2

○ Gas and oil lines must also be protected from damage and there is an open flame on both types of furnaces and on the hot water tank (if it is gas or oil) which is often located fairly close to the furnace. As a general rule, keep the storage of paint and flammable material well away from the furnace.

○ If the workshop is located near the laundry room you will have easy access to a sink for washing hands and brushes but remember to allow some space in the workshop for drying brushes and other things so that the laundry room stays clean and free of workshop clutter.

○ Concrete basement floors are cold and hard to stand on for long periods. You may want to put down carpeting to keep your feet warm. If the floor is not perfectly level, you can fill low spots with "liquid floor leveler" manufactured for this purpose. Or you can build up a new floor, placing shims under the 2x4 "sleepers" (see Fig. 1.3) where low spots exist.

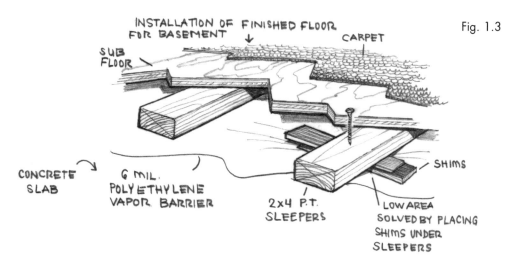

INSTALLATION OF FINISHED FLOOR FOR BASEMENT

Fig. 1.3

SUB FLOOR

CARPET

CONCRETE SLAB

6 mil. POLYETHYLENE VAPOR BARRIER

2x4 P.T. SLEEPERS

SHIMS

LOW AREA SOLVED BY PLACING SHIMS UNDER SLEEPERS

○ Basement ceilings can be covered with ½" drywall wallboard. You can either leave the pipes exposed or box them in to hide them from view. For maintenance reasons, inspection panels have to be built in, so that plumbing valves can be accessible (see Fig. 1.4).

○ Basement walls can be paneled using wallboard (sheetrock) or plywood paneling, both installed over 2x3 furring strips and 1½" thick rigid insulation, which is placed between the furring and over 6 mil polyethylene plastic sheeting.

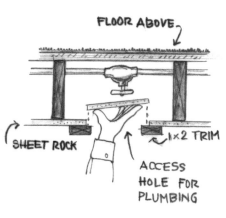

FLOOR ABOVE

SHEET ROCK

1x2 TRIM

ACCESS HOLE FOR PLUMBING

Fig. 1.4

○ Using a basement for carpentry or as a potter's studio can also create an unmanageable amount of dust that can be tracked upstairs. One solution is to install a high-powered dust collection system (see Sources), vacuuming up the dust at the end of each workday so that it is not carried upstairs to the rest of the house.

○ If you are going to construct new walls to control sound and dust, be sure to give some thought to air and heat circulation. Efficient operation of the furnace and proper heating of the basement can be dramatically changed by the installation of solid walls in what was formerly open space. Also consider traffic flow in the basement. Avoid anyone having to walk through the workshop to gain access to the family room or the laundry room.

○ Windows make the difference between a basement that is dark and uninviting and one that is a welcome extension of the living area of the house. A window of reasonable size that opens makes it possible to get lumber and materials down to your workshop without carrying them through the house and risking damage to the walls. Windows with a small fan also make it possible to exhaust paint fumes, dust and other odors quickly and easily. If at all possible, include a window in your plans for a basement workshop. Windows can be added to the basement, or made larger, if the house was built on a block foundation. Single blocks can be removed and the window opening enlarged with minimum problems. You may need to construct a window well to provide space for a window that is deeper than the original but this is not difficult if well planned in advance.

o Finding a way to get your projects out of the basement can be a major problem for the home workshop owner. Unless your projects are birdhouse size, getting them up and down stairs or out a small window severely limits what you can make. Some very old houses may have a separate entrance to the basement from the yard that will allow you to easily transport materials in and out. What usually happens, of course, is that older houses have low ceilings in the basement and limited space so the area if often not ideal for a workshop even if the outdoor access is available

Despite all these things, a workshop in the basement is probably the easiest and least expensive to build. If you decide to go this route, there are many plans for shelving, workbenches and storage in Chapter 6 that you can use to create the best possible basement workshop for your needs.

When making plans to alter any part of your house, be aware of the building code requirements in order to avoid running into trouble later on if you sell your house. You can find this information at your local library or building department. Some of the more typical requirements are:

o Headroom must be a minimum of 7½' to allow people to stand comfortably. The higher the better (see Fig. 1.5).

o Habitable rooms must have at least 70 square feet of floor space and measure a minimum of 7' in any direction.

Fig. 1.5

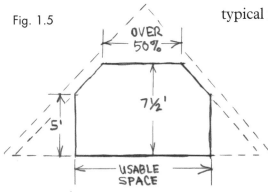

○ Floor joists must be of a size to accept the load put on them.

○ Stairways must have 6' 8" headroom measured from the top of the stair tread to the ceiling (see Fig. 1.6).

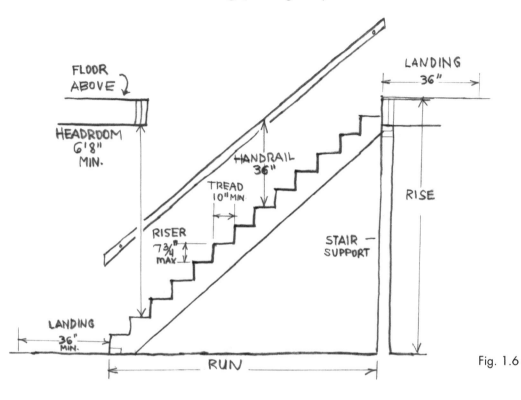

Fig. 1.6

○ Basements may require two exits in case of fire. One exit can be the interior stairs and the other can be a window with a minimum of 9 square feet of open space or a bulkhead-type exterior door.

○ Both attics and basements must have adequate ventilation, so you may need to add windows to the attic or basement (see Fig. 1.7).

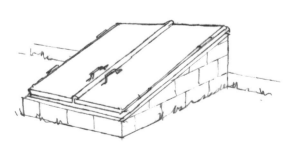

BULKHEAD

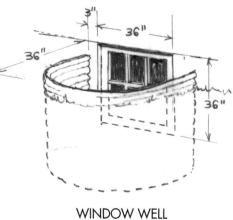

WINDOW WELL

Fig. 1.7

Basement moisture is always a problem but it can be remedied in several ways:

○ In extreme cases of water infiltration a trench can be dug around the outside perimeter of the house and coated with a waterproofing material. This requires heavy equipment and should be done by a professional.

○ The ground around the house should slope away from the house to shed rainwater.

○ Rainwater from the downspout of the roof should be diverted 6' away from the foundation.

○ Window wells should be covered with rigid plastic to allow light in and keep out water.

○ Patch any cracks in the foundation with a waterproof masonry sealant.

○ In very wet areas you may need to install a sump pump that discharges the water outside the house.

○ Paint the interior walls with a masonry waterproof paint.

○ Wrap plumbing pipes with insulation to help prevent dripping water caused by condensation.

○ Install a dehumidifier.

Hopefully you will only need to follow the last two steps in order to solve your moisture problems.

# Attics

Attics were intended to store household items, to shield the house from the heat of the summer sun and to shed the snow in winter. Many attics, such as those found in ranch houses, are too low to be of much use, but those with high-pitched roofs may be perfect for a workspace.

Attics allow you privacy, but require an extra climb to get there. Our studio/office, for example, is on the third (hayloft) floor of a converted barn and requires climbing up two sets of steep stairs to get there. If your type of work entails being in one place for hours at a time, then an attic may be a good solution for you. On the other hand, if your work requires you to move around the house, or to go inside and outside, then this may not be the best solution.

Almost all houses have slanted roofs that limit the floor area in the attic that can be used. Raising a section of the roof to make a shed dormer can alleviate this problem (see Fig. 1.8). Short knee walls can be built to enclose areas where the roof rafters meet the attic floor. Chimneys can be boxed in and integrated into a storage area. Windows and skylights can open up an otherwise dark and gloomy area, creating a bright, fresh room. New spaces are often discovered that you might never have thought existed. Many artists have found that attics can be converted into a studio for very little cost.

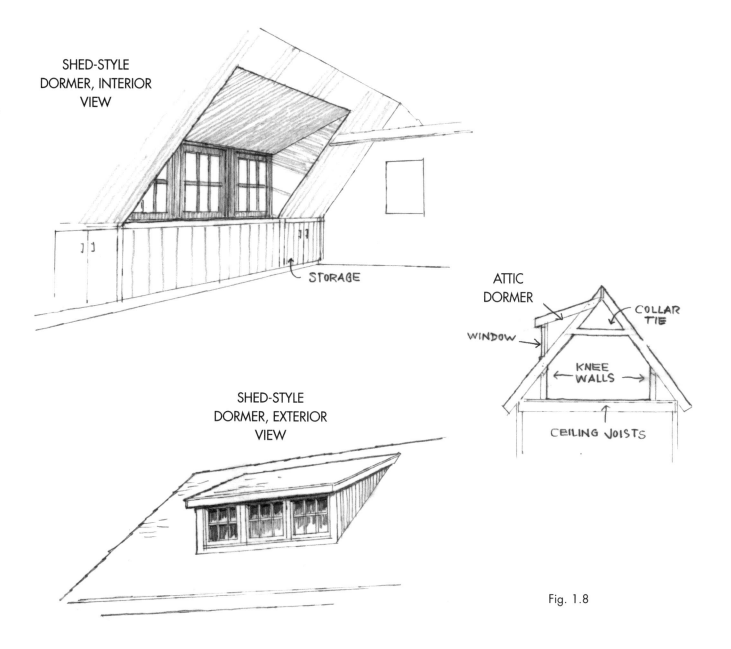

SHED-STYLE DORMER, INTERIOR VIEW

STORAGE

SHED-STYLE DORMER, EXTERIOR VIEW

ATTIC DORMER

COLLAR TIE

WINDOW

KNEE WALLS

CEILING JOISTS

Fig. 1.8

You may find that the horizontal collar ties that span the ceiling are too low. If you plan to build knee walls, as suggested, you may be able to raise the collar ties one at a time, after checking with an architect or structural engineer. At the same time, ensure the ceiling joists below the attic floor are strong enough to support the new attic workspace.

If the attic is not insulated, the rafters might have to be made deeper to accept the extra thickness of insulation. The insulating most often used is 10" (R-30) fiberglass batts (see Fig. 1.9).

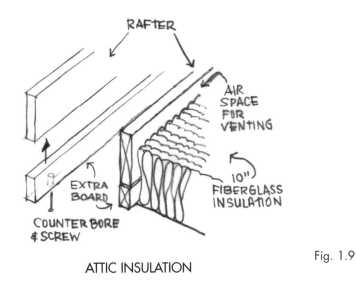

ATTIC INSULATION

Fig. 1.9

Attic walls and ceilings can be insulated and covered with drywall. The angled space directly under the eaves can be used to your advantage by building storage cupboards. Find the pitch or

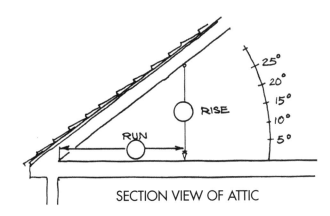

SECTION VIEW OF ATTIC

Fig. 1.10

slope of your roof by measuring out into the room from where the roof meets the floor and then vertically to the roof. This is referred to as the "run and the rise" (see Fig. 1.10). Jot down these two measurements and draw them to scale on graph paper. Lay a protractor over your drawing to find the degree of pitch, and use this number to calculate and draw the plans for your storage cupboards.

Attics can become extremely hot in the summer so it is important to provide cross-ventilation with two opposite windows or a window and an operable skylight. Ceiling or attic fans that suck out the hot air are also helpful.

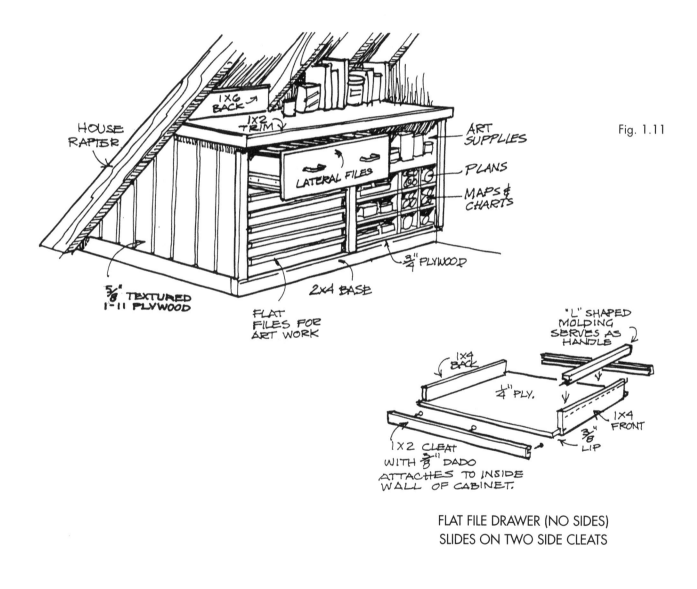

Fig. 1.11

FLAT FILE DRAWER (NO SIDES)
SLIDES ON TWO SIDE CLEATS

# Garages

After the basement, the garage is the most popular location for a home workshop. If you are lucky enough to have a freestanding garage located near the rear of your property you have a chance to make a wonderful workshop without going to the trouble to lay foundations, build walls and a roof. Even if the garage is attached to the house, as in most suburban houses built since the 1970s, there is still often room to build a nice workshop with the added benefit of often having direct access to the house without going outdoors.

Before you commit to building a workshop in your garage think carefully about where you are going to park the car and what you are going to do with all the stuff that is in the garage now. If you are like most people, your garage is full of garden equipment, toys, bikes, tools and odds and ends, and the car rarely sees the inside of the garage. The first task is usually to ruthlessly sort everything that is in the garage and dispose of anything that is not really necessary.

Once you've got the garage cleaned out, decide how much space you can devote to the workshop and how much has to be kept for storage. It will almost surely be necessary to divide the space into distinct areas – one for storage and one for your workshop. Otherwise garden tools will suddenly appear on your workbench and bicycles will be parked on top of your lumber. Consider, too, the questions of dust, dirt, privacy and security. Unless you build a wall of some sort to contain your workshop, each time the door is open dust from outside will cover every surface – annoying in a woodworking shop but obviously impossible if you are using the space for writing or as an art studio.

Most people we know make a dividing wall across the garage at the point at which the overhead door runners stop. This allows a substantial area in the garage for storage of bikes and garden and sports equipment that is accessible through the large overhead door. If you are fortunate enough to have a side door into the garage that enters the back portion of the building you have a ready entrance into the new workshop space. If there is no other door, you'll have to build one into the dividing wall and enter the garage through the overhead door. Either way, you now have two separate spaces, one for storage and one for a workshop.

Your garage almost certainly has electricity but you will want to install new outlets and lights to meet the needs of your workshop. You may also want to add insulation to the walls and even to add drywall or paneling to cover exposed studs or block construction. Regular 2x4 stud walls can be constructed. Even if these are not load bearing they will provide space for insulation and for fastening drywall. A drop ceiling will keep things cleaner, look good and make the space easier to heat; just remember to retain as much height as possible to allow for a more pleasant work area.

You will also need to decide what to do about the concrete floor. This may be stained by oil and dirt that has dropped from parked cars over the years and may also be chipped and cracked. You face the same problems here that you face when dealing with a basement floor and the same solutions apply. These range from a thorough cleaning and several coats of specially formulated concrete paint to building an insulated subfloor. Whatever you choose, be sure that the finished floor will be adequate for the tools and equipment you plan to use and will provide a clean and easy surface on which to stand and work.

# PLANNING AND DESIGN

If you don't have enough room in your house or garage to allow for a workspace and you do have room on your property, building an addition or a separate structure to create a shop for work or a hobby may be the perfect solution. The following workshop plans can be used for anything from a writer's retreat or artist's studio to a gardening shed or even an office space. Take what you need from them and modify them to fit your specific requirements. For instance, using the same basic foundation footprint, you can change the style of the workshop by simply altering the roof, giving the structure a completely different look (see Fig. 2.1).

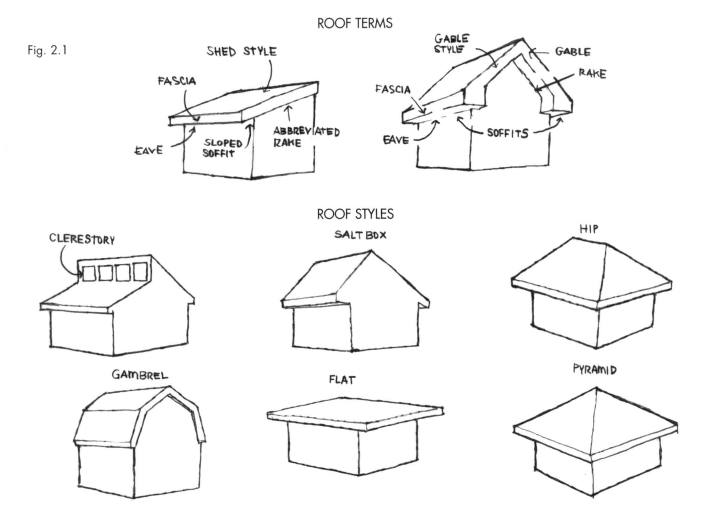

ROOF TERMS

Fig. 2.1

ROOF STYLES

There are several factors to consider when deciding where to place your workshop or studio. The first might be how far you are willing to walk from your house to get to your workshop.

Also consider the structure's orientation to the sun. Would you like sunlight to be streaming in your workshop in the morning or in the evening? Do you prefer indirect lighting? Trees are a good way of shading a structure from direct sun and can also help to block a northern wind. Keep in mind that the prevailing winds change somewhat in the summer and winter. If your workshop is in a northern region of North America you might want to position it so the wind strikes the most protected side where there are no doors or windows. On the other hand, if you live in the south, you might position your workshop to catch cool breezes. Also, ensure your front door will be positioned where the wind won't blow it open, but rather so the prevailing winds tend to close it.

If you have a large, woodsy lot, you may want your workshop tucked far away in the trees, but consider how you will be transporting building materials to your site before finalizing that decision. Are there any gates or rights of way that you will have to get through? Can a delivery truck reach your site without driving over any flowerbeds or hidden irrigation lines below grade? Are there any power lines or low-hanging tree branches that might get in the way of a large delivery truck? Consider all of these questions before deciding.

Building an addition involves matching finished floor heights and flashing the new structure into the existing siding on the house.

On the other hand, adding onto your house allows you to tap into your existing heating, plumbing, electric and telephone systems.

Before starting an addition, ask yourself

- Are there any underground electric, sewer and gas or sprinkler lines in the ground?
- Is the addition within the limits of the setback laws?
- Will you have to make great changes to landscaping, including trees or garden walls?
- Where will you enter the workshop from inside your house?

## Neighbors and Communities

Will your neighbors object if you build your workshop next to their side windows? Will they complain about the noise if you work with power tools? Will they object to the noise you make while building it? Will they complain about the style or color of your workshop?

It is usually a good idea to show a sketch of your workshop to your neighbors before beginning and get their blessing. You may even ask for their suggestions to get them enthusiastic about the idea. (You don't have to follow their suggestions, just listen to them.) Neighbors are generally the ones who complain to the building departments and get stop-work orders placed on building projects, so it is a good idea to get their approval before you begin construction.

Also, if you are part of a homeowners' association, check to see if they have restrictions that would affect your plans to build a workshop. If your community has an architectural review board or a historical preservation society they may require that you submit plans for their approval.

# Permits

In most areas of the United States and Canada you are required to apply for a building permit before you start construction. When you visit your local building department and fill out an application for a building permit, bring along a copy of your survey and show where you intend to build your workshop.

The building department will need to know if you plan to run electricity and plumbing lines to your workshop. If you intend to have running water and a working toilet, they will require you to submit an application for board of health approval from the county or region where you live. This can take several weeks (sometimes months) to receive and involves more paperwork and inspections. Many building departments are suspicious of people pretending to be building a "workshop" when they actually plan to rent out the building to tenants for extra income. Our local building department allows cold-water plumbing to be connected into the sewage disposal system, but no toilets.

Your workshop will likely be referred to by the building department as an "accessory building." You need to draw a "footprint" of the proposed building on your survey, showing the dimensions, total square footage and setbacks from your property lines, making sure you are not violating any local zoning laws or height restrictions.

You may be required to prove that you are not building near any environmentally restricted areas, such as protected wetlands. If such is the case, you might have to apply for a "variance," which could take months to complete and might even require hiring a lawyer to plead your case before a town zoning board.

Most building departments will allow you to build your own workshop without getting insurance or worker's compensation insurance because it is not likely that you will sue yourself. However, anyone you hire, including electricians or plumbers, should be licensed and have their own liability insurance. If you run electricity to your workshop, you may be required to have an electrical inspector make an inspection and sign off on the work.

Your building permit, which will expire in one year, should be posted somewhere so that it is visible from the road. When you are finished with construction, most areas will require that an "as built" survey be made, which is submitted to the building department for approval. If you fail to get this survey and decide to sell your house, not having this piece of paper can hold up a sale for months.

Depending upon your location, some building departments do not require building permits for accessory buildings if they are less than 150 square feet and are not permanently affixed to a foundation, allowing them to be moved at a future date. Zoning regulations in some areas allow an accessory building to be placed closer to the property line than a primary structure, and may waive the requirement for a permit if you can prove that it will not be used for "habitual living" or for "quartering live animals." Some building departments allow the do-it-yourself homeowner to build his or her own accessory building on their property as long as they are willing to remove it if they sell the property. We advise you to check with your local building department to find out what restrictions, if any, exist in your community and to comply with them.

# Designing Your Workshop

Planning to build a workshop may be hampered by more than just location and building codes. Don't forget to consider more personal factors. First, ask yourself how much time it will take. We recently built a 12' x 16' workshop so we could more easily work at home, but it took us six months because we could only work on it a few days a week, and only during favorable weather conditions.

Also get an idea of your budget. We built our workshop for less than $6,000, saving between $20,000 and $30,000 (the cost if we had used a local contractor). We did all the work ourselves, subcontracting only the electric.

Finally, ask yourself if you're up to the challenge physically and if you have the necessary skills. There may be parts of the job you are confident and fit enough to do yourself, like framing and wiring, but you might prefer hiring a professional for digging a foundation or installing roofing.

Here is where the fun starts. Begin by walking your property and imagining where your workshop would look best, trying to visualize it in your mind's eye. If you have a fairly good idea where it will go, stake it out with some sticks hammered in the ground. Tie a yellow mason's string around these posts to give you an idea of the footprint of your building. Don't worry if it is not exactly accurate – you should keep moving the posts until they are just right. However, do try to keep the dimensions in 2' or 4' increments to minimize your lumber cuts (as lumber comes in 2' increments).

Another way to help you visualize how your workshop will look is to take photos of the site from different angles. It is helpful if you have someone stand where the proposed doorway will be to give the photo scale. Once you have a print, place a piece of tracing paper or clear acetate over it and draw the workshop as an overlay (see Fig. 2.2).

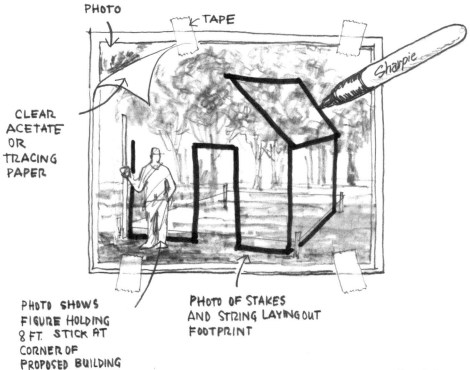

Fig. 2.2

Now is the time to commit dreams to paper. Using a pad of ¼"-grid graph paper and an architect's scale ruler, draw your plans to the scale of ¼" equals 1'. (Each square on the paper will equal one square foot.) The first view to draw is an overhead plan showing your footprint. Use this view to determine if your workshop will be the right size to hold all the things you want to include. Measure each piece of equipment and plot it on the plan using an architect's scale for accuracy. You can also use this view to show where the foundation supports will go, as well as the girders, joists and plywood subfloor.

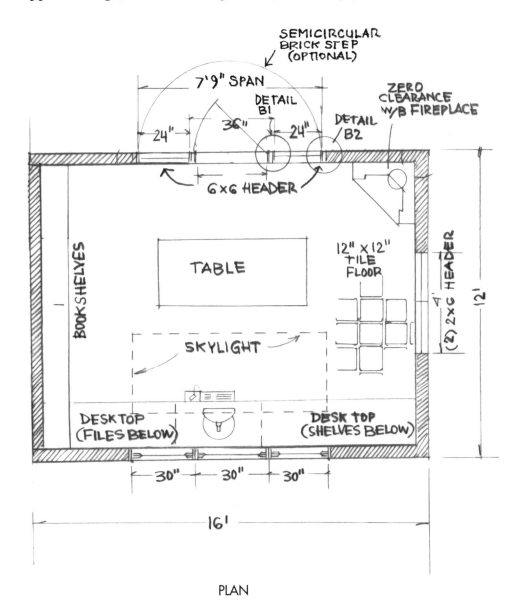

PLAN

Fig. 2.3

Fig. 2.4

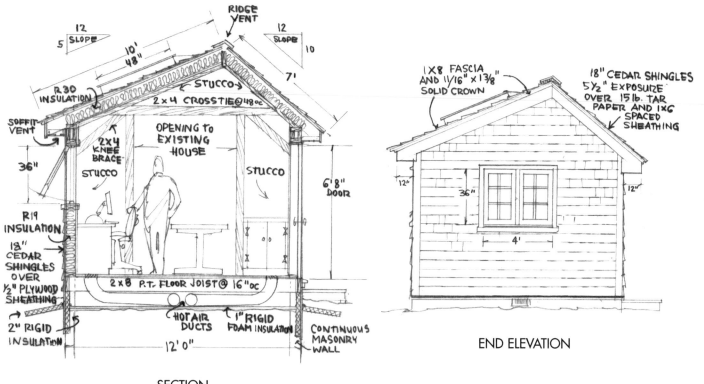

SECTION

END ELEVATION

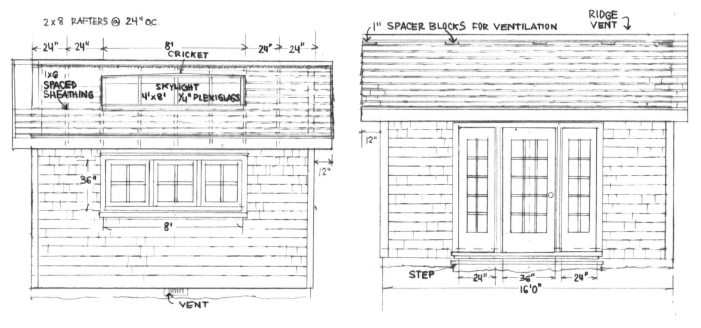

REAR ELEVATION

FRONT ELEVATION

The second most important view is the "section view" – this will help you determine the basic construction of the building. It is also useful to plot the door height, ensuring that the bottom of the roof does not interfere with the swing of the door. In addition, draw elevations of each side of the structure to scale. The following plans could be used for a workshop addition to an existing house or built as a separate structure (see Figs. 2.3 and 2.4).

When thinking about the roof design, take into account not only the style of your existing house and other architecture in your community, but also what is appropriate in your part of the country. For example, in the north where buildings must resist the weight of heavy snows, a steeply pitched roof is common, whereas in the south, especially the southwest, slightly sloping or flat roofs are more common.

Once you have finished drawing the plans, another useful technique for visualizing your finished project is to copy the side views of the plans onto stiff card stock, cut them out and glue them together. Cut and fold a piece of card stock to make the roof, completing the small scale model.

One clever homeowner we met first built his design out of cheap 1x2s and connected them together using knee braces and duct tape. In just a few hours, he had a full-size model of the structure to evaluate.

If you are building an addition to your home it is important to find the top of the finished floor inside the house and mark it on the outside of the house to determine the height of your foundation. You can find the top of the finished floor by peeling away a section of siding, and making a test hole through the side of the house using a ¼"-diameter, 8"-long drill bit (see Fig. 2.5).

Make a second test hole several yards to the right or left of the first test hole, and connect the two points by snapping a chalk line on the sheathing. To determine the correct height of your ledger and your floor frame, subtract the thickness of the materials that you will be using for the floor (that is, the finished floorboards and the subfloor) from the chalk line and snap another chalk line. Ensure you include this information on your plans.

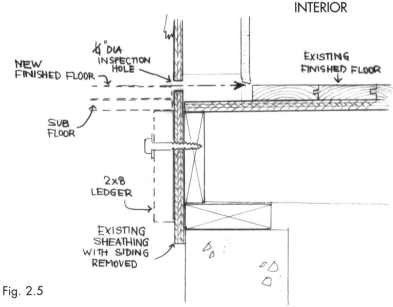

Fig. 2.5

# CHAPTER THREE

# BUILDING YOUR WORKSHOP

## Foundation

There are many ways to build a foundation (see Fig. 3.1). The easiest way to is to make the floor frame resting on concrete block piers. Start by putting together the sill beams (also referred to as rim joists), that are usually made from 2x6s or 2x8s. When measuring and cutting the beams to fit your specifications, remember that two of the beams must be 3" shorter to allow for the doubled thickness of the 1½" lumber where it butts against the other two beams. Most builders try to hide the end grain, placing it on the least visible side of the building. Nail the frame together, using three 3½" nails at each joint. Long nails are used because nails can more easily come out when nailed into the end grain (see Fig. 3.2).

Place a level on top of the frame and adjust the blocks until the frame is level on all sides. You may have to dig out the ground under the concrete blocks at certain corners to get the frame level. You can fine-tune the leveling process by inserting thin pieces of slate, which are sold expressly for this purpose at some home improvement stores. If your workshop becomes out of level in the future because of frost heave, simply jack up the low corner and insert more shims. House jacks are fairly inexpensive and can lift several tons.

If you are sure that you will never move your workshop and you want a more permanent foundation, there are several choices. One is to build a concrete slab with a thickened edge. Another method is to build a typical concrete block foundation on a cast concrete footing.

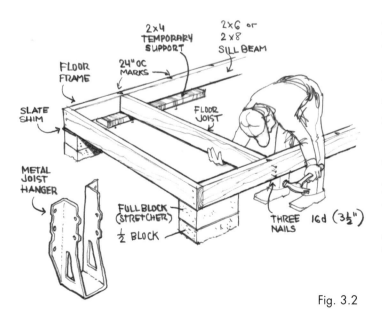

2x4 TEMPORARY SUPPORT

2x6 or 2x8 SILL BEAM

FLOOR FRAME

24" OC MARKS

FLOOR JOIST

SLATE SHIM

METAL JOIST HANGER

FULL BLOCK (STRETCHER)

½ BLOCK

THREE 16d (3½") NAILS

Fig. 3.2

Fig. 3.1

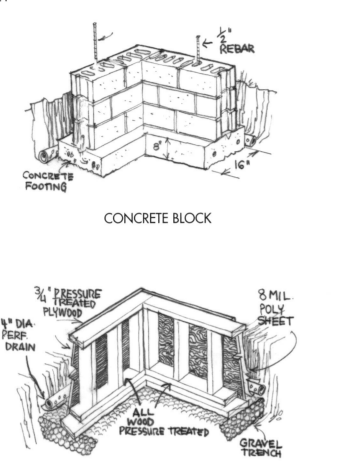

CONCRETE BLOCK

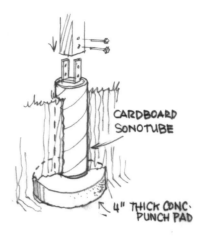

CONCRETE PIER

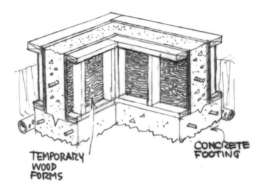

ALL-WOOD FOUNDATION

POURED CONCRETE FOUNDATION

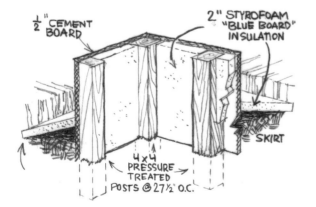

POST-AND-SKIRT FOUNDATION
(LIMITED TO ONE STORY)

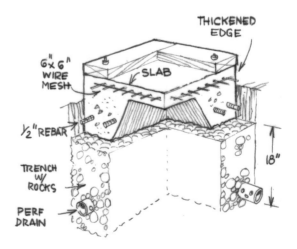

SLAB ON GRADE

# All-Wood Foundation

A foundation can also be built using just wood as long as the wood is pressure-treated. This type of foundation is also known as an "all-weather foundation," "AWWF" or "permanent wood foundation." The advantages are:

- Less expensive than masonry foundations
- Can be built in any kind of weather
- No masonry crew or heavy trucks to ruin your property
- Easier to insulate

To build an all-wood foundation, dig a deep trench that reaches below the frost line. To make this easier you can rent a backhoe or a "ditch witch" to dig the trench. A 4" perforated pipe is laid in the bottom of the trench and covered with gravel, then compacted and made level. Build 8'-long sections of stud-framed walls on the site, using pressure-treated 2x6s and pressure-treated ¾" plywood. The sections are then lowered into the gravel-covered trenches. To create a moisture barrier, glue 8-mil polyethylene plastic sheeting to the outside of the plywood wall and ensure it overlaps the footing. From this point on the procedure is the same as for any other foundation (see Fig. 3.3).

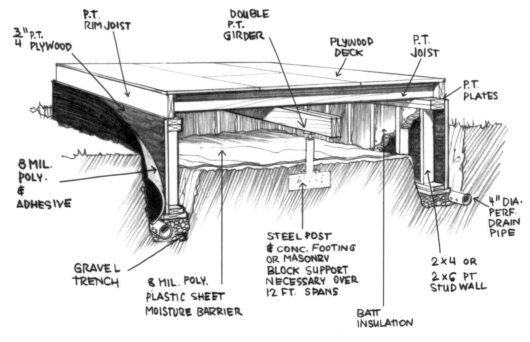

Fig. 3.3

# Post-and-Skirt Foundation

A foundation that is perfect for the do-it-yourself person working alone with limited funds and basic tools is the "post-and-skirt foundation," a combination of the "frost-protected shallow foundation" (referred to in the construction industry as FPS) and the all-wood foundation. It is made entirely of pressure-treated lumber in combination with extruded polystyrene insulation (Styrofoam "Blueboard") (see Figs. 3.4 to 3.8).

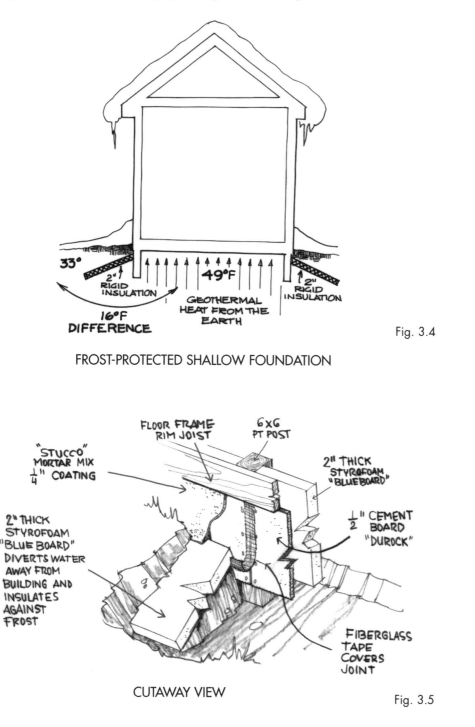

Fig. 3.4

FROST-PROTECTED SHALLOW FOUNDATION

CUTAWAY VIEW

Fig. 3.5

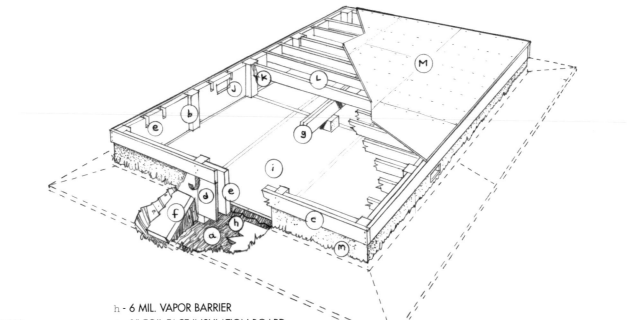

## LEGEND

a - TRENCH
b - 6X6 P.T. POSTS
c - RIM JOISTS (FLOOR FRAME)
d - ½" CEMENT BOARD
e - 2" RIGID INSULATION BOARD
f - SKIRT (2" BLUEBOARD)
g - DOUBLE GIRDER

h - 6 MIL. VAPOR BARRIER
i - 1" FOIL-FACE INSULATION BOARD
j - VENT
k - JOIST HANGER
l - FLOOR JOIST
m - ¾" PLYWOOD FLOOR

Fig. 3.6

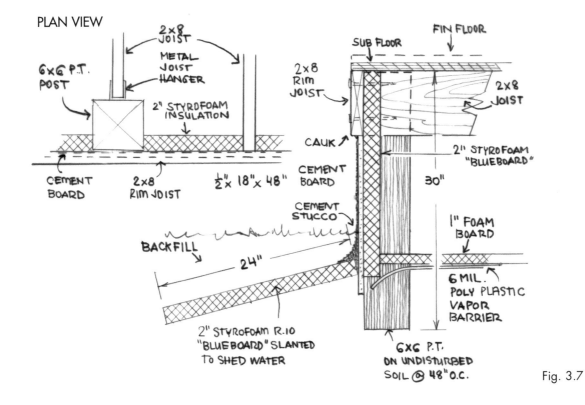

PLAN VIEW

Fig. 3.7

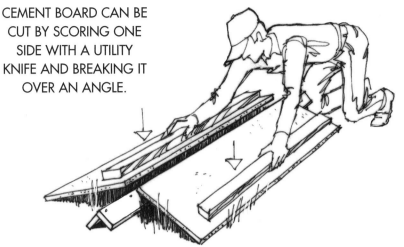

CEMENT BOARD CAN BE CUT BY SCORING ONE SIDE WITH A UTILITY KNIFE AND BREAKING IT OVER AN ANGLE.

Fig. 3.8

## Post-and-Skirt Advantages

1. Requires only hand tools to build.
2. Less excavation of soil.
3. Can be built by one person.
4. No heavy machinery or trucks to ruin the lawn.
5. Can be built in hard-to-get-into locations.
6. Provides insulation to help keep the building warm.
7. Uses nature's own "free" geothermal heat to warm the foundation.
8. Costs much less than a conventional masonry foundation.
9. Underground "skirt," rigid insulation, diverts water away from foundation.

We built this foundation for an 11'x14' addition to our house and it took only a few days of pick-and-shovel work plus two short days to complete the floor frame. The best thing about it is that it only cost us around $500 in materials as compared to the thousands we might have paid for an excavator and masonry crew to build a conventional foundation.

Once the frame is level, you must make it square. There are several ways to do this. One is using the Pythagorean theorem ($A^2 + B^2 = C^2$) that you learned in high school. Another method is to measure the diagonals, which should be equal if the frame is square. An even simpler method is to place a 4x8 sheet of plywood on top of the frame, hammering in a few temporary nails to hold it in place (see Fig. 3.9).

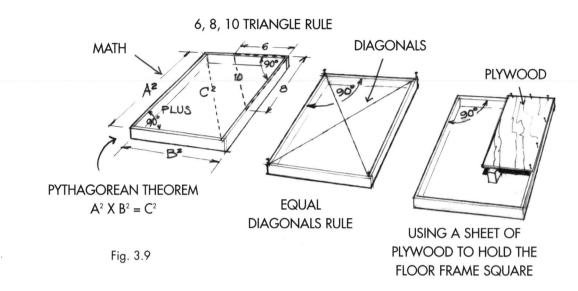

3 WAYS TO DETERMINE WHETHER THE FLOOR FRAME IS SQUARE:
USE ONE OF THE THREE METHODS SHOWN BELOW.

6, 8, 10 TRIANGLE RULE

MATH

DIAGONALS

PLYWOOD

$A^2$ $C^2$ PLUS $B^2$

PYTHAGOREAN THEOREM
$A^2 \times B^2 = C^2$

Fig. 3.9

EQUAL
DIAGONALS RULE

USING A SHEET OF
PLYWOOD TO HOLD THE
FLOOR FRAME SQUARE

Whichever way you do it, never assume that the frame will remain square during the rest of construction. Nailing the joists onto the frame quite often knocks the frame out of square, so continue to check for square as work progresses.

Measure the inside distance between the side sill beams, and cut all the floor joists exactly the same size. Make marks every 2' on the top edge of the sill beams to show where the joists will go. If you are working with another person, have him or her hold one end of the joist while you nail the joist through the side of the sill beam onto the floor frame. If you are working alone, tack a 2x4 under the bottom edge of the sill beam to hold the free end of the joist while you nail the other end to the other sill beam. You can also use metal joist hangers to hold your joists. They take a little longer to install, but they make a stronger connection and the joists can be installed by one person working alone.

## Skirt

If you are using concrete blocks to support your workshop you will be left with a large space under the floor frame. You can leave this showing, but if you work in a cold climate it will allow cold drafts to come under your floor, not to mention all the wild animals that will thank you for building them a shelter for the winter. To avoid this, buy some ½"-thick cement boards, and cut and screw them to the sill beams. The bottoms of the cement board panels should be buried at least 6" underground, which may require cutting the boards and digging a trench around the perimeter of the workshop. Special screws for attaching the cement boards to the frame are available at your lumberyard. Use fiberglass tape to cover the joints where the boards butt together and mortar cement to cover the tape and the corners (see Fig. 3.10).

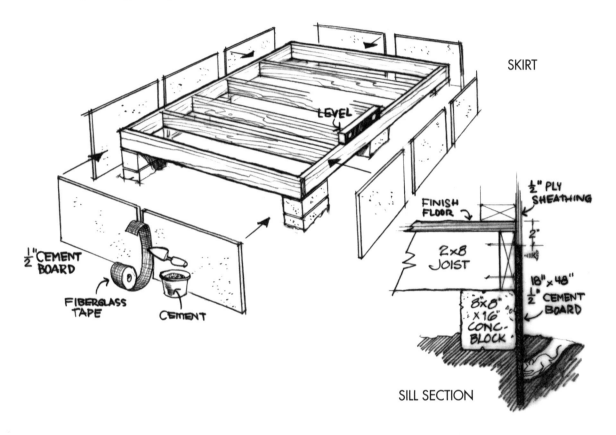

SKIRT

½" CEMENT BOARD

FIBERGLASS TAPE

CEMENT

LEVEL

FINISH FLOOR

2×8 JOIST

8"×8" ×16" CONC. BLOCK

½" PLY SHEATHING

2"

18"×48" ½" CEMENT BOARD

SILL SECTION

Fig. 3.10

# Flooring

Most outbuildings have ¾"-thick plywood floors. In some cases the plywood acts as a subfloor for a finished hardwood floor or it can be used as the finished floor. Use construction grade plywood for the former and a "finish grade," like AD plywood, for the latter. Nail the plywood flooring to the sill beams and the joists using 2½" nails every 8" to 10". Check that the floor is still level, and shim if necessary. It is very important to ensure the finished deck is level and square, as this will affect all the framing that is to come later. Now test the floor for stiffness by standing in the middle of the deck, raising your heels as high as you can off the floor and abruptly dropping them back down. You can feel the difference between a flexible floor that will "buzz" and a solid floor that will send a slight shock through your backbone.

A good alternative to a ¾" plywood floor is tongue-and-groove 2x6 decking set on 4x6 beams, spaced 4' apart. This is used as finished flooring (no subfloor is required) and is quite often seen in barn construction (see Fig. 3.11).

PLYWOOD FLOOR

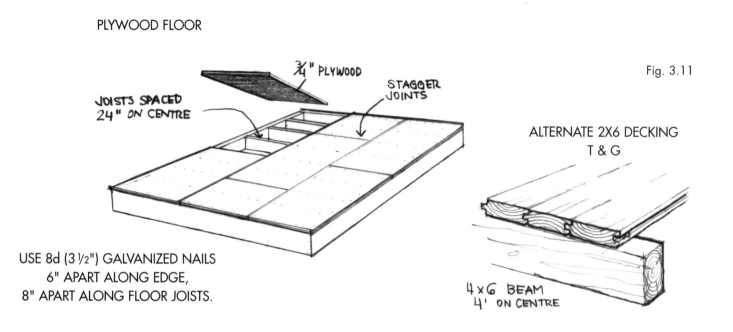

¾" PLYWOOD

STAGGER JOINTS

Fig. 3.11

JOISTS SPACED 24" ON CENTRE

ALTERNATE 2X6 DECKING T & G

USE 8d (3 ½") GALVANIZED NAILS 6" APART ALONG EDGE, 8" APART ALONG FLOOR JOISTS.

4x6 BEAM 4' ON CENTRE

# Wall Framing

Once the floor is completed you are ready to build the walls. Consider the floor as a giant worktable and use it as the space to lay out and build your walls.

Begin with one of the shorter walls, cutting the top plates and baseplates of the wall to the same width as the platform. (When you cut the two longer walls remember to allow for the thickness of the two shorter walls that they butt up against.) Cut all the wall studs to the same length and position them so they are 16" on center. In order to have a nailing surface for your drywall later on, add an extra 2x4 stud (plus blocking) at the corner (see Fig. 3.12).

Do not add the second top (cap) plate until all four walls are up. Add doubled 2x6 or 2x8 headers over the doors and windows. Any opening larger than 5' 6" should have double 2x10 headers. Leave a ½" space between the two headers or fill it with a ½" plywood spacer.

If you will be using salvaged windows, allow a ¼" space on either side of the window for shims and adjustments. If you are using pre-hung, factory-built windows or doors, follow the rough opening dimension given in the specifications.

Windows and doors typically have two 2x4s on each side. The one closest to the opening is the "trimmer" and supports the header, while the other 2x4s are called "king studs" and are attached to the upper and lower plates.

Starting at the rough openings, nail the pieces of the window framing together using 3½" nails. This gives you the room needed to swing your hammer when you are nailing the king studs to the windowsills and the headers. Let the sill plate extend across the door opening and cut it out with a handsaw after the walls are up. Check that the wall is square by measuring the diagonals. When the two measurements are the same, nail a temporary brace diagonally across the wall to hold it in place.

WALL FRAMING TERMS

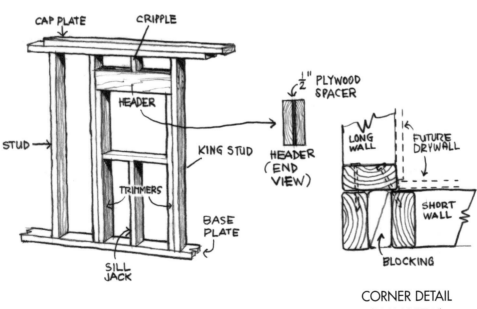

Fig. 3.12

CORNER DETAIL
(PLAN VIEW)

## Erecting the Walls

Walls that are up to 16' long can usually be lifted into position by a single person. However, if the walls are made using 2x6s instead of 2x4s, then two people are necessary. Before tilting the wall into place, nail a brace to the wall using a single nail, allowing the brace to pivot as you push the wall up. Start another nail at the other end of the brace so it is in place when it comes time to nail the wall to the platform. Lift and push the wall as if you are lifting a barbell. While holding the wall vertically, in position, nail the brace to the floor frame. This can get tricky. Don't try it in a high wind (see Fig. 3.13).

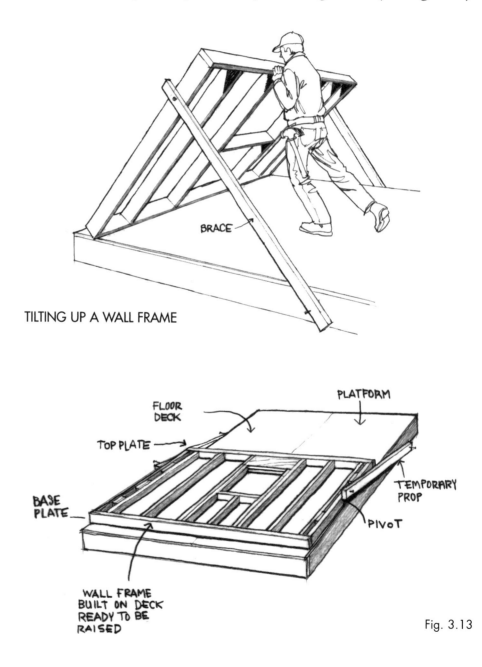

BRACE

TILTING UP A WALL FRAME

PLATFORM

FLOOR DECK

TOP PLATE

TEMPORARY PROP

BASE PLATE

PIVOT

WALL FRAME BUILT ON DECK READY TO BE RAISED

Fig. 3.13

Erect the adjoining wall and the other two walls in the same manner. As each wall is erected, nail it to the preceding wall, using 3½" nails, spaced 16" apart. Keep checking as you work to ensure that the walls are square and plumb. If a wall is out of alignment, use a rope to help you straighten it while someone else nails a temporary brace to the wall. To lock the walls in place, nail a second layer of 2x4s on top of the cap plates, and stagger the joints at each corner.

At this point, attach temporary braces to the inside of the building and remove them from the outside so you can apply the sheathing without any obstructions.

# Rafters

## Cutting the Rafters

The slope of the roof is very important and should be adjusted on the site, as scale drawings do not always show what the roof will look like when it is actually built. In an ideal world, the designer/builder who is constructing the building should make the final judgment on the slope.

Most first-time builders are confused by the process of cutting the rafters to the correct angle and cutting the notch (called bird's mouth) at the right place. Professional carpenters use their framing square to plot the correct angles, which is difficult for a beginner and sometimes results in errors.

The following solution is simpler and also allows for adjustment. Lay two 2x6 boards (1' to 2' longer than you think you will need) on the ground, crossing the tops in the shape of a wide "V." Lay a 10' 2x4 "lifting pole" over the intersection of the two 2x6s and bore 1/16" holes through the center of all three boards. Hammer a 6" nail through the holes to temporarily hold them together (see Fig. 3.14). Lift the rafter assembly up so that the ends of the rafters hang over the top plates of the workshop and the top of the lifting pole is the same distance from each side. Raise or lower the lifting pole until you think the roof angle looks just right, and temporarily nail it to the top plates. Step back and look at the angles of the rafters. If they look right to you, mark where the tail ends touch the top plates, and draw a vertical, plumb line up from that point. To plot the bird's mouth, measure up 1½" from the bottom of the mark that you just made and draw a horizontal line approximately 2" from the edge of the rafter.

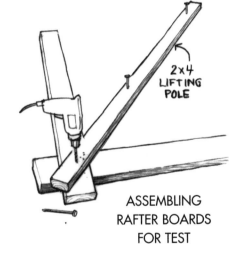

2x4 LIFTING POLE

ASSEMBLING RAFTER BOARDS FOR TEST

Fig. 3.14

Next, stand on a stepladder and draw a plumb line on both rafters at the top where they intersect. Take the assembly down, remove the temporary nail and cut the top angles and the bird's mouth cuts where marked. Don't cut the rafter tail ends until the rafters are installed (see Figs. 3.15 and 3.16).

Join the two rafters on the ground by screwing a 2x4 brace (collar tie) across them. Ensure the collar ties don't extend past the outside edge of the rafters, as this will interfere with sheathing the roof. From a piece of ½" plywood, cut a triangular "gusset plate" to hold the two rafters together at the top. Temporarily screw the gusset plate to the rafters, using 1½" screws. Lift the rafter assembly (truss) up onto the top of the plates and check to make sure the bird's-mouth notches fit perfectly. If they do, take the truss down, unscrew it and mark each piece with the word "pattern." Use these pieces as your pattern to trace onto all the other rafters, gusset plates and collar ties. Cut and nail the pieces together (see Fig. 3.17).

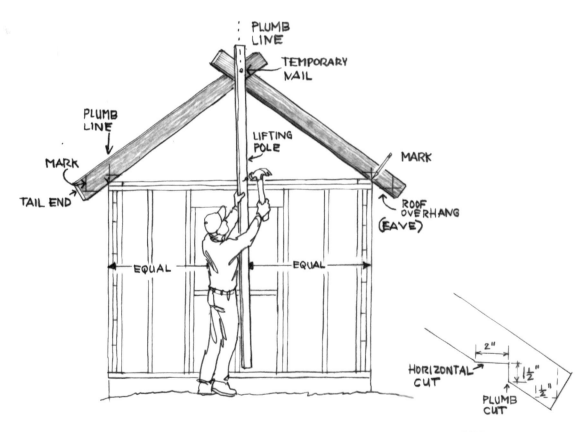

BIRD'S MOUTH

Fig. 3.15

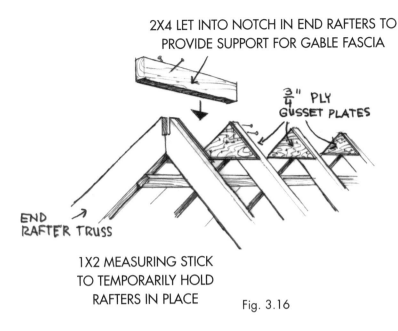

2X4 LET INTO NOTCH IN END RAFTERS TO PROVIDE SUPPORT FOR GABLE FASCIA

$\frac{3}{4}$" PLY GUSSET PLATES

END RAFTER TRUSS

1X2 MEASURING STICK TO TEMPORARILY HOLD RAFTERS IN PLACE

Fig. 3.16

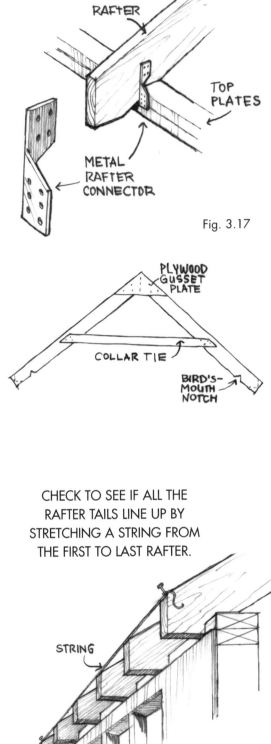

RAFTER

TOP PLATES

METAL RAFTER CONNECTOR

Fig. 3.17

PLYWOOD GUSSET PLATE

COLLAR TIE

BIRD'S-MOUTH NOTCH

Before installing the rafters, nail a temporary 2x4 collar-tie across the two walls to prevent the walls from spreading away from each other. Don't remove the collar tie until the roof is sheathed.

## Erecting the Rafters

Start by measuring and marking every 24" on the top plate where the rafters will rest. Lift the two end rafters into place one at a time, using a lifting pole, and screw them to the top plates. Make a measuring stick out of a 1x2 by marking every 24" along its length.

Temporarily nail the measuring stick to the two end rafter trusses, checking to make sure that the rafters are vertical. Lift the other rafter trusses in place and nail the measuring stick to them. This will allow you to nail the roof sheathing on top of the rafters without a problem. If you live in a windy area, attach the trusses to the top plate with metal connectors (see Fig. 3.17).

If you intend to make the roof overhang at the gable ends, remove the screws from the two end rafter gusset plates and cut out a notch before adding the sheathing. This will allow a 2x4 to extend from the next to the last rafter truss, through

CHECK TO SEE IF ALL THE RAFTER TAILS LINE UP BY STRETCHING A STRING FROM THE FIRST TO LAST RAFTER.

STRING

Fig. 3.18

the end rafter truss and out the desired distance (usually 5½"). This 2x4 supports the peak of the gable fascia (see Fig. 3.16).

After you have installed the rafters, cut the rafter (tail) ends plumb and horizontal, allowing for an overhang (see Fig 3.18). Make sure the roof overhang does not block the swing of your future door.

# Sheathing and Siding

Once the frame of your workshop is up, don't be concerned if the structure can still move a little, even with the temporary braces in place. This will be corrected when the sheathing is nailed on.

Years ago, builders nailed diagonal boards across the framed walls to make the structure rigid. Today, plywood sheathing has replaced these boards. Builders found that plywood provides bracing in many more directions and is easier and cheaper to apply.

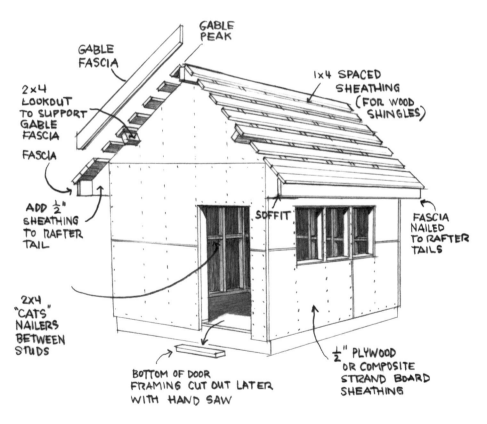

GABLE PEAK

GABLE FASCIA

1x4 SPACED SHEATHING (FOR WOOD SHINGLES)

2 x 4 LOOKOUT TO SUPPORT GABLE FASCIA

FASCIA

ADD ½" SHEATHING TO RAFTER TAIL

SOFFIT

FASCIA NAILED TO RAFTER TAILS

2X4 "CATS" NAILERS BETWEEN STUDS

BOTTOM OF DOOR FRAMING CUT OUT LATER WITH HAND SAW

½" PLYWOOD OR COMPOSITE STRAND BOARD SHEATHING

Fig. 3.19

Sheathing comes in 4x8 sheets and is usually ½" thick. It is generally a utility grade of plywood or a composition board made up of hundreds of small pieces of wood pressed and glued together (called "strand" board). Sheathing is nailed to the wall frame in a horizontal position for maximum strength and provides a base for the finished siding. It is also a good way to test whether your structure is square. Make sure each panel lines up with the framing before hammering the nails home (see Fig. 3.19).

Some accessory buildings may not require sheathing as long as their intended use is not for living and heating is not a problem. In this case, an inexpensive grade of plywood is quite often used, with a coat of paint to hide any defects and a thin 1x2 batten to hide the joints. Other choices are board-and-batten or shiplap boards, or Texture 1-11 plywood nailed directly to the frame. If the plywood you intend to use is only ⅜" thick, studs must be spaced 16" on center; however, if the plywood is ½" thick or thicker, a spacing of 24" is acceptable.

If your workshop is going to be heated, your building will need to be sheathed and then covered with a more finished grade of siding. Some common siding materials are wood shingles, beveled clapboard siding, stucco, bricks or even stone (see Fig. 3.20). All these types of siding should have some type of breathable building paper applied between the sheathing and the finished siding. Over the past years, plastic house wraps have become popular; however, they are slippery to put up and have been known to lose their strength over time. In addition, they only come in large rolls, leaving you with a lot of wasted material if your workshop is small. A good, less expensive alternative is traditional asphalt felt tar paper, stapled to the sheathing.

# Shingles

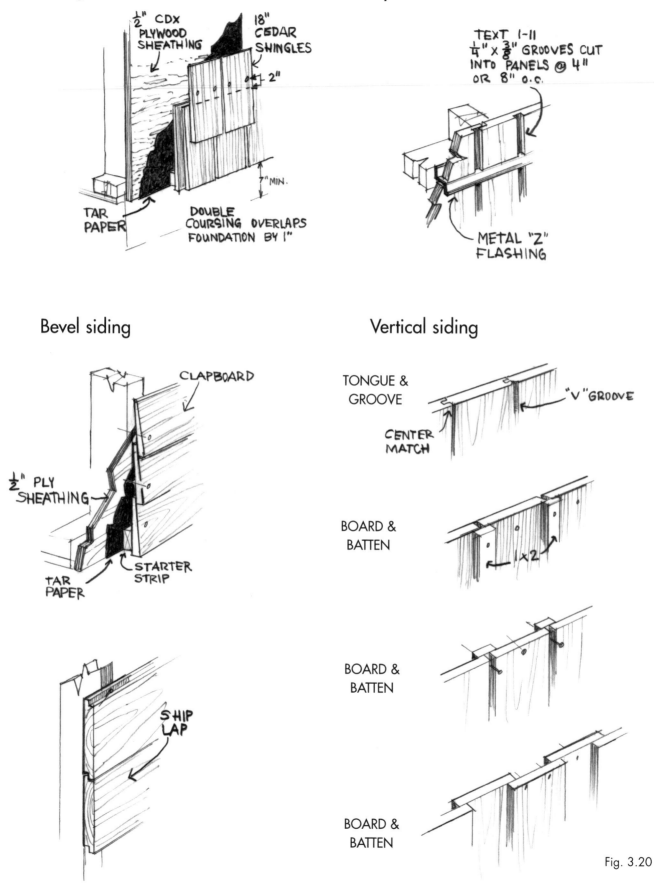

½" CDX PLYWOOD SHEATHING

18" CEDAR SHINGLES

2"

7" MIN.

TAR PAPER

DOUBLE COURSING OVERLAPS FOUNDATION BY 1"

# Plywood

TEXT 1-11 ¼" x ⅜" GROOVES CUT INTO PANELS @ 4" OR 8" O.C.

METAL "Z" FLASHING

# Bevel siding

CLAPBOARD

½" PLY SHEATHING

TAR PAPER

STARTER STRIP

SHIP LAP

# Vertical siding

TONGUE & GROOVE

"V" GROOVE

CENTER MATCH

BOARD & BATTEN

1 x 2

BOARD & BATTEN

BOARD & BATTEN

Fig. 3.20

# Fascia and Soffits

Eaves and rakes refer to the connection where the roof meets the wall of any building. Rakes are the sloped connection between the roof and the wall, while eaves are the level connection between the roof and the wall (see Fig. 3.21). Sometimes the eaves or rakes are attached flush with the building with no overhang, but usually they extend to protect the walls from rain. When the eaves and rakes are extended, the underside can be left exposed (as in the case of barns and sheds), or they can be enclosed so the rafters don't show. This requires a fascia board to cover the ends of the rafters (tails) and a soffit, which is a flat board covering the bottoms of the rafters (see Fig. 3.22). In order to hold the soffit in place, a certain amount of extra framing must be constructed and provisions made to vent the roof.

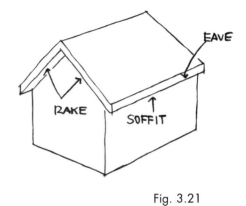

Fig. 3.21

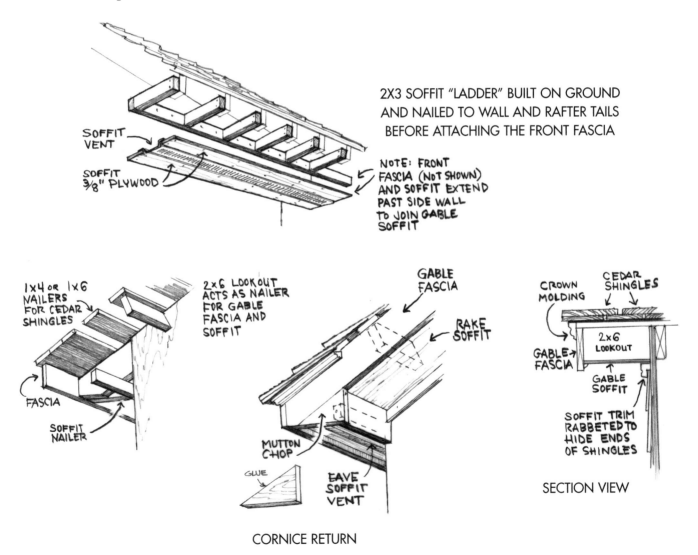

SOFFIT VENT

SOFFIT ⅜" PLYWOOD

2X3 SOFFIT "LADDER" BUILT ON GROUND AND NAILED TO WALL AND RAFTER TAILS BEFORE ATTACHING THE FRONT FASCIA

NOTE: FRONT FASCIA (NOT SHOWN) AND SOFFIT EXTEND PAST SIDE WALL TO JOIN GABLE SOFFIT

1X4 OR 1X6 NAILERS FOR CEDAR SHINGLES

FASCIA

SOFFIT NAILER

2x6 LOOKOUT ACTS AS NAILER FOR GABLE FASCIA AND SOFFIT

GABLE FASCIA

RAKE SOFFIT

MUTTON CHOP

GLUE

EAVE SOFFIT VENT

CORNICE RETURN

CROWN MOLDING

CEDAR SHINGLES

GABLE FASCIA

2x6 LOOKOUT

GABLE SOFFIT

SOFFIT TRIM RABBETED TO HIDE ENDS OF SHINGLES

SECTION VIEW

Fig. 3.22

First, you will need to extend the 2x8 ridge board the extra distance that you want your gable to overhang. This extended ridge board will eventually support the gable fascia. When you are framing the roof, cut notches in the last rafter to accept the 2x4 "lookouts." Lookouts are only necessary if the roof extension is more than 12", otherwise the extended roof can be supported by the roof sheathing. If 1x4 spaced sheathing is used for cedar shingles, a soffit board should be installed to prevent heat from escaping between the spaces of the sheathing. If the building is not to be heated, omit the soffit board and install insect screening to allow air to flow through the eaves. You may add another rafter to the end of the gable (called a "fly rafter"), but we think this adds unnecessary weight to the overhang. We prefer to add a lightweight gable fascia board, attached to the ridge board at the top and the front fascia at the bottom (see Fig. 3.23).

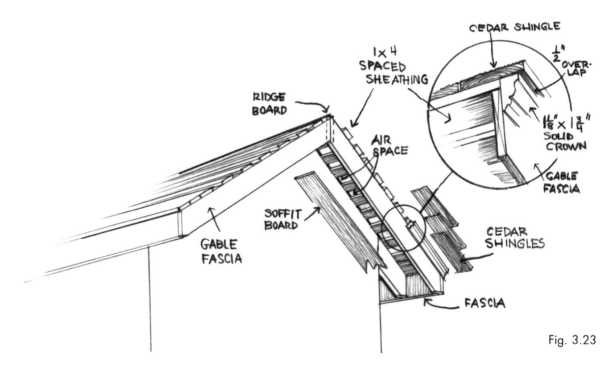

Fig. 3.23

As shown in the illustrations, the front and back roof extend over the walls by 12". Check to make sure that all the rafter ends (tails) are in line by holding a string tight from one end to the other (see Fig. 3.18). Nail a 1x8 fascia board to the rafter tails, allowing the free end of the fascia board to extend past the building and to meet the gable fascia. Carefully mark and cut the bottom end of the gable fascia so that it joins the eave fascia of the roof perfectly. The tops of the gable fascia should both be cut plumb where they meet at the ridge.

You can leave the area under the roof overhangs open, but most carpenters prefer to box them in with soffits. The soffits must be vented to allow air to flow up under the roofing and to exit out the ridge vent. To make the front and rear soffits, build a "ladder" on the ground (see Fig. 3.22) and nail it to the rafter tails and the side of the building. This provides a nailing surface for the soffit board. Cut the plywood into two long strips, allowing room for a soffit vent strip. On the gable end, the soffit does not have to be vented, and is nailed to soffit nailers. Cut a rabbeted groove out of the soffit trim to accept the top edge of your finished siding material. You will be happy that you took this small extra step when you are doing your siding, as it will give it a nice, neat appearance.

The soffit or cornice return is where the fascia turns the corner and is joined on the other side by what is sometimes called a "mutton chop" (see Fig. 3.22). Cornice returns can get quite fancy, and in some traditional styles of houses a little angled roof is added on. This job is always given to the most skilled carpenter on the job. Oddly enough, this detail is seldom shown in construction books.

The soffit return is boxed out and a triangular piece of wood (the mutton chop) is added to the bottom of the gable fascia. Over several years, this small piece of wood often separates, so take extra time to carefully glue and nail it in place using finishing nails. Also, make sure that the grain of the wood in the mutton chop follows the same direction as the grain of the gable fascia board. When you are finished, sand the cornice return flat so that it looks like it is part of the gable fascia and paint it with primer as soon as possible. You might consider priming and painting the soffit boards before you install them to avoid dripping paint on the siding.

# Roofing

Roofing material is generally sold by the "square" (10' x 10' or 100 square feet). To figure out how much roofing material you will need, multiply the length of each side of the roof by its width and divide this total by 100.

Two of the most common types of roofing material in North America are asphalt and fiberglass shingles. They are cheaper than wood shingles, last just as long and are much easier to install. There are many styles and colors to choose from and some replicate the look of real wood shingles by creating a shadow line at the butt ends. The most common types are the three-tab asphalt shingles, 36" wide by 12" long.

Asphalt shingles should not be applied directly over plywood sheathing. You will need to tack or staple down overlapping layers of asphalt-saturated felt, also referred to as 15 lb. tarpaper. It comes in 36" x 144' long rolls and each roll covers four squares. The rolls are easily cut using a utility knife, working on the ground, and then stapled to the roof sheathing. Before applying the tarpaper, tack down a metal drip edge to the bottom eave edge of the roof. Also, cover the rake side edges with metal drip edges. Allow every layer of tarpaper to overlap the one below by at least 2".

To work on the roof, you need to construct a scaffold to stand on. You can buy scaffolding boards (called staging boards) from your lumberyard and nail together some braces made from scrap pieces of 2x4 (see Fig. 3.24).

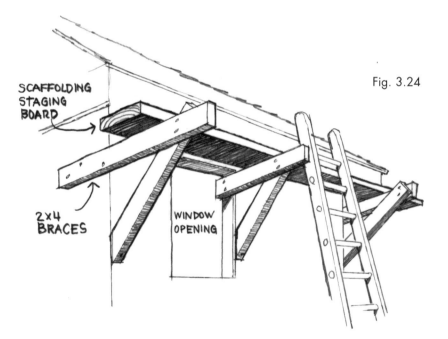

SCAFFOLDING STAGING BOARD

Fig. 3.24

2x4 BRACES

WINDOW OPENING

Nail the braces to the sides of the workshop just under the eaves. You will only be able to nail the first two rows while standing on the scaffolding. At this point, if you are not comfortable working on the roof, hire a roofer; otherwise, nail temporary 2x4s across the roof to provide a foothold. Once you have reached the top, nail 1x2 cleats to the tarpaper to keep the wind from blowing it off.

Nailing on the asphalt shingles is fairly easy. The only hard part is carrying the heavy bundles of shingles up the roof. The best way to do this is to cut the bundle open and carry one-third of the shingles up at a time. Begin nailing the shingles to the roof by overlapping the sides and the bottom by ⅜". Although it might seem strange, nail the first course of shingles with the slotted tabs pointing up. This will provide a starter course, or base, for the second layer, which is nailed directly over it. Make sure this first course of shingles is straight, as it will be used as a guide for the remaining rows.

Using four nails above each slot, start with a full shingle, overhanging ⅜" on the left, and work to the right until you come to the end. Cut the last shingle ⅜" wider, to allow for overhang. Starting at the left again, cut half of a tab off one shingle and nail it approximately 5" above the previous row so that the slots in the tabs don't line up. Cut the asphalt shingles from the back to avoid dulling your utility knife on the granular front side. Use a carpenter's square as a cutting guide to make straight cuts. Use the previous row of shingles as your guide, covering up the tops of the slots by ¼". To make sure that your rows end up even with the ridge, once you have completed half of the shingling, measure the distance from the ridge of the roof to the last row of shingles at several different points. Often they are not even, and you will have to make incremental adjustments in each row to come out even at the ridge (see Fig. 3.25).

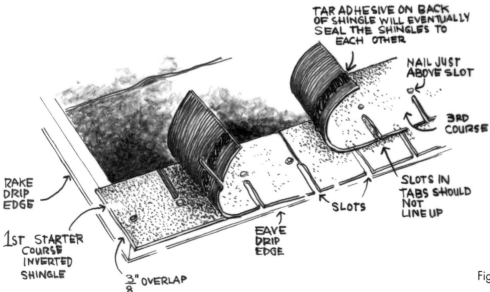

TAR ADHESIVE ON BACK OF SHINGLE WILL EVENTUALLY SEAL THE SHINGLES TO EACH OTHER

NAIL JUST ABOVE SLOT

3RD COURSE

SLOTS IN TABS SHOULD NOT LINE UP

SLOTS

RAKE DRIP EDGE

EAVE DRIP EDGE

1ST STARTER COURSE INVERTED SHINGLE

$\frac{3"}{8}$ OVERLAP

Fig. 3.25

# Doors and Windows

Compared to building a door from scratch, installing a pre-hung, factory-made door will save you 5 to 10 hours of labor. Pre-hung doors and windows can be bought from your local lumberyard or home building center. The term "pre-hung" means that the door or window comes pre-assembled at the factory, with all the hinges and stops installed. If you plan on installing a standard lock set in the door, order the door to be "bored" with holes. Most doors now come with at least three hinges to insure that the door remains straight.

Cheaper doors have a finger-jointed core underneath with a thin veneer of clear wood on top. This surface can delaminate in time if not protected with several coats of paint or sealer. Ask the salesperson before buying.

Because all doors and gates have a tendency to pull away from the top hinge and press against the bottom hinge, put aside the short screws that are provided and replace them with 2½"- or 3"-long screws (see Fig. 3.26).

When ordering doors you will have to stipulate which way the door will open – in or out, left or right. To understand this, imagine yourself standing with your back to the hinges – your right hand will be a right-hand (swing) door and your left hand a left-hand door (see Figs. 3.27 to 3.29).

We recommend that you install your exterior doors to swing out, not in, for the following reasons:

o No raised sill to sweep over or trip over
o Less prone to break-ins
o Wind presses the door tighter, eliminating cold air infiltration
o Rain drips outside the door, eliminating leaks
o Easier to exit in a fire emergency (required by law in most commercial buildings)

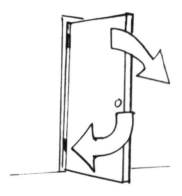

Fig. 3.26

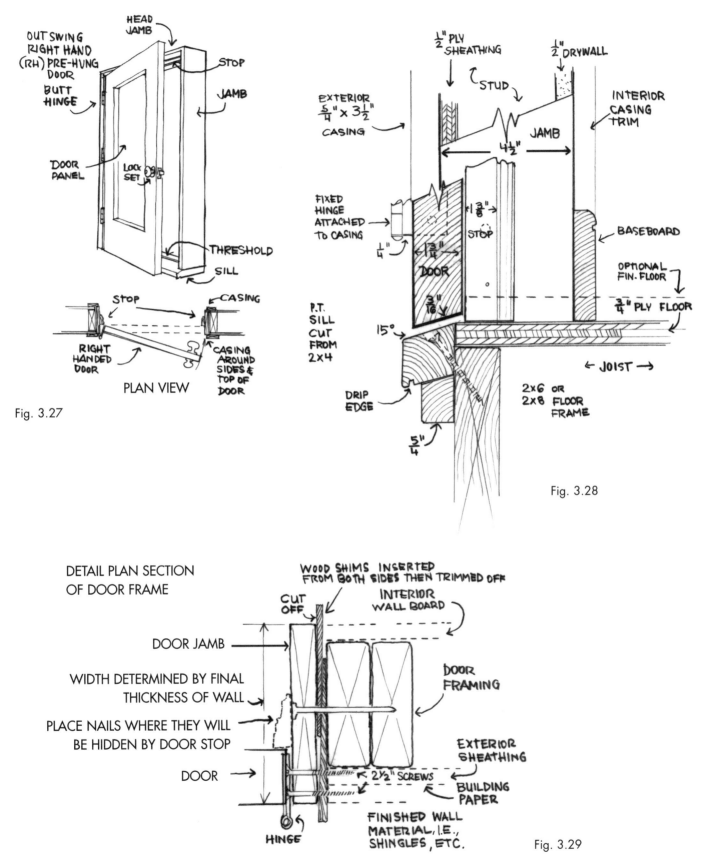

DOOR TERMS

OUT SWING
RIGHT HAND
(RH) PRE-HUNG
DOOR

BUTT
HINGE

HEAD
JAMB

STOP

JAMB

DOOR
PANEL

LOCK
SET

THRESHOLD

SILL

STOP

CASING

RIGHT
HANDED
DOOR

CASING
AROUND
SIDES &
TOP OF
DOOR

PLAN VIEW

Fig. 3.27

SECTION DETAIL FOR
DOOR HUNG ON CUSTOM-BUILT FRAME

½" PLY
SHEATHING

½" DRYWALL

STUD

EXTERIOR
5/4" X 3½"
CASING

INTERIOR
CASING
TRIM

JAMB

4½"

FIXED
HINGE
ATTACHED
TO CASING

1 3/8"

STOP

¼"

3/4"

DOOR

BASEBOARD

OPTIONAL
FIN. FLOOR

3/16"

3/4" PLY FLOOR

P.T.
SILL
CUT
FROM
2x4

15°

JOIST

DRIP
EDGE

2x6 OR
2x8 FLOOR
FRAME

5/4"

Fig. 3.28

DETAIL PLAN SECTION
OF DOOR FRAME

WOOD SHIMS INSERTED
FROM BOTH SIDES THEN TRIMMED OFF

CUT
OFF

INTERIOR
WALL BOARD

DOOR JAMB

DOOR
FRAMING

WIDTH DETERMINED BY FINAL
THICKNESS OF WALL

PLACE NAILS WHERE THEY WILL
BE HIDDEN BY DOOR STOP

EXTERIOR
SHEATHING

DOOR

2½" SCREWS

BUILDING
PAPER

HINGE

FINISHED WALL
MATERIAL, I.E.,
SHINGLES, ETC.

Fig. 3.29

Windows come in many sizes and shapes, as shown (see Fig. 3.30). Each pre-hung door or window will have its own rough opening specified in the manufacturer's catalog and on the attached installation instructions. These dimensions are generally about ¼" wider than the actual door or window, which allows for last-minute adjustments if the framing is not perfectly square or plumb. Adjustments can be made by inserting wood shims between the framing and the window or door. Before installing any window, wrap building paper or house wrap around the sides of the rough opening.

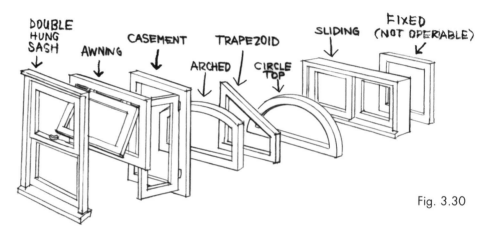

Fig. 3.30

You can install pre-hung windows by placing them in their rough openings from the outside and shimming them from the inside. This requires two people – one to do the shimming and the other to hold the window and keep it from falling out. Each window must be made level and plumb before being permanently nailed in. Remember that both window and door frames must be flush with the anticipated interior wall surface, and at the same time line up with the exterior siding. Before hammering the nails all the way in test the window to make sure it doesn't stick when it is opened, and adjust it if necessary.

Plastic-clad windows can be nailed directly to the wall through a plastic flange surrounding the window. Wooden extension jambs make up any discrepancies in the wall thickness on the interior. If you like the traditional look of muntin bars, referred to as "divided lights," across the windows, you can order removable or permanent divided-light grills for the windows. Although they are more difficult to clean and maintain, we prefer the truly divided lights found in older windows. They can be purchased new (see Sources) and come primed or unpainted.

Some building codes require you to use double-thick, insulated glass. If you are not required to use insulated glass, a good alternative is to use recycled windows found at yard sales and antique stores. As long as the glass and wood are in good condition, they can often be reused, and will cost you a fraction of the price of new windows. You can also make your own windows (if you have a table saw) for under $15 each. See *Sheds* by David Stiles, listed in Further Reading.

Inexpensive, single-pane "replacement sashes" can be ordered from many window manufacturers at one-third the cost of pre-hung windows. You can also special order "barn sash" windows from your local lumberyard's millwork shop. These are built to your exact measurements and cost less than a pre-hung manufactured window. However, you do have to frame them yourself. One of the most economical types of window you can buy are plastic window sashes made from recycled milk bottles (see Sources). They are only available in white. Since they are made of solid plastic, they are virtually indestructible.

Doors can also be handmade or bought used to save money but, like windows, they take a long time and are very difficult to hang perfectly. Don't be surprised if it takes you a whole day to build and install one door. You will need to cut and assemble the jambs, mortise and screw the hinges to the door, shim up the door in place, screw the hinges to the door jamb, drill the hole for the lock set handle and strike plate, install the lock set, cut and nail the casing trim around the door, cut and nail the stop molding to the door frame and seal and paint the wood.

Most exterior doors, except for patio doors, are 1¾" thick, while interior doors are generally 1⅜" thick. The majority of exterior doors are 36" wide, while interior doors are usually 30" wide.

# Insulation

Most building codes require you to use a minimum amount of insulation to comply with local energy conservation codes. Check with your local building department for their specific requirements. In the northeast, for instance, any inhabited dwelling must have R30 rated insulation in the ceiling and R19 in the walls. There are various types of insulation such as rigid, blown-in and even straw bale, but the most common type is fiberglass wool batts or rolls. They are sized to fit between studs and joists that are spaced either 16" or 24" apart.

Fiberglass insulation comes with either a foil face or a brown paper face, which should always face the heated side of the room. Moisture or steam inside the house can creep through the walls and settle on the fiberglass, which can make it lose its effectiveness. To prevent this, cover the interior walls with a layer of 8-mil polyethylene, stapled to the studs after you have installed the insulation. When handling fiberglass insulation, wear a long-sleeved shirt and always cut it from the paper or foil side using a utility knife and a straightedge.

One of the problems you may encounter when attempting to comply with your building department's energy code is that you may be required to have R30 insulation in the ceiling. This insulation can expand to as much as 10" after it is installed. This means that you would need to use 2x10s for your ceiling rafters, which may seem out of proportion for a small structure such as a workshop.

Fortunately, there is a high-density version of R30 insulation that measures only 8½" when installed. In addition, building suppliers sell a spacer that can fit above the insulation, which helps to insure that the air venting is not restricted.

If you are required to use R19 insulation in your walls, you will need to use 2x6s, which measure 5½" deep. Otherwise you can use rigid insulation, which requires less thickness to make up the same R-value but costs more (see Fig. 3.31). Again, check with your building department.

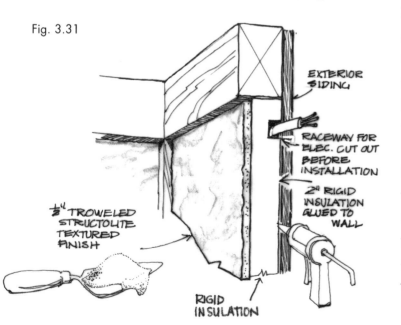

Fig. 3.31

EXTERIOR SIDING

RACEWAY FOR ELEC. CUT OUT BEFORE INSTALLATION

2" RIGID INSULATION GLUED TO WALL

½" TROWELED STRUCTOLITE TEXTURED FINISH

RIGID INSULATION

# Heat and Electricity

You will probably want your workshop to have electricity to run your lights, tools, office equipment and so on. If your electrical requirements are minimal, all you probably need is another circuit connected to your house circuit breaker box. If, however, you are planning on running an electric kiln or a heavy-duty table saw you will need 220-volt service with a 30-amp circuit breaker and a separate panel box. In either case you should hire a licensed electrician who can advise you what the local electric codes require and can do the work for you.

Make sure that you have a list of all the tools and/or appliances you want to run and a plan showing the position of all the wall outlets and lights. Most codes require an electric outlet every 6' and they are generally installed about 14" above the floor. You can save your electrician some time (and yourself some money) if you know in advance what the required amperage each piece of equipment will draw. This information is listed on the label as either amps or watts. If the label lists it in watts, convert it to amps by dividing the watts by the voltage.

As a rule of thumb, each typical 15-amp circuit can handle about 10 100-watt bulbs all on at the same time; however, if there is an electric hair dryer on the same circuit it would overload, causing the circuit breaker to trip.

If you are running electricity to a building some distance away from your home you might have to hire a contractor to dig a trench for an underground wire. He will probably use a small machine called a "ditch witch" which will happily leave very little disturbance in your lawn. If it is a short run, the electrician may dig the trench himself using a shovel. Since you are paying him to do the job, ensure he is responsible for obtaining any necessary permits and notifying the electrical inspector. Also ensure you get a signed electrical compliance certificate or you won't be able to sell your house in the future.

Heat can be provided by portable electric heaters. However, depending on your preferences, you may want to consider also heating your addition with a wood-burning stove or fireplace. There are many reasonably priced "zero clearance" fireplaces (those that have been engineered so they can be installed next to the wood framing of your workshop) on the market now, and they are fairly easy to install yourself. The flue has to be insulated with a double or triple wall and must rise a minimum of 2½' above the roof and be 10' away from the highest point of the roof. In order to get a good draft in one-story buildings, the chimney might have to rise even higher than that.

Successfully tapping into your house heating system depends on the type of foundation you have. If your house has a concrete block foundation, it is fairly easy to cut a hole in the wall using a sledgehammer and a masonry chisel. If your foundation is solid concrete, you will need a hammer drill to make the hole, in which case it might be better to call in a professional. If you have a forced air heating system, you can run flexible insulated ducts from your furnace to your addition for very little money and not much work (see Fig. 3.32).

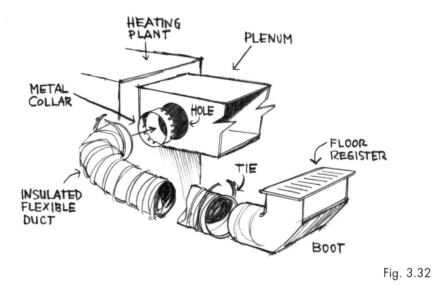

Fig. 3.32

You should check first with a heating contractor to see if your system has the capacity for one or more ducts coming from your furnace. If your house is heated by electricity, using baseboard heaters, check with an electrician to see if there are any spaces left on your circuit breaker and if the panel will accept the added load.

# Plumbing

You may want to install running water or even a toilet in your workshop. First check with your local building department to see if it is permitted in your area. Some communities allow cold water only for fear that you will turn your workshop into a guesthouse. Remember you must also provide a drainage or septic system to be connected into your house septic system. If you are attaching your new workshop to your existing house, this may not be a big problem. Otherwise, consult with your local plumber for advice and an estimate.

# Skylight

It is easy to build your own skylight, and you can save a lot of money. The only real expense is the Plexiglas, which costs $7.00 per sq. ft. The plans for this addition show a skylight that measures 4 feet by 8 feet (the dimensions of a piece of Plexiglas) (see Fig. 3.33). You can reduce the dimensions of your skylight to fit your specific situation; however, just make sure that it fits over the top of the rafters. Design

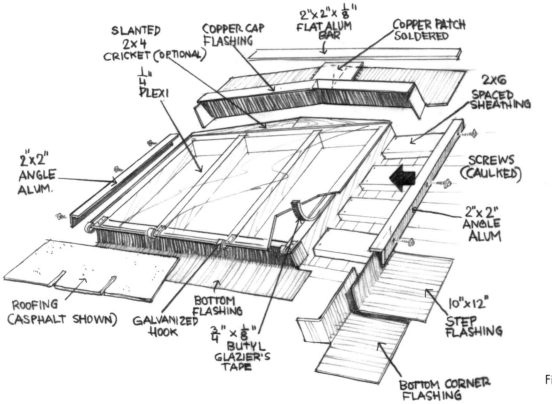

Fig. 3.33

your skylight with a "curb" that protrudes up from the top surface of the finished roof. The reason that this skylight should not leak is that it uses only one full-length piece of ¼" thick acrylic Plexiglas that extends over the top edge of the curb. Using Plexiglas rather than ¼" plate glass has the advantage of being much less heavy, plus you can install it yourself without worrying about it breaking. It is also less expensive, can be cut easily with a saw, and is safer in case a tree limb falls on it. The only trouble with acrylics is that they expand and contract quite a bit as the temperature changes. For this reason avoid drilling holes in the skylight and filling them with screws, as this can cause leaks. The Plexiglas shown in the skylight plans is held down using a strip of aluminum roof edge, and is held at the bottom by galvanized angle brackets that keep it from slipping down (see Fig. 3.34). Before the Plexiglas is set in place, a strip of butyl glazier's tape should be placed on the top edge of the skylight frame to provide a bed for the Plexiglas. It is important that the Plexiglas extends at least 1½" past the bottom edge of the skylight so that the water will run off unobstructed.

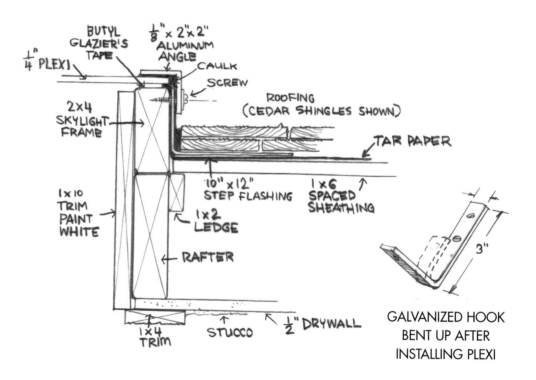

Fig. 3.34

The key to making a skylight that doesn't leak is the flashing around the curb. To install flashing around the skylight, buy a roll of aluminum flashing and cut it into 12"-long pieces, stapling them under each course of shingles as you proceed up the roof. The top edge of the stepped flashing on the sides of the skylight is covered and protected by a 6'-long, 2" x 2", ⅛"-thick aluminum angle bar, which is screwed on from the sides. Predrill the screw holes and put a dab of caulking in each hole before putting in the screw, to prevent any water from seeping through. As an added precaution, we have added a shallow V-shaped "cricket" to the top of the skylight to help direct rain water away to the sides. Depending on how much rain you get, this may or may not be necessary.

# Building a Partition

Allow at least two days to build a partition from beginning to end. To frame, drywall and tape a typical 8' x 12' partition will take you a full day, and to sand, paint and hang the door will take another day. Start by covering any doorways or openings to the rest of the house or apartment. Assemble your tools and carry all your framing material, drywall and joint compound to the job site.

Before you begin building, determine whether the proposed partition will line up with a ceiling joist or cross the joists at a right angle. If the partition is going to be parallel with the joist, it should lie directly under it, giving you something solid to nail into (see Fig. 3.35). Use a stud finder to determine the location of the joists, or check construction plans if they are available. (Ceiling joists generally run across the width of the room.)

The most important thing to keep in mind when you are putting up the framing for a partition wall is that all edges of the drywall panel must be backed up and supported by framing members. It should be backed up a minimum of every two feet so that it will remain rigid and flat. That means a typical vertical sheet of drywall should be supported by at least three (preferably four) studs. It is essential that where two pieces of drywall meet at the same stud, they share the 1½" face of the stud equally (¾" for each panel), allowing enough room for each panel to be nailed or screwed into the stud. This is the reason it is important that the studs are set exactly on center (see Fig. 3.36).

CEILING JOISTS PARALLEL WITH PARTITION

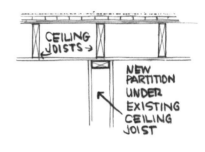

Fig. 3.35

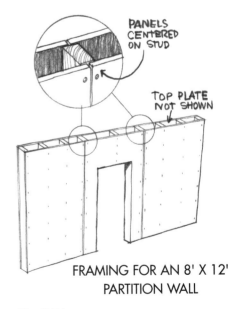

FRAMING FOR AN 8' X 12' PARTITION WALL

Fig. 3.36

## Drywall

Drywall, Sheetrock, gypsum board and wallboard are different names for a plaster panel covered on both sides with a layer of light gray paper. It is sold in ¼", ⅜", ½" and ⅝" thickness, 48" wide and from 8' to 16' long. The most common size used by the majority of do-it-yourselfers is ½" x 4' x 8', because it is easier to handle and requires only one person to lift. One sheet weighs about 54 pounds. Since it comes two pieces to a bundle, you will need to strip them apart at the ends before moving individual pieces.

Drywall panels have a slight taper on the long edges to allow the joint compound and tape to end up flush with the surface of the panels (see Fig. 3.37). Drywall is usually hung vertically rather than horizontally.

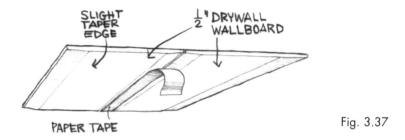

Fig. 3.37

Drywall is very easy to cut. All you need is a long drywall T-square and a utility knife. Once you have measured the piece to be cut, place the head of the T-square on top of the drywall panel and, while bracing the bottom of the T-square with your foot, cut the surface paper of the drywall panel, using the T-square as a guide (see Fig. 3.38). Holding the panel with one hand, bend the part to be cut

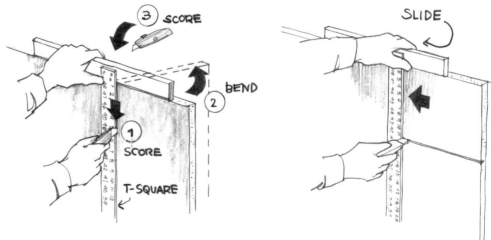

Fig. 3.38

off until it snaps open. Keep the panel in its folded position, walk around to the back and cut the paper along the crease. Cutting drywall on the long dimension can be done by holding your knife at the desired measurement on the T-square and sliding it along the length of the panel, cutting the panel at the same time.

To install the drywall onto wood framing, use type "W" self-drilling screws. If you are using nails to hang drywall onto wood studs, you should use special ringed Sheetrock nails that are designed to resist pullout (see Fig. 3.39).

Be careful not to hammer the nails or set the screws so deep that they break the paper on the surface of the panel. On the other hand, make sure they are set slightly below the surface of the panel, making a shallow dimple that will be filled in later with joint compound.

Joint compound, called "mud" by the pros, comes in plastic buckets that are also useful once the job is finished. A 2½ gallon bucket should be enough for an 8' x 12' wall. Buy the "setting type" compound for most jobs. Mix it thoroughly before using and never let it freeze. Also, don't use old joint compound, as it could contain tiny pieces of dried compound that have fallen into the mix, which could ruin your job.

Taping and finishing drywall involves the following steps. First, use a 4" or 6" taping knife to cover the drywall seam with a thick coat of "embedding" compound. Cut a piece of paper tape the same length as the joint and press the tape into the wet coat using your fingers and a 6" taping knife. Lightly squeeze the joint compound out from underneath the tape. If you see any blisters (air pockets), remove the tape, add more joint compound, and resume taping. Remove any excess joint compound, making sure that the joint is smooth, and let it dry for several hours.

Apply a second coat of joint compound using a 10" taping knife, making a smooth 8" or 9" wide joint. Once again, let this coat dry. Before applying the third finishing coat, pass your 10" knife over the joints to knock off any high spots, and then apply a thin, smooth finish coat. Then, after allowing everything to dry overnight, lightly sand the joint using 120-grit sandpaper placed over a wide sanding block. Fill the dimples left by the screws or nails, using no less than three coats of joint compound (see Fig. 3.40).

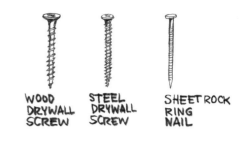

WOOD DRYWALL SCREW   STEEL DRYWALL SCREW   SHEET ROCK RING NAIL

Fig. 3.39

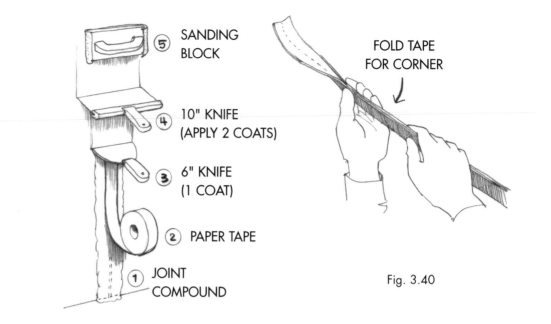

⑤ SANDING BLOCK

④ 10" KNIFE (APPLY 2 COATS)

③ 6" KNIFE (1 COAT)

② PAPER TAPE

① JOINT COMPOUND

FOLD TAPE FOR CORNER

Fig. 3.40

## Framing a Partition Wall

When framing a partition wall there are two choices of material – steel or wood. Lightweight steel framing is most often used in commercial buildings where fire ratings and economy are the main factors, whereas wood framing is more popular in residential housing. Steel studs are good because they are lighter in weight, are quick to install and remain very stable; however, you need to wear gloves to prevent the sharp steel edges from cutting your hands. Wood studs, on the other hand, produce a more solid wall and require only basic carpentry skills. The disadvantage of using wood studs is that they can warp, bow, rot or harbor termites.

### Steel studs

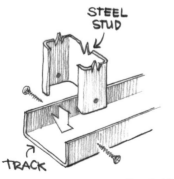

STEEL STUD

TRACK

Fig. 3.41

Steel studs are 20-gauge steel bent into approximately the same shape as a 2x4 with one side open. The studs are designed to fit into "tracks" that have been screwed into the floor and ceiling. The studs are screwed to the track from both sides using special "bugle head" screws and are spaced 16" on center (measured from the wall) (see Fig. 3.41). The steel studs on either side of the door and the header above the door have to be reinforced with wood by sliding a 2x4 into the channel and securing it with screws.

## Wood studs

When buying wood studs make sure they are absolutely straight by sighting down the length. (Don't forget to turn them ¼ turn to inspect the other side.) It is a good idea to buy this lumber at a home supply center where the lumber has been kept out of the rain, making it less likely to warp. This is to prevent the drywall from bulging out or creating a recess once the drywall is installed.

Doorways will require two studs on each side – a king stud and a jack stud, which supports the header, generally attached 81" up from the floor. The header in a non-load-bearing partition only requires a 2x4 since it only supports the weight of the material above it. Check the local building code for your specific situation, as building codes differ on this. A short "cripple" stud is necessary above the door to provide support for the drywall (see Figs. 3.42 and 3.43).

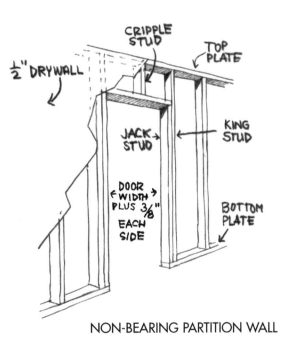

NON-BEARING PARTITION WALL

Fig. 3.42

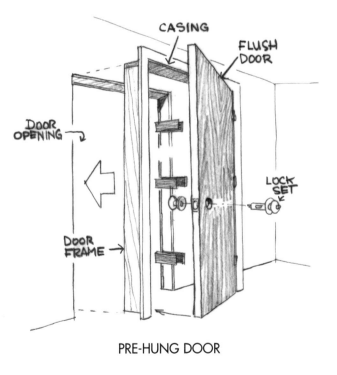

PRE-HUNG DOOR

Fig. 3.43

## Exposed Beams

You can skip this part if your workshop is going to be covered in drywall and painted. For those of you whose tastes run toward a rustic style here is a way of achieving the timber-framed barn look without going through all the trouble of cutting mortise and tenon joints.

At your lumberyard, buy cheap rough-sawn scaffolding (staging) boards, which come about 13' long, 2" thick and about 9" wide. The older the better; in fact, you might find some builders who will trade you their old beat-up boards for new ones. Since they will be used for decoration only, they don't have to be structural. These boards can be ripped into any widths you want. We found that 2⅛"-wide boards made good rafters. Four of these can be ripped from one board. You will need to coat the freshly cut edges with a gray wood stain. The best way to do this is to buy a gray stain that comes close to matching the weathered wood color of your beams and fine-tune it by adding tinting pigments. Apply the stain with a brush or roller. To make the beams look hand-hewn, "distress" or shape them with an adze (see Fig. 3.44). For more instructions on hand hewing, see our book *Cabins*, published by Firefly Books.

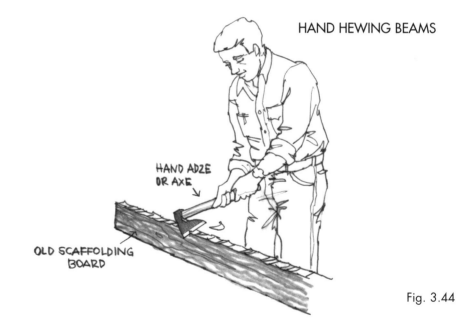

HAND HEWING BEAMS

HAND ADZE OR AXE

OLD SCAFFOLDING BOARD

Fig. 3.44

Cut and screw the "faux" rafters to the ceiling every 4 feet so that they hide the drywall joints. This will save you the messy job of taping and spackling the overhead joints. Cut the bottom ends of the rafters at an angle so that they meet the horizontal beams. Rip some of the scaffolding boards into 4"-wide pieces and install these as knee braces, with a 45° angle at each end. The horizontal beams should be about 7" to 8" wide so that they appear structural (see Fig. 3.45).

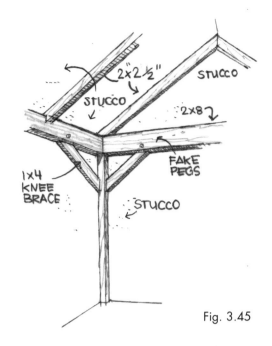

Fig. 3.45

## Stucco

A layer of stucco covering the drywall gives a nice effect and covers up any mistakes you may have made. Before applying the stucco it is important to tape all the joints with fiberglass tape, as this will keep the joints from cracking later on. A second or third coat of drywall compound is not necessary, as the stucco will cover the joint up.

The stucco we recommend here is not the "true" stucco that is used on traditional houses, but is a simple combination of two ingredients premixed – wet drywall compound and dry "Structolite." The drywall compound

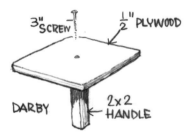

TO KEEP FROM BENDING OVER TO LOAD YOUR TROWEL, MAKE THIS DARBY OUT OF A 12" X 12" PIECE OF PLYWOOD AND A 6"-LONG PIECE OF 2X2.

Fig. 3.46

keeps the mixture glued to the wall and the Structolite gives the stucco the rough-textured look. Before applying the stucco, tape all the beams with blue 1½" painter's masking tape. Mix the two ingredients together in equal proportions and apply it to the wall with a mason's trowel (see Fig. 3.46). The trick to making stucco look good is to try not to repeat the direction of any strokes, making it look as haphazard as possible. Don't try to smooth it out flat; rather, try to give the wall some texture. Mix the stucco in a small plastic mason's mortar pan, in batches approximately the size of one drywall bucket, and transfer it to a "darby" (see Fig. 3.46). The mixture will begin to harden after half an hour, so mix only as much as you need for that amount of time. One ¼"-thick coat is sufficient to give the walls and ceiling the effect that you need.

# CHAPTER FOUR

# THREE DETAILED DESIGNS

## Cotswold Cottage Office/Workshop

This 12' by 12' 6" office/workshop was designed and built for Roger Bates, a self-employed airport consultant who had worked for several years from his home. He decided to build a separate workspace on his property that would reflect the architecture of his existing house.

The house had exposed beams and brick walls, reminiscent of the architecture in the Cotswolds, England. He wanted his new office (see photo page 162) to be built in the same style, while at the same time incorporating all his office requirements (see Figs. 4.1 to 4.6).

Photo: Karl Sarpalius

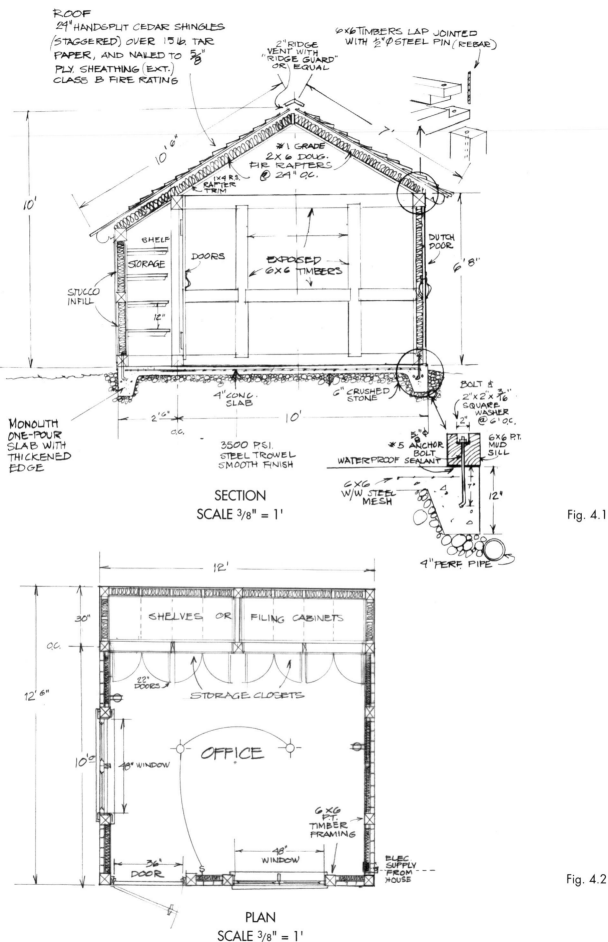

ROOF
24" HANDSPLIT CEDAR SHINGLES
(STAGGERED) OVER 15 lb. TAR
PAPER, AND NAILED TO 5/8"
PLY. SHEATHING (EXT.)
CLASS B FIRE RATING

2" RIDGE
VENT WITH
"RIDGE GUARD"
OR EQUAL

6×6 TIMBERS LAP JOINTED
WITH 1/2"Ø STEEL PIN (REBAR)

#1 GRADE
2×6 DOUG.
FIR RAFTERS
@ 24" O.C.

10'6"

1×4 R.S.
RAFTER
TRIM

SHELF

STORAGE

DOORS

EXPOSED
6×6 TIMBERS

DUTCH
DOOR

10'

6'8"

STUCCO
INFILL

12"

MONOLITH
ONE-POUR
SLAB WITH
THICKENED
EDGE

2'6"

O.C.

4" CONC.
SLAB

10'

6" CRUSHED
STONE

3500 PSI.
STEEL TROWEL
SMOOTH FINISH

BOLT &
2"×2"×3/16"
SQUARE
WASHER
@ 6' O.C.

2"

5/8"Ø
#5 ANCHOR
BOLT
WATERPROOF SEALANT

6×6 P.T.
MUD
SILL

6×6
W/W STEEL
MESH

7"

12"

4" PERF. PIPE

SECTION
SCALE 3/8" = 1'

Fig. 4.1

12'

30"

SHELVES   OR   FILING CABINETS

O.C.

12'6"

22"
DOORS

STORAGE CLOSETS

10'0"

48" WINDOW

OFFICE

6×6
P.T.
TIMBER
FRAMING

36"
DOOR

48"
WINDOW

ELEC.
SUPPLY
FROM
HOUSE

Fig. 4.2

PLAN
SCALE 3/8" = 1'

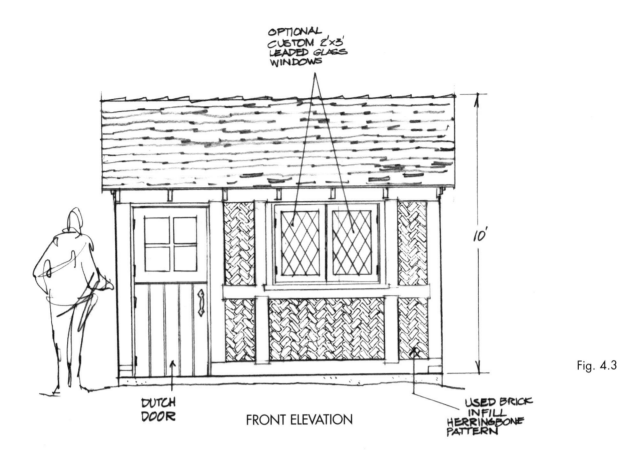

OPTIONAL
CUSTOM 2'x3'
LEADED GLASS
WINDOWS

10'

DUTCH
DOOR

FRONT ELEVATION

USED BRICK
INFILL
HERRINGBONE
PATTERN

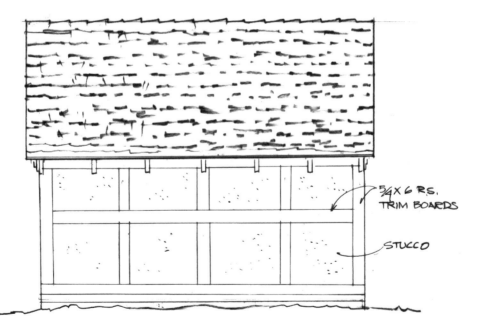

3/4 X 6 R.S.
TRIM BOARDS

STUCCO

REAR ELEVATION

Fig. 4.3

Fig. 4.4

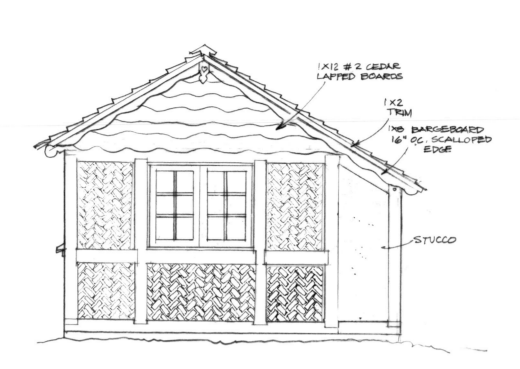

1X12 #2 CEDAR
LAPPED BOARDS

1×2 TRIM

1×8 BARGEBOARD
16" O.C. SCALLOPED
EDGE

STUCCO

SOUTH SIDE ELEVATION

Fig. 4.5

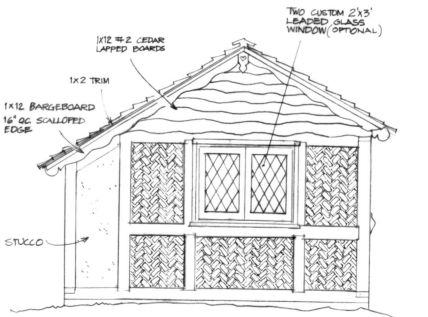

TWO CUSTOM 2'x3'
LEADED GLASS
WINDOW (OPTIONAL)

1X12 #2 CEDAR
LAPPED BOARDS

1×2 TRIM

1×12 BARGEBOARD
16" O.C. SCALLOPED
EDGE

STUCCO

NORTH SIDE ELEVATION

Fig. 4.6

# Concrete Floor

There are several types of concrete foundations – the one that most people are familiar with is the typical poured or block foundation used in most homes in the United States and Canada. This type of foundation generally has a full basement or a shallow crawl space, which is unnecessary for a small building. The foundation we recommend, and one that is easy to build, is the monolithic slab foundation, which is only 4" thick everywhere, except at the edges, where it is 24" thick. This thickened edge, called the "footing," keeps the slab from shifting and supports the weight of the wall above it. The nice thing about it is that it can all be poured at one time by only two or three people. To keep it from cracking in the future, 6" x 6" welded wire mesh and ½" reinforcing bar are embedded in the concrete during the pour. In severely cold climates, stone or gravel is laid in a trench under the slab to drain off any water that might accumulate and freeze, causing the foundation to heave.

To pour the slab, remember that the chute on the concrete truck will reach no farther than 20 feet from the building site. Check to make sure there are no underground plumbing pipes or electric lines that could be damaged and that you have clearance of 8' wide and 15' high for the concrete truck to pass under tree branches. You can help protect your lawn by laying sheets of ¾" plywood on the grass to distribute the weight of the truck's wheels.

Don't be afraid to pour your own slab foundation. We did it with no previous experience and with good results. Simply follow the steps below.

Start by clearing the area where the workshop will go by removing any roots, bushes, rocks or stumps. Level the site by removing soil from any high areas and placing it on lower areas. Clear a 3'-wide area around the intended building site to allow room for working and to make a level surface for your ladder later on during construction. Locate the four corners of your workshop by establishing one corner as a constant.

The next step is to dig a 30"-wide trench around the perimeter of the footprint and to remove a layer of soil inside the footprint. How much soil you remove depends on the frost level in your area and how much gravel you will be using under the slab. For example, if you plan on using 6" of gravel, your finished slab is 4" thick and the top of the slab will be 8" above the original grade, then you only need to remove 2" of dirt from inside the perimeter footprint. Check with your building department to determine what is recommended in your area. The 4"-diameter drainpipe will be situated outside and slightly below the footing. The trench around the footprint should be wide enough to fit both the form boards and the drainpipe. In addition, the footing needs to be 12" wide at the bottom, sloping up to 24" wide at the top, to provide for the thickened edge of the slab.

Once the area is excavated, the next step is to tamp down or compact the soil, especially any areas that have been disturbed, for instance, where stumps or large rocks have been dug up and backfilled. Once this is done, lay down a sheet of 4-mil plastic to act as a moisture barrier, then fill the excavated area with 6" of gravel.

The forms are built using either ¾" plywood or stacked-up 2x8 boards. Build the forms so that the inside dimension is exactly the same as the intended outside dimension of your workshop.

Ensure that the forms are level and square, as this will affect the remaining construction. Use 2x4s to back up the joint where the form boards are joined together and use 2x4s as braces (kickers) every 4' (see Fig. 4.7). When the forms are complete give them a coat of recycled motor oil to make it easier to strip the forms when the concrete has hardened.

Before you consider mixing the concrete by hand and transporting it by wheelbarrow, take into consideration that concrete weighs 150 pounds per cubic foot, or over two tons per cubic yard. A wheelbarrow filled with wet concrete can weigh as much as 220 pounds! My first attempt at lifting a full wheelbarrow of concrete tipped over, leaving a hardened puddle of concrete on the ground.

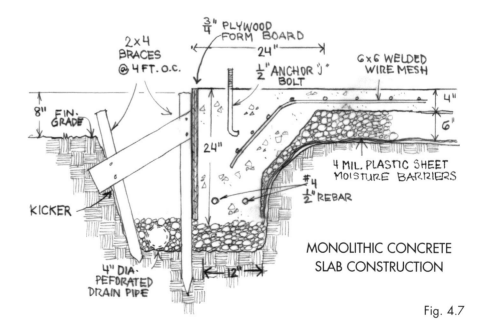

MONOLITHIC CONCRETE SLAB CONSTRUCTION

Fig. 4.7

Next comes the rebar and the 6x6 welded wire mesh, which should be delivered before the cement arrives. Rebar comes in 20' lengths and the 6x6 welded wire mesh comes in 4'-wide, 150'-long rolls. You can cut the rebar to the required lengths fairly easily using a hacksaw, or have it cut at the masonry yard with a mechanical cutter. Space the reinforcing bars 6" apart and parallel to each other near the bottom of the trench. Bend the pieces to fit around the corners and tie them with wire so they overlap the straight pieces of rebar by 12". Prop the rebar up with pieces of stone or bricks so that the bars will be totally embedded in the concrete once it is poured.

Unroll the wire mesh and cut it with bolt cutters so that it covers the entire length of the foundation hole and angles down into the footing. Overlap the edges of the mesh strips by 6". Place bricks under the mesh as you did under the rebar. To strengthen the connection of the footing to the slab, use wire to tie pieces of bent rebar to the wire mesh and the bar into the footing trench.

## Ordering concrete

The concrete is delivered in ready-mix concrete trucks and should be ordered the day before, after you are sure of the weather (over 50°F/10°C) and have lined up your helpers. You will probably need Type 1 concrete with a PSI rating of 35,000 pounds. If you are mixing it yourself, you will most likely need a ratio of 1 part Portland cement, 2 parts sand and 4 parts gravel; however, this can vary from area to area. Call your concrete supplier in advance, tell him what you are building and get his advice. Also, tell him to send an experienced driver with the load who can direct you and your crew on the "pour," and tip him when you are finished. Another option is to hire an experienced mason for the few hours it takes to do the pour and finish the surface.

Most concrete trucks come with troughs, or "chutes," that can reach 10 to 12 feet from the truck. If you need the truck to reach a longer distance, they can bring along extra troughs. But you must tell them in advance. Also, ask them how much time they will give you to make the pour, and if there is an extra fee if it takes longer. Note: Concrete typically begins to harden in two to three hours, depending on the conditions.

Concrete is sold by the cubic yard. To figure out how much concrete to order, use the following formula. Multiply length x width x thickness of the slab. Add another cubic foot times the perimeter of the footing, and an additional 8 percent to play it safe. Divide the total number by 27 to convert the amount into cubic yards.

## Preparation for the pour

You will need one or two helpers, depending on the size of the slab. Ensure you have a cell phone or access to a phone to confirm delivery of the transit mix.

Be prepared to get right to work when the truck arrives. Wet cement invariably gets on your hands, so rub moisturizing cream on them before putting on your gloves. Start pouring at the far end. Have your helpers push the concrete around with rakes so it is a little high and, using two people, strike off the top with a straight 2x4 screed, using a zigzag motion (see Fig. 4.8). Use shovels to fill in any

STRIKING OFF CONCRETE WITH A SCREED          Fig. 4.8

low spots and tap the sides of the forms lightly to get rid of any air bubbles. After a few minutes, the aggregate in the pour will begin to

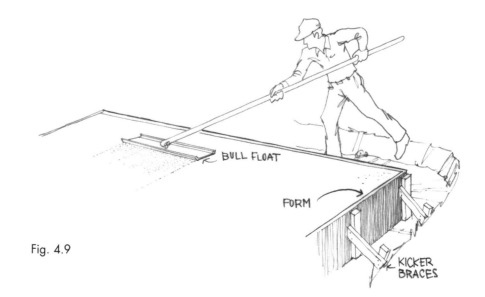

Fig. 4.9

settle, leaving a slushy residue on the surface. This is your signal to use the bull float to begin smoothing the surface with a slow forward and backward motion (see Fig. 4.9).

Before the concrete hardens, sink ½" anchor "J" bolts into it 1' from the end of each corner, and 4' to 6' on center. Make sure to leave enough of the anchor bolt exposed so that it can reach through a sill baseplate and a washer and nut can be screwed onto it. Make sure not to put anchor bolts where there will be any studs or a doorway.

## Drying

Concrete doesn't need air to dry. In fact, it can harden under water and actually "cures" due to a chemical reaction. Depending on the weather, concrete can harden to "walk-on condition" in several hours, but it is best to wait a day. Unlike almost all other materials it actually gains in strength the longer it remains in place; however, its near maximum strength is 28 days. In the meantime it is important to keep it moist during the first week by covering it with a sheet of plastic. Check it periodically to make sure it is not drying out, and sprinkle it with water if necessary.

## *Post-and-Beam Construction*

This Cotswold office/workshop is built using post-and-beam framing, not to be confused with timber framing. The latter is a traditional, highly respected method of framing that uses mortise-and-tenon joints and is more difficult to construct (see Figs. 4.10 and 4.11). Post-and-beam framing uses very simple joints that can be made in a matter of minutes, using either large nails, lag screws, pegs or rebar to hold the beams together. The basic post-and-beam joint is a simple lap joint, used where two beams come together (see Fig. 4.12). All the necessary joints can be cut quickly using a portable circular saw and chisel, and fewer pieces of lumber are required than when building a wall out of 2x4s. However, it still costs about three times more to build a post-and-beam wall using 4x6s than to build the same size wall using 2x4s. You will need to use a large circular saw since a 7½" blade will not cut through a full 4" timber.

EXAMPLE OF TIMBER FRAMING

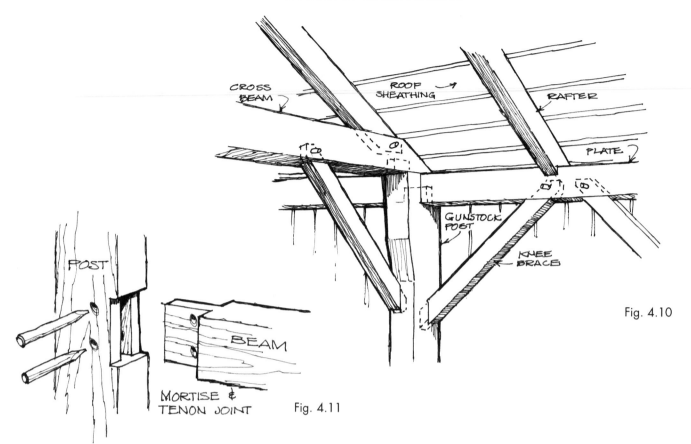

CROSS BEAM

ROOF SHEATHING

RAFTER

PLATE

GUNSTOCK POST

KNEE BRACE

Fig. 4.10

POST

BEAM

MORTISE & TENON JOINT

Fig. 4.11

Knee braces are an essential part of post-and-beam framing and give it the lateral strength needed to resist wind pressure. In timber framing, these are painstakingly mortised and pegged into the beams, while in post-and-beam framing, you can simply attach the 4x4 braces using lag screws and, if you like, cover up the screw heads with wooden pegs (see Fig. 4.12).

POST-AND-BEAM FRAMING

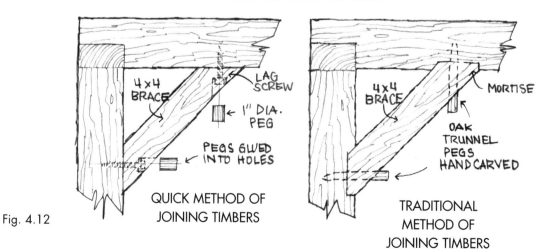

4x4 BRACE

LAG SCREW

1" DIA. PEG

PEGS GLUED INTO HOLES

QUICK METHOD OF JOINING TIMBERS

4x4 BRACE

MORTISE

OAK TRUNNEL PEGS HANDCARVED

TRADITIONAL METHOD OF JOINING TIMBERS

Fig. 4.12

Based on the dimensions of your slab, begin framing the structure by cutting all the sill timbers to length. Lay them next to the slab and mark where the anchor bolts will extend through the sill beams. Drill slightly oversized holes to receive the anchor bolts. Set the beams on sawhorses and cut the end lap joints (see Fig. 4.13).

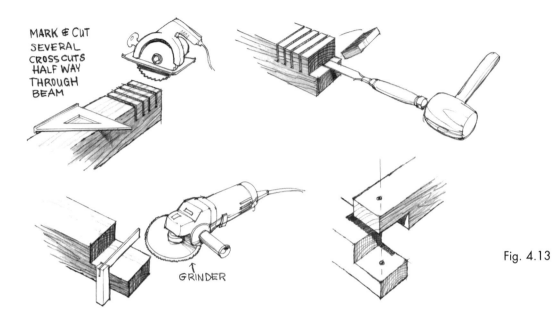

MARK & CUT SEVERAL CROSS CUTS HALF WAY THROUGH BEAM

GRINDER

Fig. 4.13

After chipping out the waste wood with a chisel, use a coarse grinder or rasp to smooth the surface. Put a strip of sill sealer around the

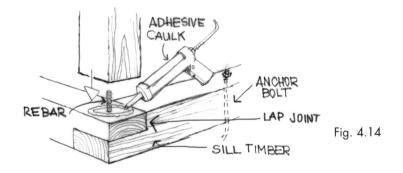

ADHESIVE CAULK

ANCHOR BOLT

REBAR

LAP JOINT

SILL TIMBER

Fig. 4.14

perimeter of the slab to keep out drafts and prevent insects from crawling into the workshop. Lay the sill beams over the sealer strips and tighten the anchor bolts. Drill ½"-diameter holes in the corners, where the sill timbers meet, and pound a 10" piece of ½"-diameter rebar into each hole (see Fig. 4.14). Cut the four corner posts to length and drill oversized-diameter holes in the ends of the posts to accept the rebar. Squeeze polyurethane caulking into the holes and drop the posts onto the rebar that extends up from the surface. Adjust the posts slightly so that they line up plumb with the corners. Use two sticks to brace each post (see Fig. 4.15). Cut the "laps" on the ends of the top beams, and cut the ½"-deep mortises to accept the vertical posts for door and window openings.

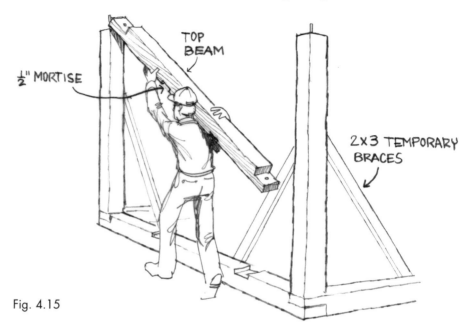

Fig. 4.15

Place the beams on the posts. Drill ½"-diameter holes through the lapped ends of the beams and into the tops of the posts, and hammer a 10" piece of rebar into the holes to lock them together. Measure, mark and cut the posts that will frame the doors and windows. Cut, mortise and install the windowsills.

## Brick Walls

Before filling in the walls of the workshop with bricks it is necessary to fill in the space between the beams with a light framing of 2x3s and ½" cement board as a backup for the herringbone brick facing. Once this is done, you are ready to lay the bricks. We recommend using recycled old bricks. Because these bricks are salvaged from buildings that are torn down, inspect them before buying them to make sure that the cement has been removed from the back (see Figs. 4.16 to 4.18).

Because of the labor involved to clean old brick, it is slightly more expensive than new brick. Standard-size bricks weigh approximately

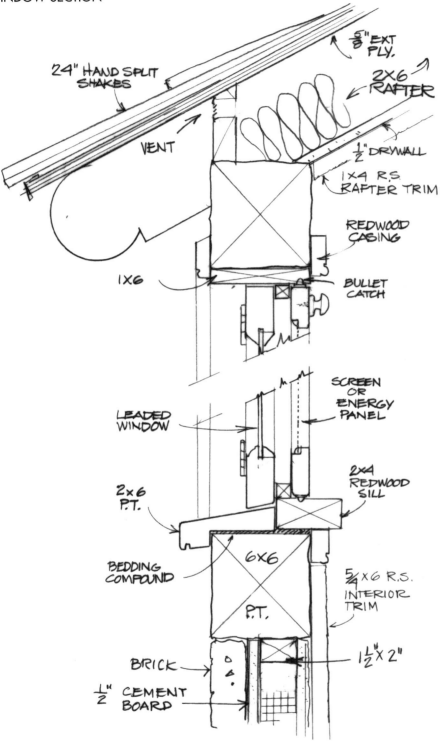

$\frac{5}{8}$" EXT PLY.

24" HAND SPLIT SHAKES

2x6 RAFTER

VENT

$\frac{1}{2}$" DRYWALL

1X4 R.S. RAFTER TRIM

REDWOOD CASING

1X6

BULLET CATCH

SCREEN OR ENERGY PANEL

LEADED WINDOW

2x4 REDWOOD SILL

2x6 P.T.

BEDDING COMPOUND

6X6

P.T.

$\frac{5}{4}$ X6 R.S. INTERIOR TRIM

BRICK

$1\frac{1}{2}$" X 2"

$\frac{1}{2}$" CEMENT BOARD

**Masonry tools you will need**

- 4' level
- Yellow mason's string
- Measuring tape
- Wooden mallet
- 11" mason's trowel
- Plastic mortar-mixing pan
- Mason's hoe
- Jointer or "strike" tool
- 24" x 24" mortar board
- Stiff brush
- Bags of mortar cement
- Carrying tongs (optional)

Fig. 4.16

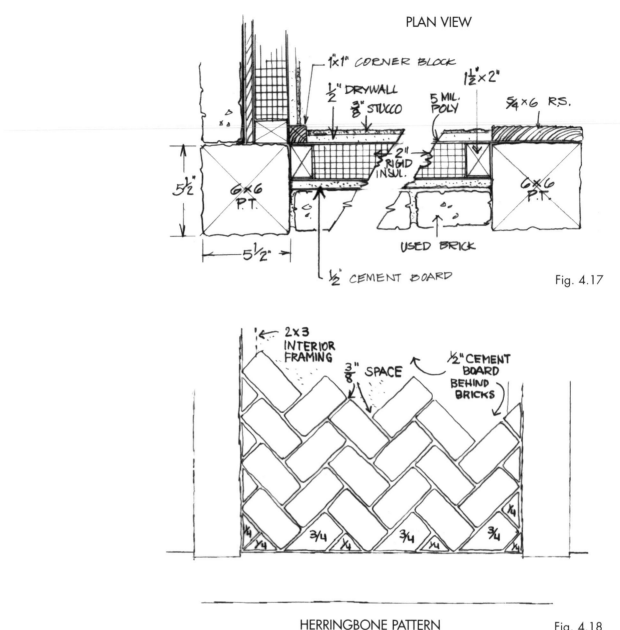

PLAN VIEW

1"x1" CORNER BLOCK
1½" DRYWALL
⅜" STUCCO
5 MIL. POLY
1½"x2"
⅝x6 R.S.
5½"
6x6 P.T.
2" RIGID INSUL.
6x6 P.T.
5½"
USED BRICK
½" CEMENT BOARD

Fig. 4.17

2x3 INTERIOR FRAMING
⅜" SPACE
½" CEMENT BOARD BEHIND BRICKS
¼
¾
¼
¾
¼
¾
¼

HERRINGBONE PATTERN

Fig. 4.18

4½ pounds and measure approximately 8" long, 3¾" wide and 2½" high. They can, however, vary slightly in size from one manufacturer to another. Bricks are usually sold by the pallet. One pallet contains approximately 500 bricks, and pallets can be delivered by a masonry supplier for a delivery charge. When you are planning how many bricks you will need, figure on seven bricks per square foot of wall. One 70-pound bag of mortar mix should be enough to cement 125 bricks to a wall.

Mix the mortar with water by forming a depression in a pile of cement and adding water a little at a time. Fold the dry mortar into the pool of water and mix with a hoe. Gradually add more water until the mix is the consistency of soft ice cream, not too dry or sloppy (wet). While you are working, add a little water periodically and mix it in to keep the same consistency.

Unless you are a skilled mason, you are probably better off cutting the bricks with a masonry saw rather than a trowel or chisel. To do this, either rent a masonry saw or make your own by buying a masonry saw blade and attaching it to your circular saw (see Fig. 4.19). Set up a makeshift table on sawhorses and construct a jig to hold the bricks while you cut them. Use a hose with a fine spray nozzle, fixed to the table, so that you can direct a light spray of water onto the masonry blade while you are cutting the bricks. This will eliminate a great deal of dust and reduce the amount of wear on your blade. Mark and cut the bricks on both sides partway through, and break the bricks apart using a wooden mallet.

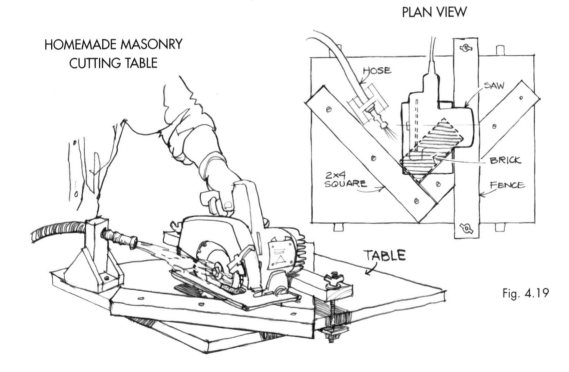

PLAN VIEW

HOMEMADE MASONRY
CUTTING TABLE

HOSE

SAW

2x4
SQUARE

BRICK

FENCE

TABLE

Fig. 4.19

If you are working in the sun or on a hot day, sprinkle the bricks with water before laying them up to prevent them from soaking up the water in the mortar too fast, thus causing a weak joint. Starting at either of the bottom corners of the wall, and taking into account that there will be a small space filled with mortar around each brick, mark and cut a triangular brick to fill the corner space. Cover (butter) one end, the bottom and the back of each brick before placing it in the wall. Continue along the bottom until you reach the other side, then continue up the wall, adding bricks in a herringbone pattern and filling in with triangle pieces on the sides. Check periodically to make sure that you are laying the bricks at a 45° angle. Granted, the herringbone pattern is more time-consuming, but it is well worth the effort when you are finished. A week later, after the cement has dried, use masonry cleaner to scrub off any splatters that have fallen on the face of the bricks.

## Finishing

The roof, windows and doors are built in the same manner as the workshop addition (see pages 47–53). Unlike other workshops, however, the interior walls are filled with 2" rigid foam insulation, covered with drywall and plastered with stucco. Built-in closets and shelves can be added to store office files. Add desks, chairs and a coffee maker and you are ready to get to work.

We encourage you to modify the basic plan to suit your requirements. Here are some options that you might consider:

- Increase the length by 4' to make it 16' wide or even longer.
- Extend the sloping rear roof to provide an open storage area for bicycles, lawn equipment or firewood.
- Reduce the side windows from double to single to reduce cost.
- Change the roof from a double-pitched gable to a single-pitched shed (see Roof Styles, page 20).
- Use 2x6 studs instead of 6x6 posts and beams to reduce cost.
- Make the roof flat, not double-pitched as shown.
- Use radiant heating in the floor.
- Add a skylight to the roof.
- Build the workshop on blocks instead of a concrete slab.

# Writer's Retreat

This writer's retreat was built for our friends Shari and Art, who wanted a small structure separate from their house where they could write without interruption. This small cabin (see photo page 162) would also be an ideal space for a musician to practice or a jeweler to work in. Although small in size, the workshop could be enlarged without compromising the proportions (see Figs. 4.20 and 4.21).

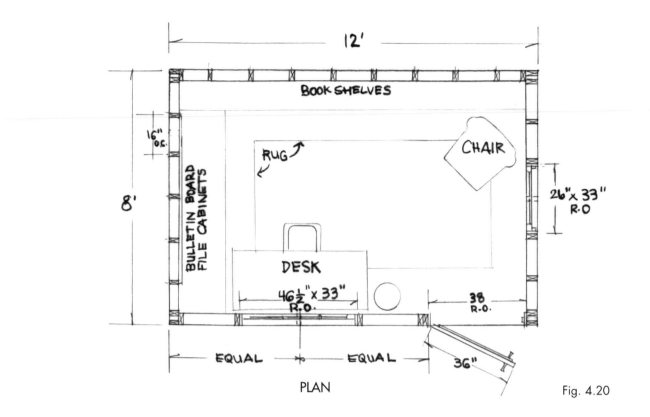

PLAN

Fig. 4.20

From the outside it appears to be timber-framed (to match the owner's house), but is actually built using conventional 2x4s to reduce the cost and simplify construction. The entire structure is sheathed in ½"-thick cement board. Since the cement board measures 3' x 4', 2x4 "cats" (nailers) are installed between the studs 3' up from the floor. Special cement-board screws are required for this purpose. They should be countersunk slightly so they are flush with the surface of the board.

After sheathing the building in cement board, 1x6 rough-sawn cedar is nailed (using 3" finishing nails) to the corners and across the sides and back to create the timber-framed look. The cedar trim is stained a gray-brown to match the main house, then a ¼" to ⅜" coat of stucco is applied to the cement board. To keep the stucco from getting on the stained boards, we used 1"-wide blue painter's tape. As a final touch, ¾"-diameter pegs are cut and glued into holes to simulate timber-pegged construction.

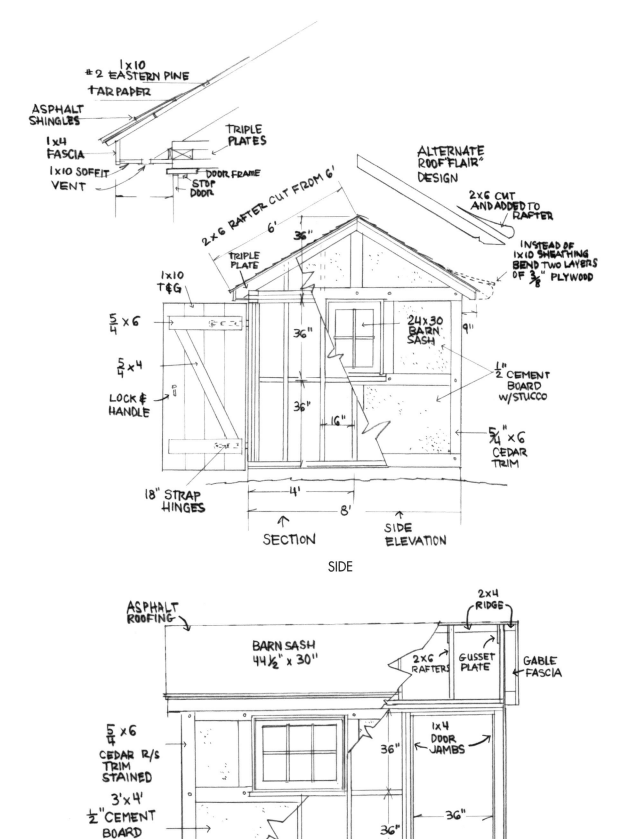

1x10
#2 EASTERN PINE
TAR PAPER

ASPHALT
SHINGLES

1x4
FASCIA

1x10 SOFFIT
VENT

TRIPLE
PLATES

DOOR FRAME
STOP
DOOR

ALTERNATE
ROOF "FLAIR"
DESIGN

2x6 CUT
AND ADDED TO
RAFTER

INSTEAD OF
1x10 SHEATHING
BEND TWO LAYERS
OF $\frac{3}{8}$" PLYWOOD

2x6 RAFTER CUT FROM 6'

6'

36"

TRIPLE
PLATE

1x10
T&G

$\frac{5}{4}$ x 6

$\frac{5}{4}$ x 4

LOCK &
HANDLE

36"

36"

16"

24x30
BARN
SASH

9"

$\frac{1}{2}$" CEMENT
BOARD
w/STUCCO

$\frac{5}{4}$" x 6
CEDAR
TRIM

18" STRAP
HINGES

4'

8'

SECTION

SIDE
ELEVATION

SIDE

ASPHALT
ROOFING

2x4
RIDGE

BARN SASH
44½" x 30"

2x6
RAFTERS

GUSSET
PLATE

GABLE
FASCIA

$\frac{5}{4}$ x 6
CEDAR R/S
TRIM
STAINED

3' x 4'
½" CEMENT
BOARD
w/STUCCO

36"

36"

1x4
DOOR
JAMBS

36"

48"

FRONT

Fig. 4.21

# Asphalt Roofing

Red asphalt shingles were used to match the owner's house. Since the roof is left exposed inside the building, we used rough-sawn 1"-thick eastern pine boards. These produce a more traditional look than plywood and provide enough thickness for the roofing nails to hold the asphalt shingles without poking through the pine. This, of course, is not necessary if you plan on insulating and paneling the interior with drywall or some other material.

Asphalt shingles come in many different styles and colors; each is rated with a different "life" depending on the cost and the material. To give the impression of weathered wood shingles, you can purchase "architectural style" shingles that create an undulating shadow line at the bottom edge of the shingle.

Before you start shingling, make sure your fascia and cove moldings are in place, and the gable and eaves are edged with aluminum drip edge strips (sold in 10' lengths at your local lumberyard). Once the drip edge is on, cover the entire roof surface with 15-pound tarpaper.

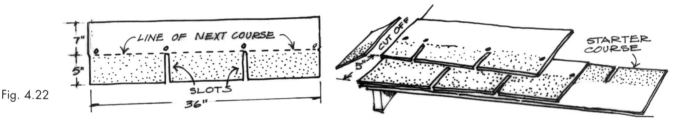

Fig. 4.22

Begin by nailing the first course of shingles on upside down (with the tabs pointing up), allowing a slight overlap at the edges and sides. Using a framing square, cut any remaining material off with a utility knife. This starter course provides an unbroken base for the next course, which is applied directly over the first course, but with the tabs pointing down (see Fig. 4.22). Nail four galvanized roofing nails just above the slots of each shingle. Before starting the next row, cut the first shingle in half so that the joints are staggered from row to row. Each row must be offset by one-half a tab from the preceding row so that the slots do not line up. Each row of shingles should be 5" above the preceding one and just barely covering the top of the slots. Once you have put on six or seven rows, measure down from the ridge to see if the rows are even. If they are not, adjust each remaining row slightly so that the rows end up even at the top.

To cover the top ridge, cut the shingles into thirds and taper the top portion of the shingle so the edges will be hidden. Starting at one end, bend each ridge tab over the top and secure with two nails (see Fig. 4.23).

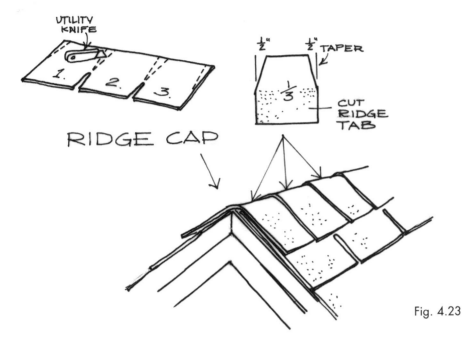

Fig. 4.23

## Homemade Windows and Screens

The windows are handmade, both to save time in ordering them and for aesthetic reasons. For approximately $25 in materials and five hours in the shop, the two windows rival anything you could buy. Because very little wood is required, you can afford to buy the very best type of wood, even mahogany. We chose clear cedar because of its resistance to weather. Using a table saw, you can rip all the pieces needed out of a single piece of 2x6 (see Fig. 4.24).

The reason we like this design is because the windows can be easily removed for cleaning, painting or maintenance and at the same time can be held securely in place by a simple transom catch. Since the window tilts in at the top, it can be left open in the summer without fear of rain coming in. Although it looks like four separate

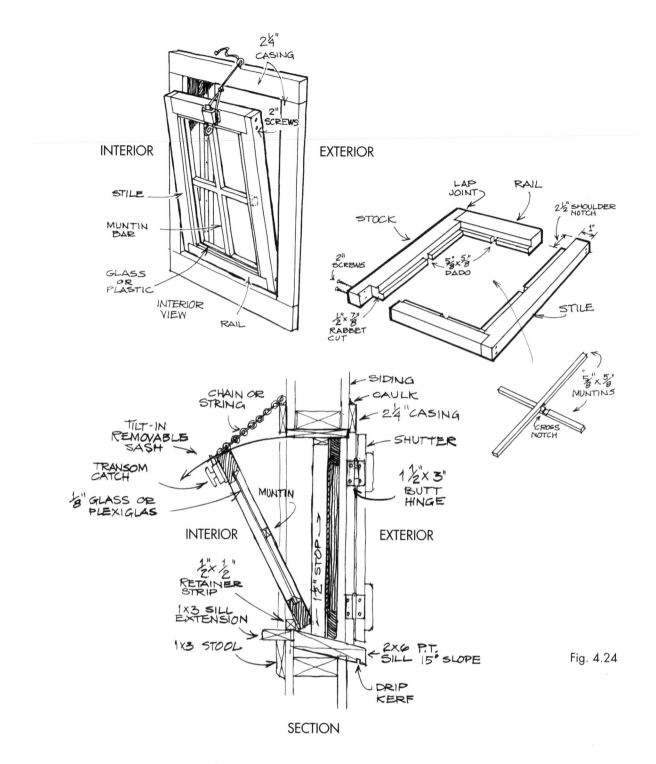

Fig. 4.24

panes, it's actually just one piece of Plexiglas, which can easily be cut with a table saw using a blade with many small teeth designed to cut plywood. The muntins or grilles are cut from the same piece of 2x6 cedar and are mortised to the rails and stiles on the outside of the Plexiglas. This makes the construction and the installation much simpler, and the windows, lacking muntins on one side, are easier to clean than most.

To make your own screens, use 1x3 boards (preferably red cedar) and join the boards at the corners using lap joints. Before assembling the pieces, cut a ⅛"-wide, ¼"-deep dado groove ½" from the inside edge of all the pieces. Then join the pieces together using waterproof glue and brass brads. Once the glue has dried, cut a piece

MAKING SCREENS

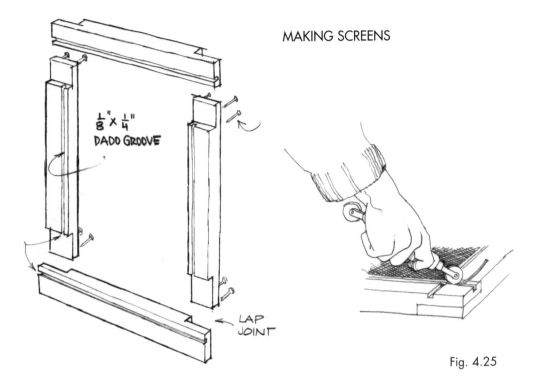

Fig. 4.25

of insect screening 1" wider on all sides than the inside opening of the window frame. Fit a flexible rope, called "screen retaining spline," into the groove. Use the tool sold particularly for this purpose to press the rope and the screen into the groove of the window frame. It may help to have someone hold the screening taut while you are doing this. Cut off any excess screening with a utility knife (see Fig. 4.25).

# Carpenter's Workshop

This 18' x 14' workshop is suitable for many different types of activities. Although here it is a woodworking shop, it can easily be adapted to be used as a pottery shop, an antique car repair shop or a sculpture studio, just to mention a few uses. We know of one couple that has built this workshop and are using it as a blacksmith shop (see Figs. 4.26 and 4.27).

Fig. 4.26

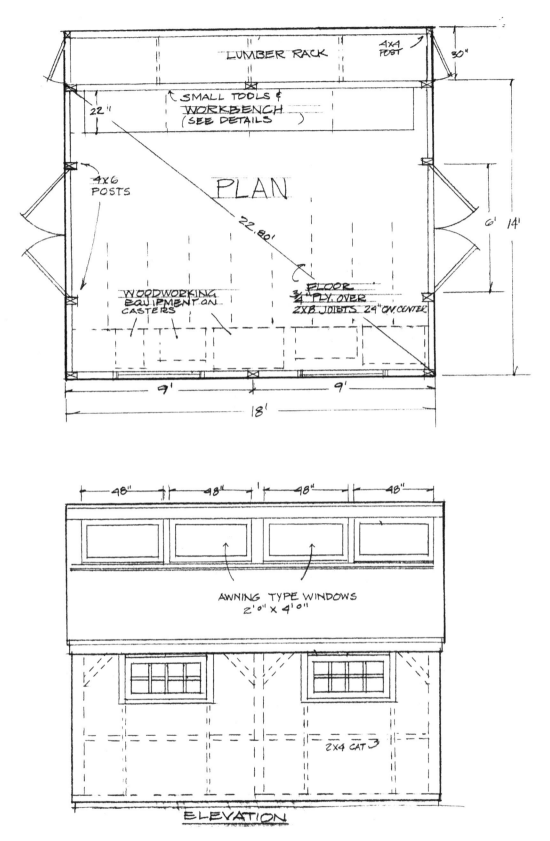

LUMBER RACK          4X4 POST          30"

SMALL TOOLS &
WORKBENCH
(SEE DETAILS)

22"

4X6 POSTS

PLAN

22.80'

6'   14'

WOODWORKING
EQUIPMENT ON
CASTERS

FLOOR
¾" PLY OVER
2X8 JOISTS 24" ON CENTER

9'          9'

18'

48"          48"          48"          48"

AWNING TYPE WINDOWS
2'0" X 4'0"

2X4 CAT 3

ELEVATION

Fig. 4.27

In our design, as a carpenter's workshop, we have suggested a layout for woodworking tools and equipment. The large doors on opposite ends of the building can be opened, allowing long boards to be rip cut without running into a wall. Keeping the doors open also makes it nice for anyone working in the shop on a hot summer day. For added ventilation a vent could be installed on both ends near the roof peak, allowing hot air to escape. In the winter the doors can be closed and the workshop heated by a wood-burning stove, using leftover scraps of lumber (see Fig. 4.28).

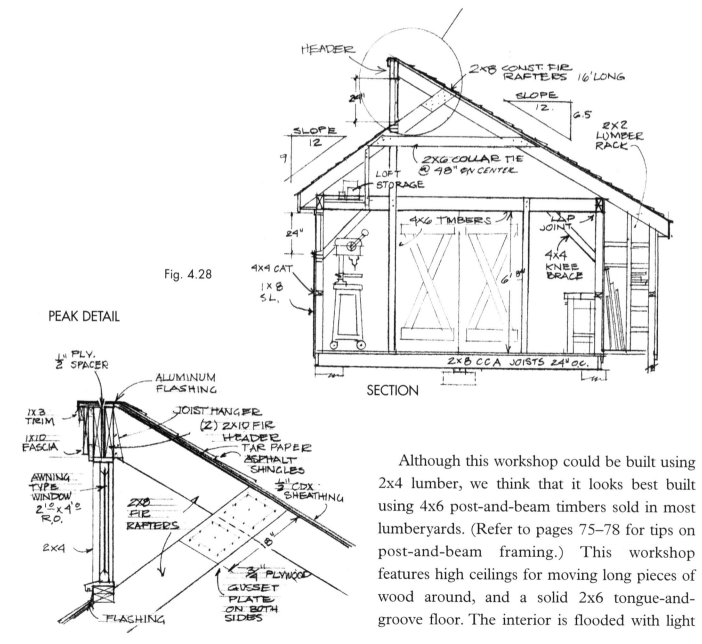

Fig. 4.28

Although this workshop could be built using 2x4 lumber, we think that it looks best built using 4x6 post-and-beam timbers sold in most lumberyards. (Refer to pages 75–78 for tips on post-and-beam framing.) This workshop features high ceilings for moving long pieces of wood around, and a solid 2x6 tongue-and-groove floor. The interior is flooded with light from the clerestory windows and the two side windows along the long wall. Awning windows can be bought at your local lumberyard or home building supply center, or you can make your own fixed glass windows to keep within a more modest budget. More light can be brought in by installing additional skylights (see page 57).

## *Interior Layout*

There is also room for benches and shelves, and an extra 30"-wide "lumber library" for storing long boards and panels of plywood. It

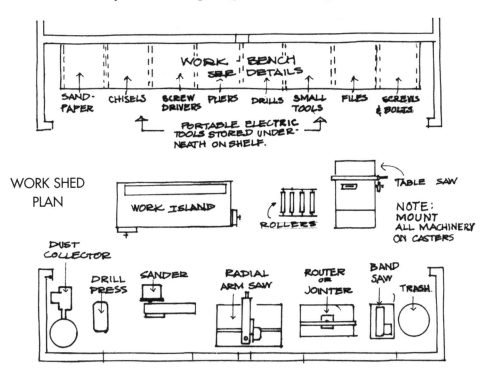

Fig. 4.29

can be accessed from both ends of the building, or this area can be left open to store firewood and other materials (see Fig. 4.29).

Start with a solid, level floor – either poured concrete slab or a simple wooden floor. Frame the shed using a lap joints and knee braces. Rough cedar timbers are lighter and look nice but any construction fir will also do. The rafters are butt-jointed near the peak with ½"-thick plywood gusset plates. The header at the peak (or ridge) is a combination of two pieces of 2x10 fir, 18' long, with a piece of ½"-thick plywood sandwiched between them. Build the trusses first, then build the header once the rafters are in place. You should have an assistant and safe scaffolding to build this part of the shed (see Fig. 4.30).

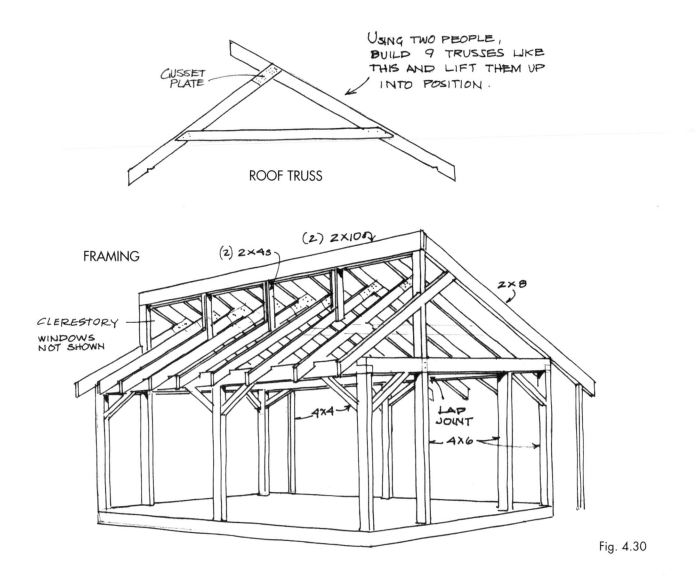

GUSSET PLATE

Using two people, build 9 trusses like this and lift them up into position.

ROOF TRUSS

FRAMING

(2) 2X4s

(2) 2X10s

2X8

CLERESTORY WINDOWS NOT SHOWN

4X4

LAP JOINT

4X6

Fig. 4.30

Cover the roof with plywood and shingle it with asphalt shingles. Buy six 4' x 2' rough-opening awning-type windows. Install two in the lower front wall and four in the clerestory. The two lower windows (sometimes called "stable windows") look nicer divided into eight panes; however, this does increase the cost.

Install 4x4 "cats" around the outside walls and cover the walls with 1x8 shiplapped northern pine. Build the doors out of exterior plywood braced with 5/4" x 6" battens. Use the leftover 2'-wide plywood for the doors in the lumber storage area. Build the lumber racks out of 2x2s, making sure to provide an area for large sheets of material.

## Carpenter's Workbench

You can build a workbench using 2x4s for frames and 3x12s for the top. Make drawers out of 1x6s and ¼" plywood. Attach 1x2 "cleats" to act as extensions so the drawer won't drop if it is pulled out too far (see Fig. 4.31).

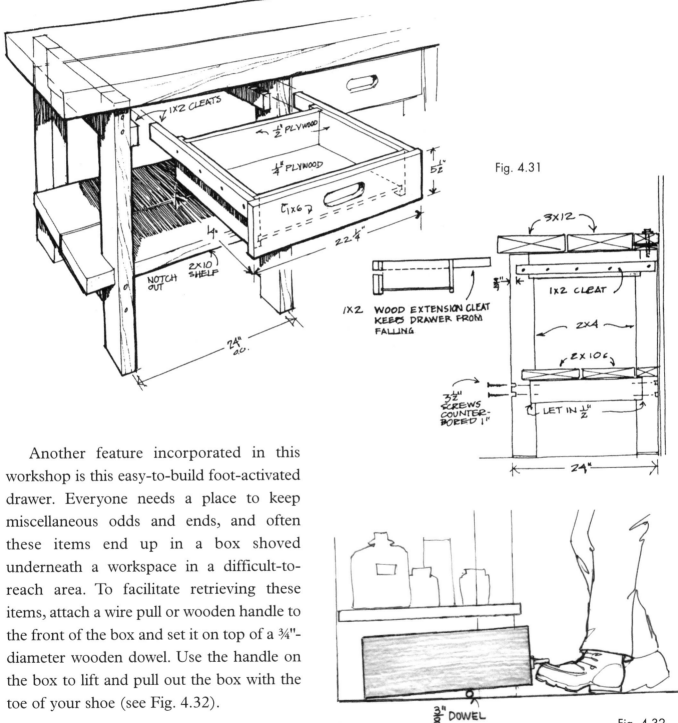

Fig. 4.31

Another feature incorporated in this workshop is this easy-to-build foot-activated drawer. Everyone needs a place to keep miscellaneous odds and ends, and often these items end up in a box shoved underneath a workspace in a difficult-to-reach area. To facilitate retrieving these items, attach a wire pull or wooden handle to the front of the box and set it on top of a ¾"-diameter wooden dowel. Use the handle on the box to lift and pull out the box with the toe of your shoe (see Fig. 4.32).

Fig. 4.32

# MORE WORKSHOPS AND STUDIOS

This chapter describes a variety of workshops, including some that are very specialized. But you can combine parts of one workshop and used them in another. For instance, the painting storage shown in the art studio might be used in the darkroom to store large photographs, and the layout of the architect's studio would be perfectly suitable for a home office. These workshop designs are intended to inspire the reader to design his or her own projects, altering the dimensions that follow when necessary, to suit their specific situation.

## Small Wookworking Shop

This woodworking shop (see photo page 176) is suitable for a weekend carpenter who has acquired enough tools to make repairs around the house and then some. It is 14' long and 10' wide. By extending the roof of the workshop on one side, a covered storage area for lumber, or "lumber library," is provided that is accessible from the front and back of the shop. This extension also gives the workshop a more interesting "saltbox" shape, which was compatible with the architecture of the area. The heavy woodworking equipment is lined up on the right side of the shop so that pieces of lumber can either be ripped on the table saw, cross-cut on a Hitachi sliding compound miter saw, cut on the band saw or sanded on the belt sander. All these pieces of equipment are at the same height, making it easy to slide boards across them. With the exception of the drill press, the other side of the workshop is devoted to hand tools, storage shelves and drawers. Both front and rear doors open for access and ventilation. Because the doors open at both ends, we can rip a board of any length without running into a wall (see Fig. 5.1).

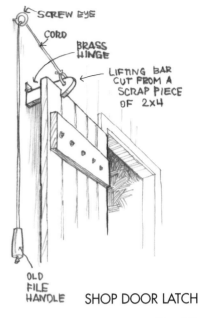

SHOP DOOR LATCH

Fig. 5.2

To prevent the shop door from banging in the wind, David built this nifty door latch. A notched wooden arm hinged to the outside of the workshop pivots up and catches the top edge of the door. Pulling on a rope with an old file handle at the end lifts up the arm and frees the door (see Fig. 5.2).

Fig. 5.1

There is plenty of lighting as a result of a row of windows on one side, plus an overhead skylight in the roof and a fixed triangular window at each peak. The windows are made from Plexiglas and, to date, have never leaked. There is also an exterior workbench for working outdoors when the weather is favorable. The building is framed with 4x6 cedar beams, covered with panels of 1" Homasote board insulation and sheathed with exterior plywood. The floor is covered with plywood. A wood floor has the advantage of becoming a "nailing jig" if you are bending or holding wood assemblies. Because this is a relatively small shop, it heats up quickly with only one portable electric heater.

# Dream Woodworking Shop

For the woodworker with enough property, and the energy and supplies to build a dream workshop, this 24' x 44' design is perfect. It is a unique one-man woodworking shop (see photo page 174) with plenty of light, room for all kinds of tools and machinery, and a 13' x 24' loft/gallery on the gable end of the structure opposite the front door. It is here that John Sutton displays his lanterns, handcrafted furniture and frames, and his wife, Leyla, displays her watercolors.

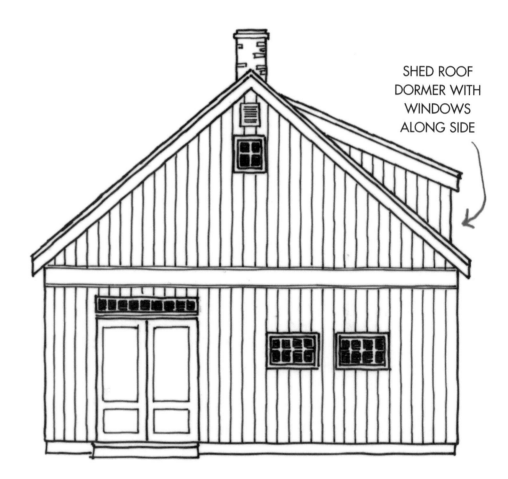

SHED ROOF
DORMER WITH
WINDOWS
ALONG SIDE

FRONT VIEW OF
JOHN SUTTON'S DREAM WOODWORKING SHOP
24' X 44'

Fig. 5.3

This shop was built by John, his brother and a few friends. It has 2x6 stud walls and 2x10 rafters and is heavily insulated. It is heated with a wood-burning stove, which keeps the shop at about 62°F to 65°F during winter days. The fire goes out at the end of the day, and the next morning the temperature is around 42°F; it takes approximately four hours to get the space back up to optimal temperature. Because of the high-efficiency dust collection system, the interior of the shop is, for the most part, dust-free (see Figs. 5.3 and 5.4).

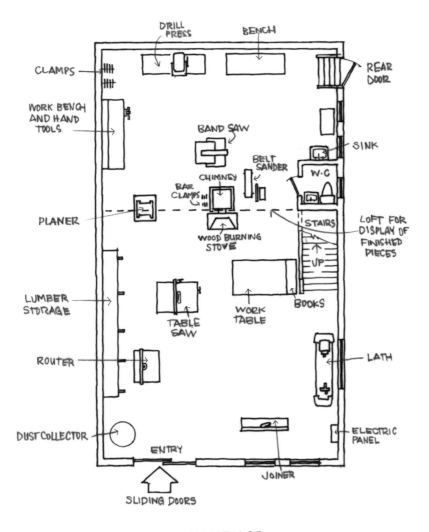

PLAN VIEW OF
JOHN SUTTON'S WOODWORKING SHOP
24' X 44'

Fig. 5.4

# Garage Woodworking Shop

Sam Meade, who lives and works at home in a traditional house in Massachusetts, needed space for a woodworking shop. A background of living on a farm as a boy and working as a carpenter during the summers gave him the necessary skills to tackle practically anything in the way of light construction.

Behind Sam's house stood an old, dilapidated one-car garage in need of new doors and some wall strengthening. The perfect place to build a new shop (see photo page 171) was alongside the garage; however, its low one-story roof didn't allow enough height for a sloped roof for the shop. Sam's solution was to raise the existing garage roof 4'. This would give the garage a loft where he could store extra furniture and lumber, while also allowing enough extra height for a sloping roof on the workshop (see Fig. 5.5).

After obtaining a building permit, Sam braced the interior of the garage with diagonal supports in preparation for the big lift. With the help of a good friend he cut the embedded nails that held the two top plates together, using a reciprocating saw. This left one 2x4 plate connected to the roof and the other 2x4 plate connected to the walls. Hydraulic jacks were put in place and the process of raising the roof began.

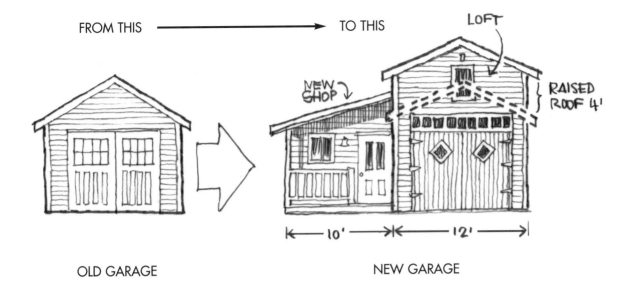

FROM THIS ⟶ TO THIS

LOFT

NEW SHOP ↓

RAISED ROOF 4'

OLD GARAGE

NEW GARAGE

⟵ 10' ⟶ ⟵ 12' ⟶

Fig. 5.5

After the roof was raised 6", previously prepared "shoring boxes" were slipped into place and the jacks were moved to a higher position. After working into the night, the roof was finally raised by 4'. Two 4'-high walls that had been previously built were slipped under the roof and nailed in place. The next day they began building the shop next to the garage. By the following weekend, the shop was framed out and new doors for the garage were set in place. By raising and using the same roof section, Sam saved money on materials; however, the job ultimately took about 10 hours.

With the structure completed, they were ready to move in the heavy woodworking equipment, which included a 3-horsepower, 220-amp table saw. Shelves on the attached side hold books and some small hand and power tools, plus projects in various stages of repair or construction.

During the planning stages, Sam cleverly positioned a window in the rear of the shop so those extra-long pieces of lumber could be cut on the table saw without running into a wall. He added a front porch, both for appearance and to create a place for his family to sit and enjoy the evening sunsets. Sam now has a fine woodworking shop, which cost under $2,500 in materials.

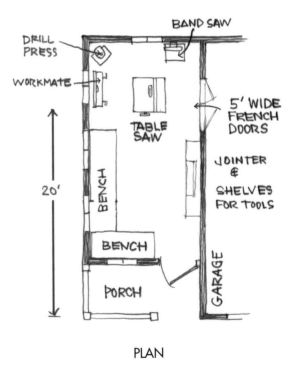

BAND SAW

DRILL PRESS

WORKMATE

TABLE SAW

20'

BENCH

BENCH

PORCH

5' WIDE FRENCH DOORS

JOINTER & SHELVES FOR TOOLS

GARAGE

PLAN

Fig. 5.6

# Ceramic Studios

We interviewed several ceramists and potters, all very different in their styles, and found that they share many of the same basic requirements for a working studio. The need for storage space comes first. Shelves are important to hold finished work, and should ideally be at least 16" deep to prevent pieces from falling off. One potter made shelves using reinforcement rods and ½" plywood. The shelves are adjustable and bracketed to the wall in order to keep them steady. Work tables on casters and shelving units help to create a versatile workspace that can be redesigned as different projects are being developed. And, of course, good ventilation and lighting are essential.

Several ceramic artists that we met had converted garages into workspaces. Nancy Robbins, of the Clay Art Guild in Sag Harbor, converted a garage into a potter's studio, doing the work herself. Her priority was separating the studio into three separate spaces: a clay room for "throwing" pots, a kiln and glazing room for firing and an office with a library and display shelves for finished work. One-third of the floor space is used for the art studio, kiln and glazing room; she also has private students and classes in the studio.

Isador Schiffman, another ceramics artist, also converted a garage into a workspace. Because the view looking out of the garage was a pleasing one, for most of the year he wanted to leave the garage door up. In order to enjoy the view and keep bugs and animals out, he stapled two fixed screen panels to a 1x2 nonstructural frame and installed a screen door. This also gave the room excellent ventilation, especially when the kiln was fired up to 220°F. (Many ceramists prefer to have the kiln outside, especially if they have a small workshop.)

Every studio needs a lot of wall space and tables that can be worked on or used for display. A worktable should be long enough to comfortably work with clay, apply glazes and throw pots. Six feet seems to be a good length. A damp room is important to keep clay moist while you are working on pieces before they are fired.

After interviewing several ceramists and potters, the voice of one, Connie Sherman, stands out: "It is important for any artist to design his or her own space, not an architect. You need to assess your specific needs and requirements and design and build them into your workspace to make it work for you." Another good tip: "Never store any ceramic pieces so high up that they can fall and give you a concussion!"

# Garage/Studio

This contemporary ceramic/painting studio (see photo page 175) sits on top of a 24' x 24' two-car garage. The challenge was to design a combination garage/workspace that would complement the architecture of Pamela Abrahams' existing house, and to build it for an affordable price. After several attempts to reconfigure the typical 24' x 24' gabled garage, we discovered that by turning the ridge 45° so that it rested on two diagonal corners, a totally different shape emerged, more compatible with the existing house (see Figs. 5.9 and 5.10). This could be done without adding to the cost of materials or sacrificing any space. By using the same materials and window treatment as the original house, the garage/studio ended up relating perfectly to the main house and looking as though it had been there forever.

Because of the steep slope of the land, three sides of the garage are set into the ground, and the fourth side (with the two garage doors) is at ground level. The foundation is concrete blocks covered with stucco. We built a deck outside of the workspace to provide a place to work during warm weather.

The studio has cold water plumbing with a drain that can be connected either to the house drain or to a septic system. The garage has room for two cars plus enough space to store some garden equipment (see Figs. 5.8, 5.11 and 5.12).

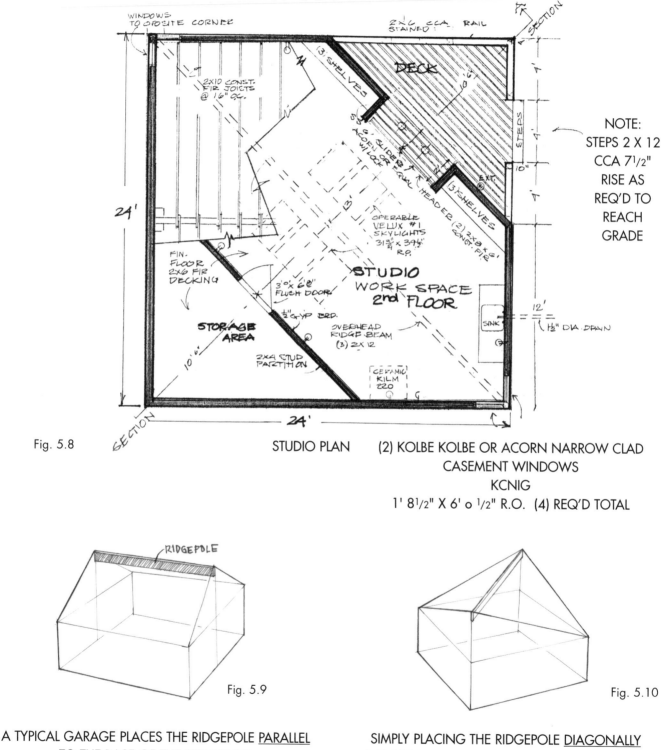

Fig. 5.8          STUDIO PLAN          (2) KOLBE KOLBE OR ACORN NARROW CLAD
CASEMENT WINDOWS
KCNIG
1' 8 1/2" X 6' o 1/2" R.O.  (4) REQ'D TOTAL

Fig. 5.9

A TYPICAL GARAGE PLACES THE RIDGEPOLE <u>PARALLEL</u>
TO THE BASE OF THE STRUCTURE.

Fig. 5.10

SIMPLY PLACING THE RIDGEPOLE <u>DIAGONALLY</u>
ACROSS THE BASE (FROM CORNER TO CORNER)
MAKES A MUCH MORE INTERESTING SHAPE EVOLVE.

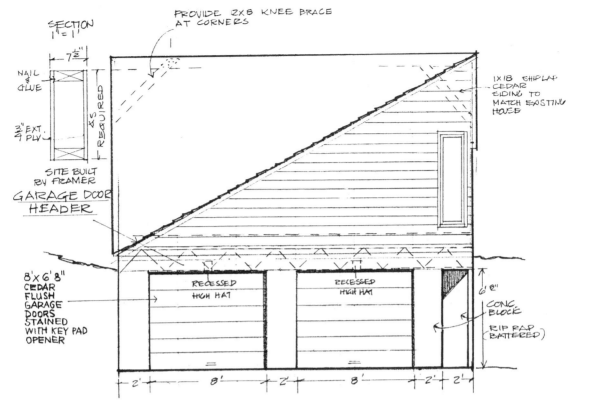

PROVIDE 2X8 KNEE BRACE AT CORNERS

SECTION
1"=1'

7½"

NAIL & GLUE

⅜" EXT. PLY.

X5 REQUIRED

SITE BUILT BY FRAMER
GARAGE DOOR HEADER

1X18 SHIPLAP CEDAR SIDING TO MATCH EXISTING HOUSE

8'x6'8" CEDAR FLUSH GARAGE DOORS STAINED WITH KEY PAD OPENER

RECESSED HIGH HAT

RECESSED HIGH HAT

6'8"

CONC. BLOCK

RIP RAP (BATTERED)

2'    8'    2'    8'    2'  2'

**SOUTH ELEVATION**

Fig. 5.11

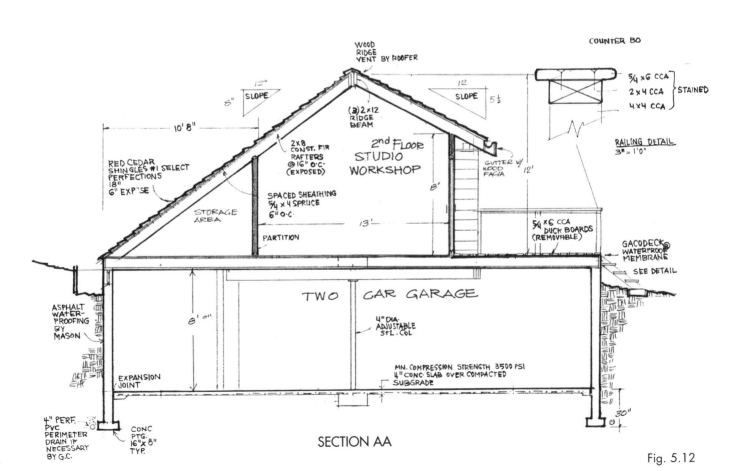

WOOD RIDGE VENT BY ROOFER

COUNTER BO

12"    8"    SLOPE

12    SLOPE    5½

5/4 x6 CCA
2 x4 CCA        STAINED
4 x4 CCA

10'8"

(3) 2x12 RIDGE BEAM

2nd FLOOR STUDIO WORKSHOP

RAILING DETAIL
3"=1'0"

RED CEDAR SHINGLES #1 SELECT PERFECTIONS 18" 6" EXP"SE

2x8 CONST. FIR RAFTERS @ 16" O.C. (EXPOSED)

GUTTER W/ WOOD FACIA

12'

8'

SPACED SHEATHING 5/4 x 4 SPRUCE 6" O.C.

STORAGE AREA

PARTITION

13'

5/4 x6 CCA DUCK BOARDS (REMOVABLE)

GACODECK® WATERPROOF MEMBRANE

SEE DETAIL

ASPHALT WATER-PROOFING BY MASON

TWO    CAR    GARAGE

8'-0"

4" DIA. ADJUSTABLE STL. COL.

EXPANSION JOINT

MIN. COMPRESSION STRENGTH 3500 PSI 4" CONC. SLAB OVER COMPACTED SUBGRADE

30"

4" PERF. PVC PERIMETER DRAIN IF NECESSARY BY G.C.

CONC. FTG. 16"X 8" TYP.

**SECTION AA**

Fig. 5.12

# Art Studio

When Ann and John Hulsey decided to move from the East Coast back to the Midwest, they began looking for a suitable place to set up their art studios. After an exhausting, fruitless search for a house with room for a workspace, a friend offered to sell them 14 acres of rural farmland outside of Lawrence, Kansas. This was the answer to their dreams, as they both wanted to be close to nature, both for their artwork (landscape painting) and to pursue their interest in gardening and landscaping (see Fig. 5.13).

Fig. 5.13

They set to work, on a limited budget, designing a house that would have adequate space for each of them to have a studio of their own. Their requirements included

○ several oversized windows on the north side of the house (to allow indirect light to fall on their canvases)
○ tall ceilings
○ thick, well-insulated walls
○ a small office on the top floor for their landscaping business
○ a cupola with an operating fan that would exhaust turpentine fumes

They designed a three-level house (see photo page 168) with a walkout lower level that serves as their living quarters. The second level, as viewed from the front, is the studio; it is divided into two separate workspaces separated by a central utility core and bathroom. The third level, accessed by a unique set of stairs, leads to their loft office. One of their friends, a local architect, helped to finalize their plans. Working with limited funds, they soon realized they could not afford to hand over the job to a general contractor, and consequently decided to contract out the bigger jobs and to do the remaining work themselves (see Fig. 5.14).

They began by making forms and pouring their own concrete floors, then relinquished the next phase, framing the house, to professional carpenters, electricians and insulation installers. They built and installed their own cabinets, doors and window trim, finished floors and plumbing. They hired professionals to drywall the walls, then painted them themselves with three coats of white paint. The result was a beautiful, bright, warm house to both live and work in.

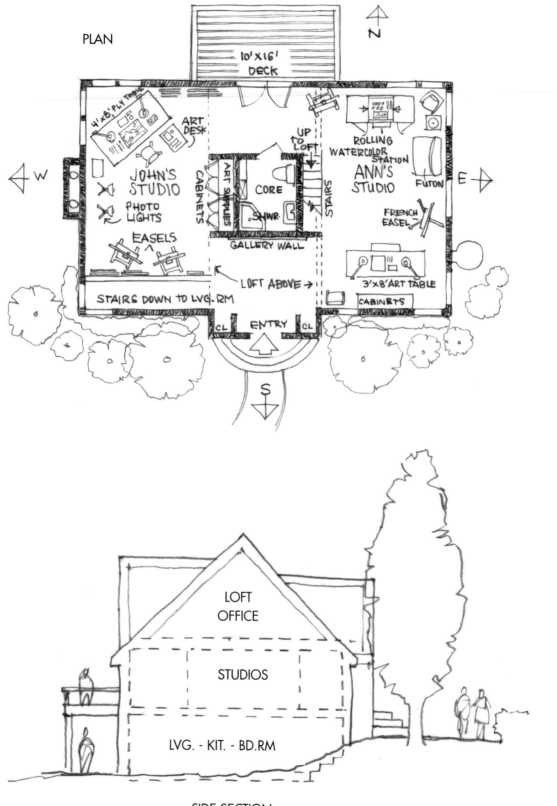

PLAN

N

10'X16'
DECK

W

4'x8' PLY TABLE
ART
DESK

JOHN'S
STUDIO

PHOTO
LIGHTS

EASELS

STAIRS DOWN TO LVG. RM

CABINETS

ART SUPPLIES

CORE

SHWR.

GALLERY WALL

UP
TO
LOFT

STAIRS

ROLLING
WATERCOLOR
STATION

ANN'S
STUDIO

FUTON

E

FRENCH
EASEL

3'x8' ART TABLE

CABINETS

LOFT ABOVE →

CL   ENTRY   CL

S

LOFT
OFFICE

STUDIOS

LVG. - KIT. - BD.RM

SIDE SECTION

Fig. 5.14

# Design Studio

When you are planning your design studio, take into consideration the equipment that you use and what your priorities are. Although computers and CAD systems have revolutionized the workspaces of many designers and architects, most offices still need a drafting table to spread out plans, even if they have been drawn up on the computer. Worktables are also essential for meetings and doing reference work.

The basic plan for this design studio (see Fig 5.15) is typical for an architectural firm. It allows room for both a drafting table and a computer center and adds a second desk that can be used for meetings or as a spot to look at final plans.

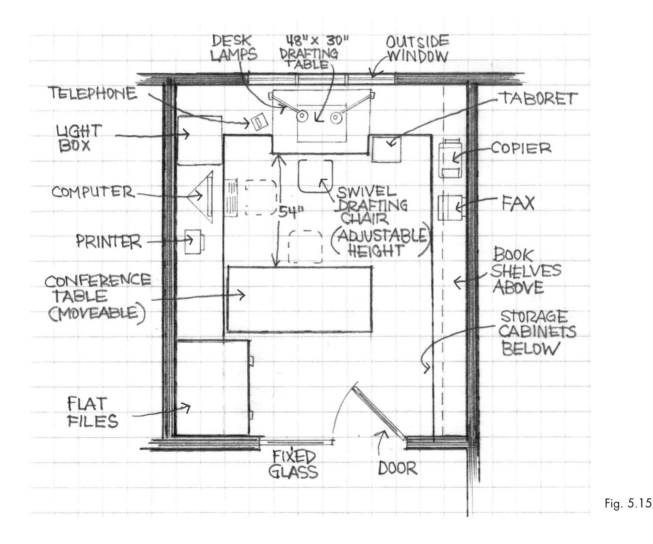

Fig. 5.15

# Architect's and Writer's Workspace

Sharing a workspace can be tricky, but it can work if both parties understand the rules. It is essential for each person to have his or her own office equipment, including a computer, phone line, storage space and shelves. In this case, Dan and Coco Rowen, a married couple with different professions, converted the long, narrow shed that was attached to a garage into an office for two (see Fig. 5.16 and photo page 172).

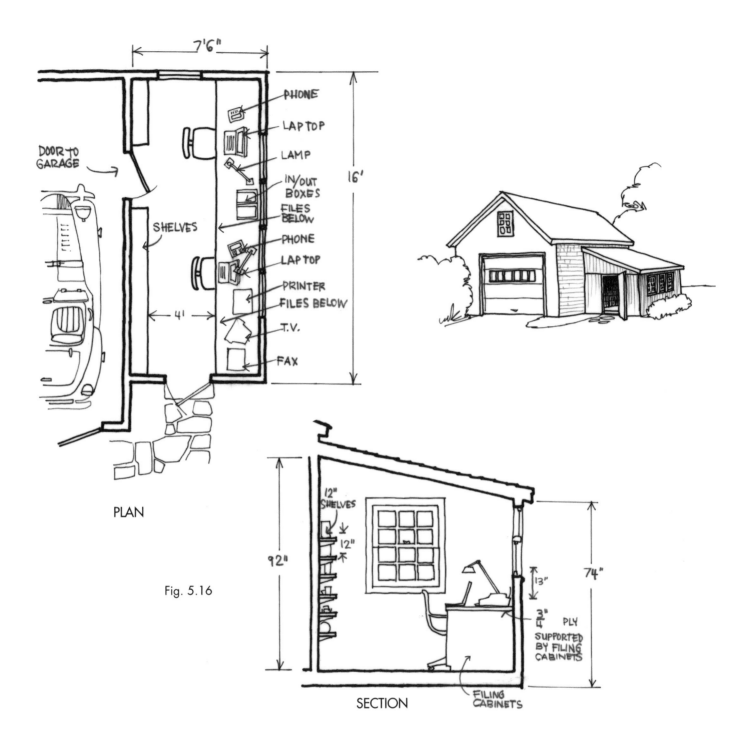

PHONE
LAPTOP
LAMP
IN/OUT BOXES
FILES BELOW
PHONE
LAPTOP
PRINTER
FILES BELOW
T.V.
FAX

7'6"

16'

DOOR TO GARAGE

SHELVES

4'

PLAN

Fig. 5.16

12" SHELVES
12"
92"
13"
74"
3/4" PLY
SUPPORTED BY FILING CABINETS

FILING CABINETS

SECTION

When Dan, an architect, and Coco, a writer and editor, began renovating their house, it was important for them to have an office outside of their home. With three young children, separating their work from their family time was essential. Fortunately, their shingled house is surrounded by several outbuildings, including a tool shed, a playhouse for the kids and an old barn that had once been a butcher's shop.

On one side of the barn, the former owners had built a long, narrow shed measuring 7½' wide x 16' deep x 8' high. Dan chose this structure, the outbuilding closest to the main house, as the one to transform into a small but efficient space, accommodating two people working at two different professions. He covered what had been a dirt floor with plywood, put drywall on the walls and installed a propane furnace. The wall that connects to the garage is covered with shelves, while the opposite wall has a desk surface made from ¾" Finply, which extends from one end to the other. Each person has a computer, phone and slide-out keyboard tray.

The studio is hard to recognize from the outside, with its shed roof and nondescript, almost secret, gray door. In fact, there is no handle, doorknob or casing around the door, just a tiny wing nut holding it shut. When the door opens, however, an efficient workspace is revealed – contemporary, brightly lit and perfectly designed for two – filled with state-of-the-art computer equipment and a small but efficient sound system.

Inexpensive six-paned windows wrap around two sides of the studio, offering a panoramic view of the side and backyard at just the right height to keep an eye on the children when they are playing outside. A 13" wall extends up from the back edge of the desk to the bottom of the windowsill, creating a backsplash for the computer equipment and hiding the workspace from view from the outside.

Dan's experience as an architect includes designing several structures for people who need workspaces in or next to their homes. He strongly recommends having your workspace in a building separate from your living space and feels that the physical act of going outside and walking from one space to another helps define the two distinct parts of your life – the domestic space versus your workspace. Dan feels that people act and think differently when they are working, and he designs their working space differently than their home. "You pick different art for a workspace, wear different clothes, deal with time differently." And, of course, your family is less likely to interrupt you if you have an office in a separate structure.

# Tack Room

For the rider who has more than one horse, it can be impractical to store tack and tools in the same space as the horses are housed. A good solution is to build a separate tack room (see photo page 164) to store blankets, saddles, bridles, stirrups, brushes, riding boots and vet and cleaning supplies.

The key is not how big the space is, but how well you can organize it. Wooden trunks can store blankets and sheets and make a convenient place to sit while putting on your riding boots. Hooks on the walls are used to hang bridles, saddle racks hold saddles and cabinets can store any supplies needed for vets and for grooming.

This is a place where you will spend much time, so it is a good idea to insulate the walls and cover them with wood paneling, keeping the workspace cooler in the summer and warmer in the winter. A small portable heater is also a good idea. A sink is helpful but not essential. The floor should be either cement or wood. Having a finished floor and walls and a strong door helps to keep out rodents and any other animals that might stray in for a good chew on a piece of leather.

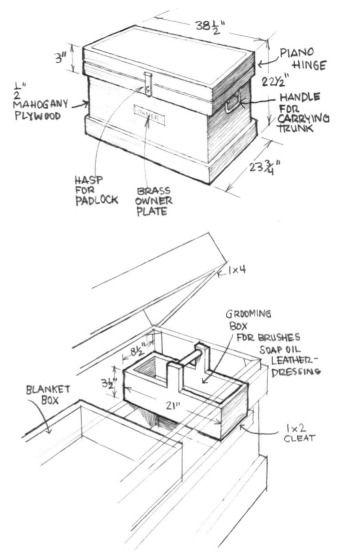

STORAGE BOX

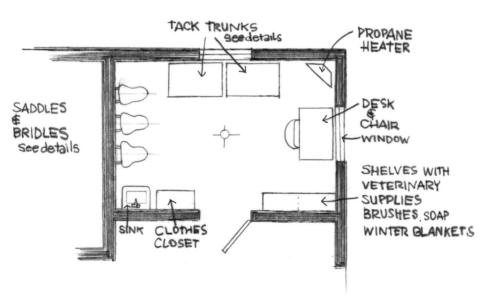

# Gardener's Workshop

This garden workshop is perfect for a vegetable or flower gardener, or it can be used as a simple potting shed. It is built out of 4x6 cedar and features timber framing and 1x8 cedar lap joint siding. The basic requirements of gardeners we interviewed included

- storage space for grass seed and fertilizer
- wall space for hanging spades, shovels and rakes
- storage space for smaller garden tools
- adequate natural light
- a door wide enough to allow a wheelbarrow, a lawn mower or even a small tractor to fit through it.

With these requirements in mind, we designed the garden workshop with a skylight to fill the space with enough light so that not too many windows are required. This allows more wall space for hooks and storage shelves.

In order to fit large equipment inside, we have suggested installing two doors, one 36" wide and the other 20" wide. When maneuvering a large wheelbarrow or lawn mower through the doors, both can be opened to allow for a 56"-wide opening; otherwise, the smaller door can remain shut (see Figs. 5.17 to 5.19).

Fig. 5.17

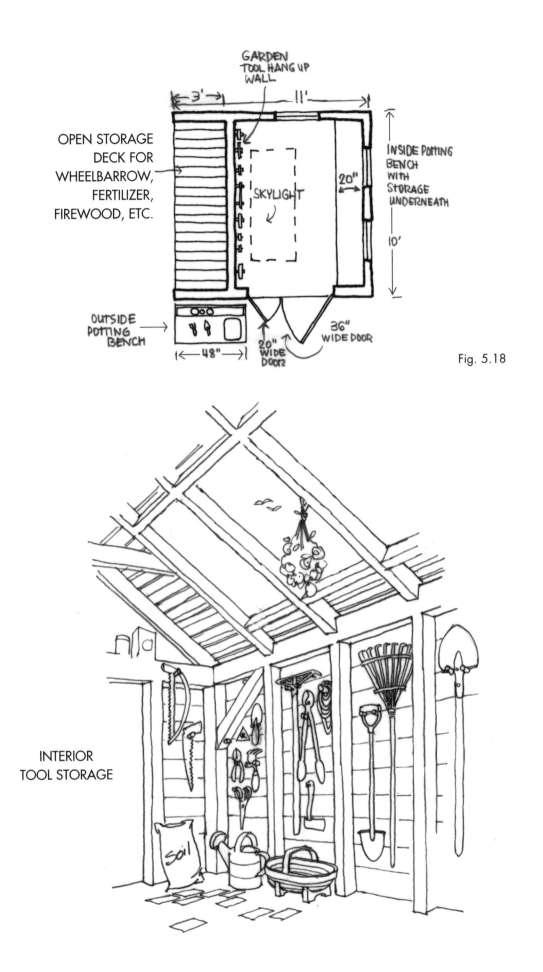

GARDEN TOOL HANG UP WALL

3'

11'

OPEN STORAGE
DECK FOR
WHEELBARROW,
FERTILIZER,
FIREWOOD, ETC.

SKYLIGHT

20"

INSIDE POTTING
BENCH
WITH
STORAGE
UNDERNEATH

10'

OUTSIDE
POTTING
BENCH

48"

20"
WIDE
DOOR

36"
WIDE DOOR

Fig. 5.18

INTERIOR
TOOL STORAGE

soil

Fig. 5.19

# Boatbuilding Workshop

This 24' x 44' boathouse is designed to accommodate a small group of wooden boatbuilders. The overall size can be reduced or enlarged depending on the size of the boats that will be built. We recommend that the boathouse be constructed using timber framing because of its inherent strength, and also to inspire the craft of traditional woodworking. Between the posts are panels of 4"-thick rigid insulation, covered with unseasoned horizontal planks of rough lumber. The exterior of the workshop is covered with vertical shiplap 1x10" in #2 red cedar (see Fig 5.20).

Fig. 5.20

Inside there is room for moving oversized planks of wood around, and there is a long bench for working on masts and spars. All the heavy power tools are resting on lockable casters and can be rolled out of the way when necessary. The roof framing is designed to be self-supporting, eliminating the need for interior posts that could get in the way (see Figs. 5.22 and 5.23).

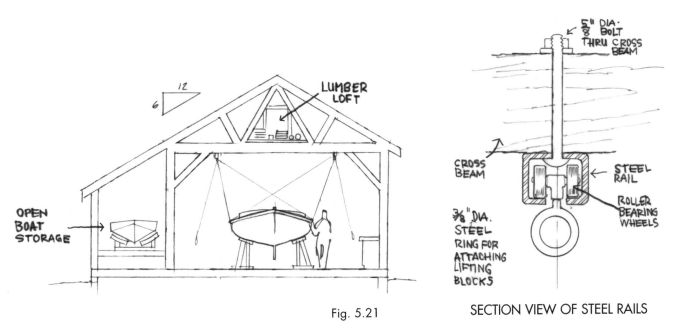

Fig. 5.21

SECTION VIEW OF STEEL RAILS

Fig. 5.22

The two steel rails that run the length of the boathouse are used to hoist and turn over the partially finished boats, using a block and tackle. A narrow loft, with ladder access, provides a place to store lumber and spars. Lighting is provided by a row of barn sash windows (see Sources) as well as three skylights on each side of the roof.

To deal with the sawdust, a flexible filtering system is attached to each major power tool and ducted through the floor into the crawl space. The boathouse workshop is heated by two overhead gas or kerosene heaters, as well as an iron stove to burn leftover wood scraps.

Extending the eaves on one side allows finished boats to be stored and displayed in the winter, while in the summer this area can be used to varnish spars. An enclosed bathroom completes the boathouse, with a slop sink just outside for washing up or mixing glues.

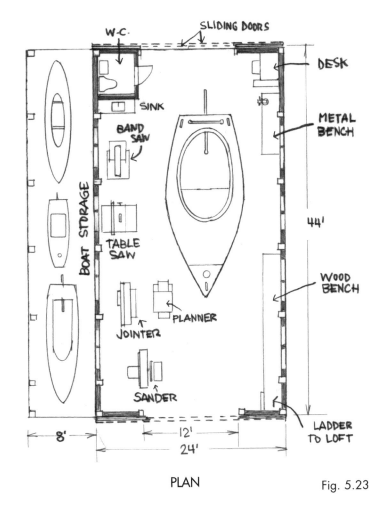

PLAN

Fig. 5.23

# PORTABLE AND MINI-WORKSHOPS

Don't despair; even if you have no room or extra land for your own workspace, there are wonderful portable workshops that can hold all the basic necessities. The object is to make your workspace work for you. The following ideas describe mini-workshops for carpenters, home office workers and even kids. Although all of these projects can be used in workshops or studios, they also enable the artist, carpenter, writer, etc. who doesn't have a separate space to work in the means to store or do their craft or work using a portable or mini-workshop.

## Workbench

This utility bench can serve many purposes, ranging from woodworking to household repairs to gardening projects. It requires only straight cuts, and can easily be built in a Saturday morning. We suggest attaching it to a wall with lag screws to make it sturdy and secure enough for carpentry projects (see Figs. 6.1 and 6.2)

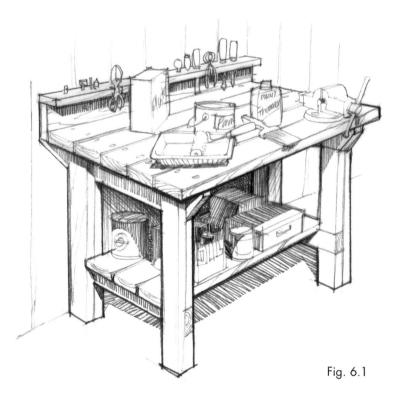

Fig. 6.1

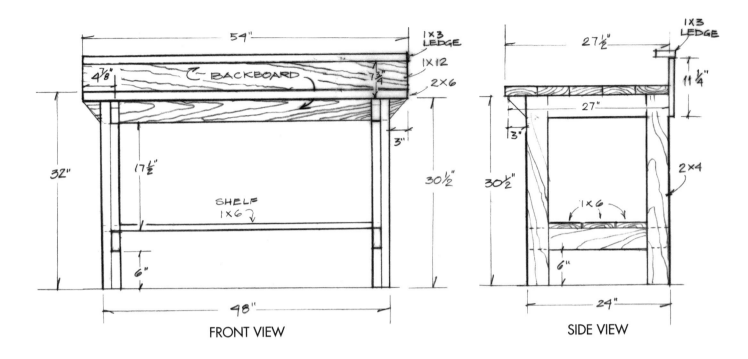

FRONT VIEW

SIDE VIEW

The work surface consists of 2x6 fir boards that overhang two sides by 3", enabling you to clamp boards to the top of the bench. The bottom shelf is deep enough to hold large items, storing them out of the way while keeping them visible and accessible. The top ledge provides a convenient place for chisels, screwdrivers, drill bits, trowels, clippers and other frequently used small hand tools.

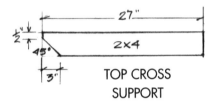

TOP CROSS
SUPPORT

Fig. 6.2

Begin by building the two leg sets. The leg pieces for each set can be cut from one 10'-long 2x4, and all the top and bottom cross supports for both sides can be cut from another 10'-long 2x4. Consequently, you will need to buy a total of three 10'-long 2x4s.

Refer to the cutting plan (see Fig. 6.3) as you cut out the individual pieces. Rest the first 2x4 on top of two sawhorses or other work surface. Use a tape measure and pencil to mark the first 6"-long leg piece, draw a cut line with a combination square and saw the piece off where marked, using a handsaw or a portable circular saw. Measure, mark and cut each of the leg pieces separately, using the same procedure. You will be cutting two 6" pieces, two 17½" pieces and two 30 ½" pieces from two of the 10'-long 2x4s. After all the leg pieces have been cut, measure, mark and cut the two 27" top cross supports and the two 24" bottom cross supports out of the third 10'-long 2x4.

## Materials List

| Quantity | Size | Description | Use |
|---|---|---|---|
| 5 | 54" | 2x6 fir | tabletop |
| 4 | 30 1/2" | 2x4 fir | legs |
| 4 | 17 1/2" | 2x4 fir | legs |
| 4 | 6" | 2x4 fir | legs |
| 2 | 27" | 2x4 fir | top cross supports |
| 2 | 24" | 2x4 fir | bottom cross supports |
| 3 | 48" | 1x6 #2 common pine | bottom shelf |
| 1 | 54" | 1x12 #2 common pine | backboard |
| 1 | 54" | 1x3 #2 common pine | top ledge |
| 1 box | 2 1/2" | #10 galvanized deck screws | |
| 1 box | 1 1/2" | #8 galvanized deck screws | |
| 20 | 1/2" diameter x 1/4" | wood plugs | |
| 1 belt | 6" x 48" | 40-grit sandpaper | tabletop |
| 1 belt | 6" x 48" | 60-grit sandpaper | tabletop |
| 1 sheet | 9" x 11" | 60-grit sandpaper | top ledge |

One at a time, clamp each of the two 27" cross support pieces to a sturdy work surface and use a combination square to mark a 45° angle 1/2" down from the corner of the top cross support. Use a handsaw to cut off the piece so that the bottom of the cut is 3" in from the end of the top cross support. After all the pieces that make up the leg sets are cut to size, temporarily assemble them on the floor, laying them side by side (see Fig. 6.4). When you assemble the leg sets, be careful that the cross supports of each set will face inside the bench once it is built.

After you have checked to see that the leg assemblies fit together, use an electric drill with a Phillips screwdriver bit to screw together all eight pieces of each leg set with 2½" galvanized deck screws. Space the screws approximately 5" apart and stagger them, placing two in each bottom section of the leg and three in each top section.

To make the bottom shelf, cut three 48"-long pieces out of one 12' piece of 1x6 #2 pine. Stand the two leg sets up with the help of an assistant (or prop them up against a wall if you are alone) and use a Phillips screwdriver to temporarily screw the three 1x6 bottom shelf pieces to the bottom cross supports, so that the ends of the shelf boards overhang the cross-braces by 1½" (see Fig. 6.5). Drill in the screws only halfway to allow you to make any necessary adjustments before the workbench is completed.

To make the tabletop pieces, cut five pieces of 2x6 fir, each 54" long. Temporarily screw one of these boards across the front of the top cross supports to stabilize the unit.

Next, make the backboard by cutting one piece of 1x12 #2 pine 54" long. Temporarily hold the backboard in position by placing two screws through the backboard and into the back of the legs. The backboard should extend 7¾" above the top of the cross supports. Place a mark 7¾" down from each top corner of the backboard and mark a diagonal line from this point to where the backboard meets the legs (approximately a 45° angle). Remove the backboard and cut this triangular section off each end (see Fig. 6.6).

Screw the backboard on again, using the same temporary screw holes. Before going on to the next step, use a framing square to check that the unit is plumb (vertically straight) and square. Make sure that the legs line up at right angles with the floor and the bottom and top shelves. Check the top work surface by measuring the diagonals with

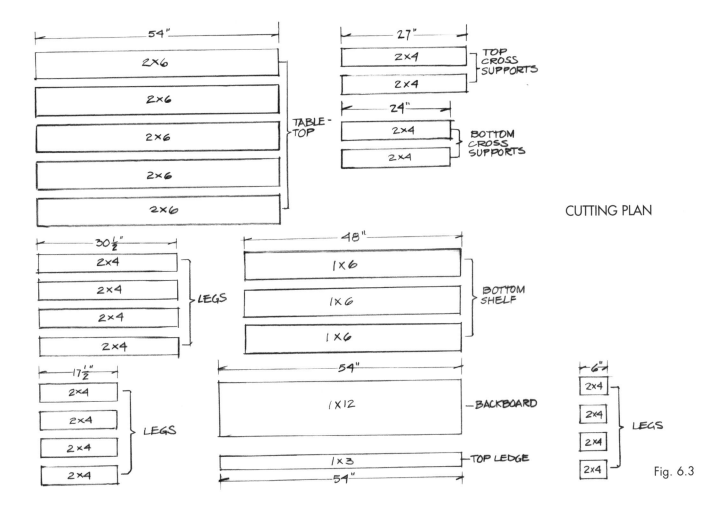

CUTTING PLAN

Fig. 6.3

LEG SETS

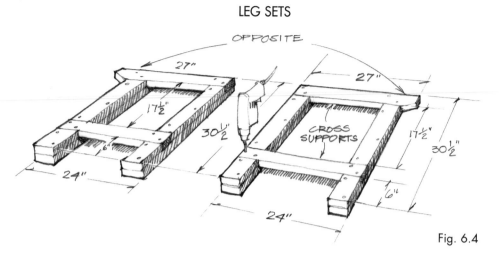

Fig. 6.4

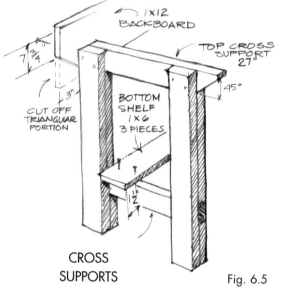

CROSS
SUPPORTS

Fig. 6.5

a tape measure – they should be the same length. If the tabletop is not square, make adjustments by twisting it into the correct position.

Position the four remaining 2x6 tabletop boards on top of the two crosspieces so that their ends are lined up evenly. Make sure that there is an equal amount of space between each board. To mark where you should place your screw

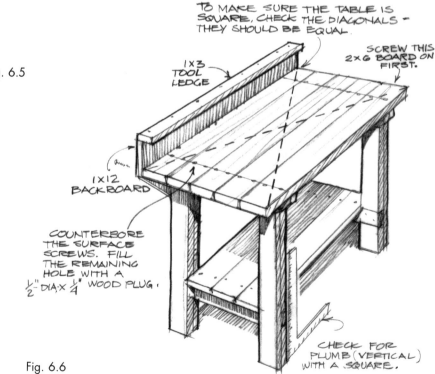

Fig. 6.6

holes, measure in 4⁷⁄₈" from each side of the tabletop and, using a framing square as your guide, draw a line from back to front. Make sure that the lines are over the center of each cross support. Use a ½" spade bit to counterbore ¼"-deep holes for the screws. This will prevent the screw heads in the work surface from marring anything placed on top of the bench. Drive 2½" #8 screws, equally spaced, through the backboard and into the tabletop edge. Tighten all the screws. Fill the screw holes in the work surface with ½"-diameter ¼"-thick wood plugs (see Fig. 6.7). Sand the tabletop surface across the grain, using a belt sander fitted with 40-grit sandpaper.

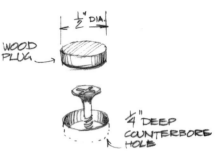

Fig. 6.7

To make the top tool ledge, cut a 54"-long piece of 1x3 and screw it to the top of the 1x12 backboard with 1½" #8 galvanized deck screws, spaced 6" apart (see Fig. 6.8). Lay the hand tools that you

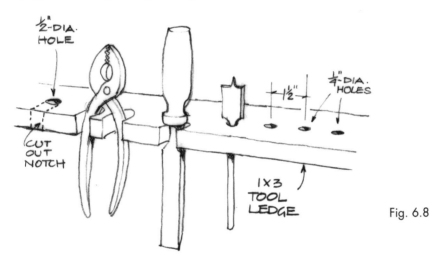

Fig. 6.8

expect to use most often on the tabletop and mark where they should go on the 1x3. Some tools, such as drill bits and screwdrivers, need only a hole drilled, while others, like pliers and chisels, require notches to be cut out of the front of the tool shelf to hold them. Use a ½" spade bit to drill holes for the notches. Cut out the material in front of the hole with an electric jigsaw. Make sure that each notch or hole is at least 1½" on center from the next hole. Sand the inside of the notches and holes with a rolled-up piece of 60-grit sandpaper (see Fig. 6.9).

To finish the work surface and make it perfectly level, sand with the grain, using a belt sander fitted with 60-grit sandpaper. This project does not need to be finished with wood sealer, paint or stain.

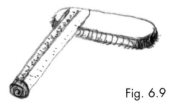

Fig. 6.9

# Wall-Mounted Tool Chest

Having your tools well organized, ready to use, will ultimately save you a lot of time. One solution is to have a wall-mounted tool cabinet that stores all your tools in a neat, orderly manner (see Fig. 6.10). This tool chest is a terrific design for anyone who is serious about carpentry and cares about tools. The tool chest can be permanently attached to the wall or closed up and transported to a job. New tools fit into the chest easily, since new pegs can be added by boring and gluing them into the backboard.

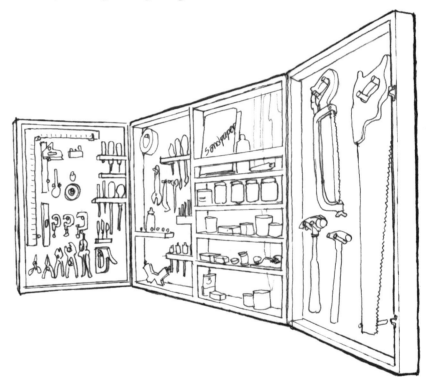

Fig. 6.10

This project is easy to make, but it does require an electric router or table saw to cut the joints. Clear pine 1x4s and birch plywood are preferred, though cheaper grades of lumber can do a perfectly adequate job.

Cut all the lumber to size, making sure that the panels are square. Make a ½"-wide, ¼"-deep dado groove ⅛" from the outside edge of the top and side pieces. Next the sides are rabbeted to accept the top and bottom pieces (see Fig. 6.13).

Mark the shelf positions according to the height of the glass jars you are using to store nails and other fasteners. Cut the dado grooves for the right sidepiece and the center divider at the same time. Before the final assembly, place all the pieces into their

| Materials List | | | |
|---|---|---|---|
| **Quantity** | **Size** | **Description** | **Use** |
| 2 | 8' long | 1x4 | tops and bottoms (cut into 23" long pieces) |
| 3 | 6' long | 1x4 | sides (cut into 36" pieces) |
| 1 | 34 1/2" long | 1x4 | center divider |
| 4 | 23 3/8" long | 1x4 | shelves |
| 2 | 22 3/8" long | 1x2 | rail |
| 1 | 48" long | 1x2 | wall support |
| 1 | 47" x 35" | 1/2"-thick ply | back panel |
| 2 | 23" x 35" | 1/2"-thick ply | side panels |
| glass jars to store nails and screws | | | |

proper positions and check to see that everything fits, making sure that the shelves fit into the grooves.

Using 1½" finishing nails and glue, assemble the cabinet and doors. Check frequently for squareness. When the glue is dry, screw the center divider into the cabinet and slide the shelves into place. It's better not to glue them, since you may want to remove them later and rearrange your storage space. Glue and nail the 1x2 rail in place. Add friction catches, door handles and a piece of ¼"-thick leather for a carrying handle (see Fig. 6.12).

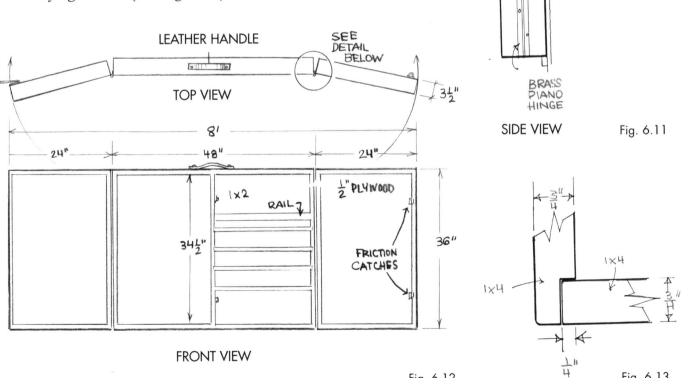

SIDE VIEW     Fig. 6.11

FRONT VIEW

Fig. 6.12

Fig. 6.13

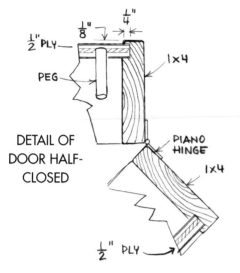

DETAIL OF DOOR HALF-CLOSED

Fig. 6.14

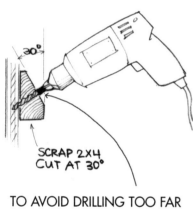

TO AVOID DRILLING TOO FAR MARK THE DRILL BIT WITH TAPE AT THE CORRECT DEPTH

Fig. 6.15

Now comes the fun part. Gather together your tool collection and lay the tool chest down on the floor. Begin placing your tools in the chest, marking with a light pencil where they will be stored. Leave space for tools that you plan to buy in the future. Most of the tools can be hung on pegs inserted at a slight angle into holes bored into the plywood (see Figs. 6.14 and 6.15).

We chose wood pegs to hang the tools on rather than pegboard wire brackets because they are cheaper and make a nice "thud" when the tool is returned to its place rather than a "clank."

Cut dozens of 2"-long pegs from a ¼" dowel, keeping those you don't use in a jar for future use. Spread some white glue in the holes and hammer in the pegs where you want them. You have three choices for showing where your tools belong in the tool chest: (1) Outline the tool on the backboard and paint in the silhouette (this requires a steady hand); (2) cut the tool profile out of contact paper and press on, after first sanding and varnishing the underlying wood surface; or (3) label the position of the tool with a labeling gun. Certain tools like drills, screwdrivers, chisels and files are difficult to hang on pegs and require a different solution.

Many years ago, some clever person discovered that hanging glass jars on the underside of a shelf was a good way to store screws, nuts and bolts. The only difficulty is finding enough jars of the same size. Baby-food jars or small mayonnaise jars seem to work well, but who can eat 18 jars of mayonnaise? It's almost worth it to buy new mason jars all the same size.

To keep the tools in place, make a wooden crossbar from a piece of scrap wood and an old thread spool and screw it to the backboard. To store sandpaper, make a folder out of cardboard. Provide two sections, one for coarse sandpaper and one for fine. Finish by covering the wood with three coats of polyurethane.

To hang the tool chest on the wall, first locate two 2x4 wood studs behind the wall. Bore ½"-diameter holes in each stud about 5' to 6' above the floor. Make sure they are level and at the same angle. Drive a ½" wood dowel into each hole. Bore two larger ¾"-diameter holes in the back of the cabinet to correspond with those in the wall and hang the tool chest on the pegs. As a safeguard against falling, nail a 1x2 support to the wall under the tool chest.

# Adjustable Sawhorse

One of the most important yet overlooked items that a woodworker needs is a solid support to hold wood while it is being cut. Sawhorses can be bought; however, the ready-made ones are difficult to store, hard to transport and not adjustable. A better alternative is to build your own. Two inexpensive sawhorses can be made from a single sheet of plywood, with the leftover piece serving as a work surface or tabletop. They are adjustable and can be easily folded up and stored away when not in use (see Fig. 6.17).

Fig. 6.16

The bottoms of each pair of folding plywood legs are connected with ropes so that the height of the sawhorses can be raised or lowered. The sawhorses can also be used as a support for a tabletop. We use ours on Thanksgiving when we need more table space.

Referring to the cutting plan, use a T-square or tape measure and a pencil to mark the sawhorse dimensions on the plywood. Rest the sheet of plywood on three 2x4s laid on edge on the floor, and be sure there is enough room for the jigsaw blade to cut through the plywood

## Materials List

| Quantity | Size | Description | Use |
|----------|------|-------------|-----|
| 4 | 24" x 36" | 3/4" exterior-grade plywood | leg supports |
| 1 | 24" x 48" | 3/4" exterior-grade plywood | tabletop |
| 4 | 1" x 3" | butt hinges with screws | leg supports |
| 1 sheet | 9" x 11" | 60-grit sandpaper | handholds |
| 1 | 14' | 1/4"-diameter rope | leg supports |
| 4 | 2" | Phillips-head screws | tabletop |

Handholds can be cut from the top of each panel. Measure down 2¼" from the top and 10¼" from the sides of each panel and make two pencil marks to indicate where drill holes should be made. To prevent tear-out from the back of the wood, place a piece of scrap wood under the panel before you begin drilling your holes. Using a 1½"-diameter hole saw or a 1½" spade bit in an electric drill, bore two holes in each panel at the pencil marks. Use an electric jigsaw to cut out the section between each of the two holes, making an elongated slot. To keep the blade of the jigsaw from hitting the floor, rest the two panels on two 2x4s, placed on edge. Smooth the inside edges of the handholds with 60-grit sandpaper.

without touching the floor. Clamp an 8' piece of a scrap 1x6 to act as a straightedge while cutting and make four identical pieces, each measuring 24" x 36", from a 4x8 sheet of exterior plywood. When joined together, these pieces form the legs of the sawhorses. The 24" x 48" leftover piece of plywood will serve as the tabletop (see Fig. 6.18).

If you plan on using the sawhorses outside, cut out a 1½" x 18" section from the bottom of each panel with an electric jigsaw. Begin and end the cuts 3" in from each side of the two 24" x 36" panels. Lay two panels (with the good side facing down) end to end and join them together, using 1" x 3" butt hinges placed 3" in from the outside edge of the plywood. When screwing the hinges onto the plywood, be sure that the pin of each hinge is centered between the two pieces of plywood. Repeat this procedure for the other two panels.

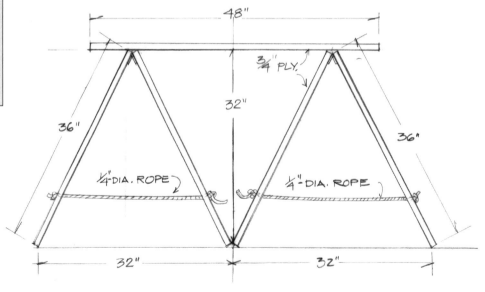

Fig. 6.17

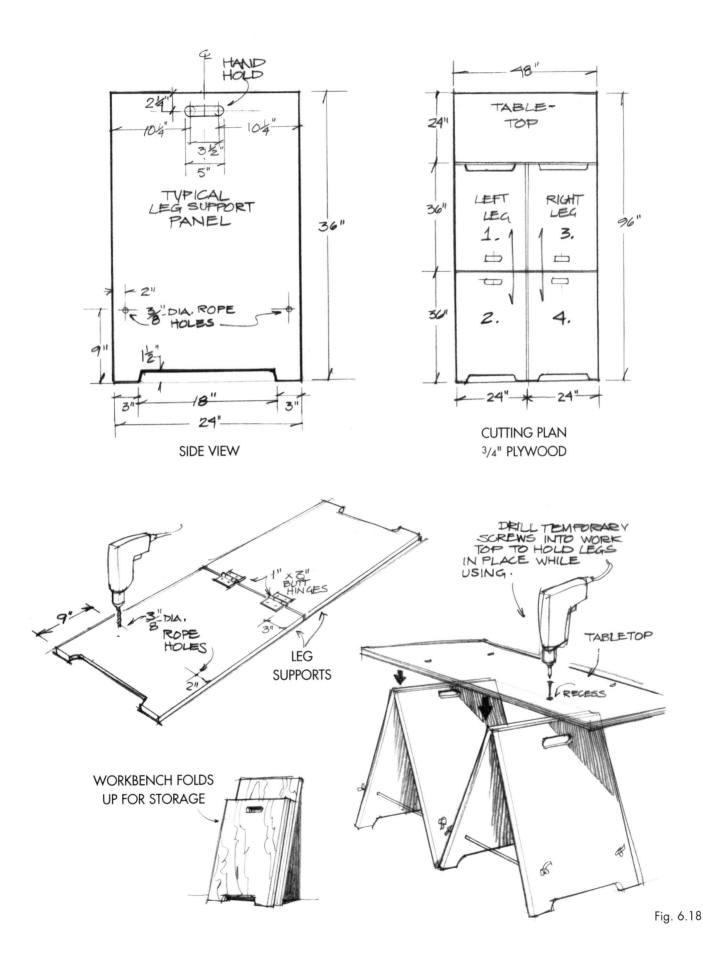

HAND HOLD

2¼"

10¼"    10¼"

3½"

5"

TYPICAL
LEG SUPPORT
PANEL

36"

2"

⅜" DIA. ROPE
HOLES

9"

1½"

3"    18"    3"

24"

SIDE VIEW

48"

24"

TABLE-
TOP

36"

LEFT
LEG

1.

RIGHT
LEG

3.

2.    4.

96"

36"

24"    24"

CUTTING PLAN
3/4" PLYWOOD

9"

⅜" DIA.
ROPE
HOLES

1" x 3"
BUTT
HINGES

2"

LEG
SUPPORTS

DRILL TEMPORARY
SCREWS INTO WORK
TOP TO HOLD LEGS
IN PLACE WHILE
USING.

TABLETOP

RECESS

WORKBENCH FOLDS
UP FOR STORAGE

Fig. 6.18

# Closet Workshop

For apartments and small homes, a closet can easily be converted into a small workshop – useful when small repairs and maintenance are necessary. The one shown here uses the back of the closet door to store and display small hand tools, making them easily accessible.

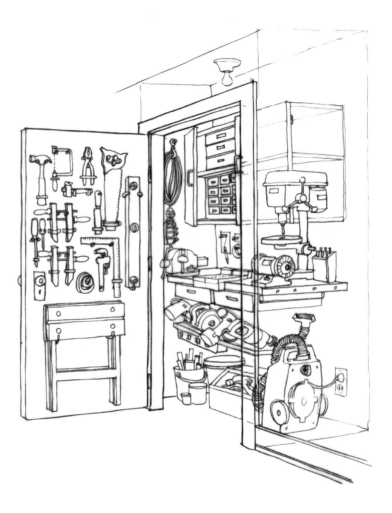

Make a list of the tools you will be storing and draw a scale plan on paper before attaching any hooks permanently. Draw the outline of each tool on the door so that you can return them easily. Place the tools you use the most often in the most accessible spots.

# Potting Table

Although a potting bench may at first glance seem like a luxury, once you have built one, you will consider it a necessity. This design gives you a convenient place to pot plants without bending over, hooks to hang the essential potting tools on and a storage shelf below for heavy bags of potting soil and fertilizer. The removable bin for soil frees up the rest of the bench top for plants and pots while you are working (see Fig. 6.19).

Fig. 6.19

Begin by cutting the 2x4 front and rear legs 35" and 54" long, respectively. Cut four 2x4 crosspieces, each 22" long, to hold the legs together. Before attaching the crosspieces, use a carpenter's square to check that all the pieces are at right angles to each other. Glue and screw the top crosspieces to the insides of the legs, 35" up from the bottom of each rear leg and flush with the top of the front leg, using 2½" galvanized deck screws. Glue and screw the bottom crosspieces to the front and rear legs so that their tops are 15" from the bottom of the legs (see Fig. 6.20).

## Materials List

| Quantity | Size | Description | Use |
|---|---|---|---|
| 2 | 8' | 2x4 redwood or P.T. lumber | legs and crosspieces |
| 1 | 12' | 2x4 redwood or P.T. lumber | crosspieces |
| 8 | 8' | 5/4x4 redwood or P.T. lumber | top and bottom decking and trim |
| 2 | 8' | 5/4x8 redwood or P.T. lumber | backsplash, top shelf and shelf backboard |
| 1 | 6' | 1x4 redwood or P.T. lumber | back braces |
| 1 lb. | 1 1/2 " | galvanized deck screws | |
| 1 lb. | 2 1/2" | galvanized deck screws | |
| 1 | 16 qt. | 12 3/4" x 15 1/2" plastic dishpan (optional) | |
| 1 bottle | 8 oz. | waterproof yellow glue | |

In preparation for building the top and bottom decking, cut 14 pieces of 5/4x4, each exactly 48" long. Stand up the assembled legs and attach the front and back 5/4x4 decking boards to the crosspieces, using 2½" countersunk deck screws. The back decking board will have to be cut 3" shorter to fit between the two rear legs.

To build the backsplash, cut a 5/4x8, 48" long. Tip the structure over and screw the backsplash to the rear leg posts so that the bottom edge of the backsplash is 1" above the bottom edge of the crosspieces (see Fig. 6.21).

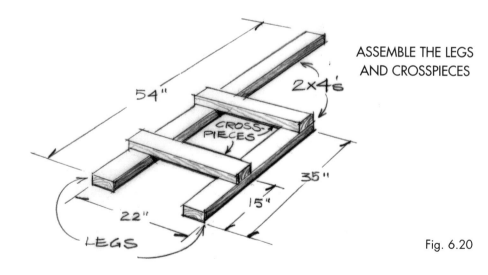

ASSEMBLE THE LEGS AND CROSSPIECES

Fig. 6.20

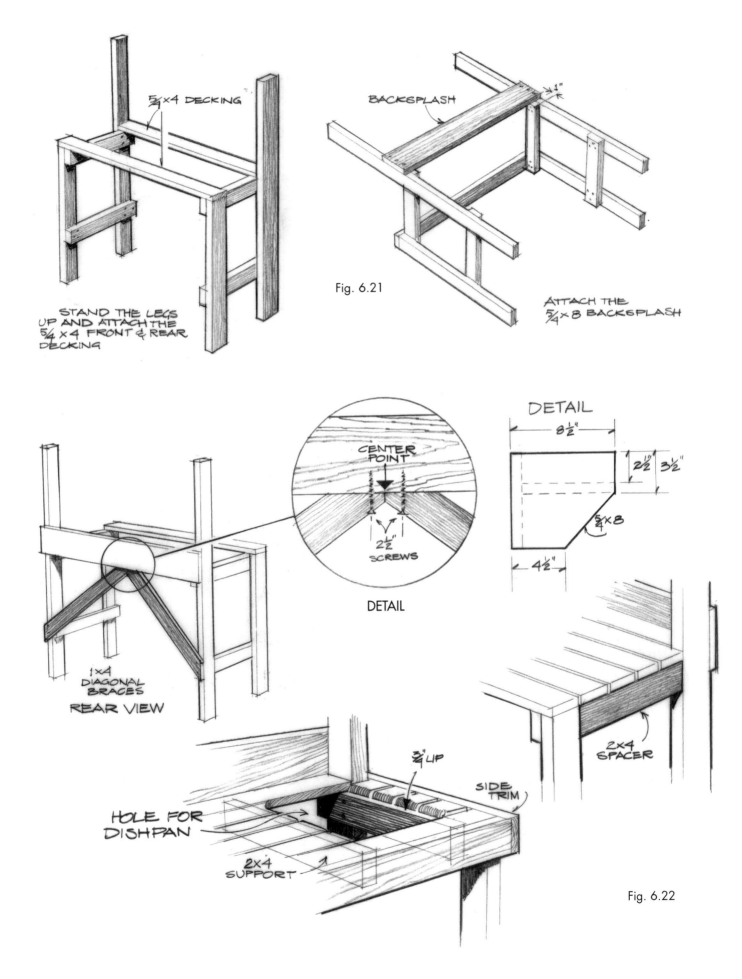

$\frac{5}{4} \times 4$ DECKING

STAND THE LEGS UP AND ATTACH THE $\frac{5}{4} \times 4$ FRONT & REAR DECKING

BACKSPLASH

1"

Fig. 6.21

ATTACH THE $\frac{5}{4} \times 8$ BACKSPLASH

CENTER POINT

DETAIL

$2\frac{1}{2}$" SCREWS

DETAIL

$8\frac{1}{2}$"

$2\frac{1}{2}$" $3\frac{1}{2}$"

$\frac{5}{4} \times 8$

$4\frac{1}{2}$"

$1 \times 4$ DIAGONAL BRACES

REAR VIEW

$\frac{3}{4}$" LIP

SIDE TRIM

$2 \times 4$ SPACER

HOLE FOR DISHPAN

$2 \times 4$ SUPPORT

Fig. 6.22

To build the diagonal back braces, cut two 1x4s, each 32" long. Find and mark the center of the bottom edge of the backsplash. Hold each piece of 1x4 (one at a time) diagonally, one end touching the center of the backsplash, the other end touching the leg, and trace the angle where the pieces meet at the center. Also trace the angle where the bottom edge of each brace will overlap the rear leg, and cut the braces at these angles (see Fig. 6.22).

Using 1½" galvanized deck screws, screw the 48" long 5/4x4 decking to the bottom crosspieces, leaving approximately a ¼" gap between each board. Install the top decking in the same way, unless you are installing the dishpan; if so, do not screw the top decking at this time.

Select the 5/4x4 with the nicest grain for the front edge trim, and screw it every 10" to the top front of the legs and the front edge of the deck board. Cut two pieces of 5/4x4 approximately 24" long to trim off the two sides of the top decking, and screw them to the 2x4 legs.

To build the top shelf, cut a piece of 5/4x8, 48" long, and screw it to the tops of the two rear legs. To make the backboard for the top shelf, cut another 48"-long piece from the same board and screw it to the back of the shelf and to the backs of the two rear legs. Allow the backboard to extend 2½" above the top of the shelf.

To prevent pots from falling off the ends of the top shelf, cut two 8½"-long pieces of 5/4x8 and make a diagonal cut 4¼" from the bottom corner and 3½" from the top front corner. Screw these side pieces to each end of the shelf.

Gardening tools and implements can be hung on the backboard under the shelf by attaching wooden pegs, hooks and nails to the wood, depending upon your gardening needs.

# Corner Desk

This L-shaped desk (see photo page 165) is useful for small workspaces because it doesn't take up too much space but allows for a good deal of desktop room for office equipment. Before buying your lumber, draw plans up on ¼"-square grid paper. This is a convenient size, since four squares equal one foot and each square equals 3". Try out different designs by photographing your existing space and sketching various design possibilities on tracing paper or acetate placed on top of the photograph. Adapt the dimensions of the following plans to fit your space as needed (see Fig. 6.23).

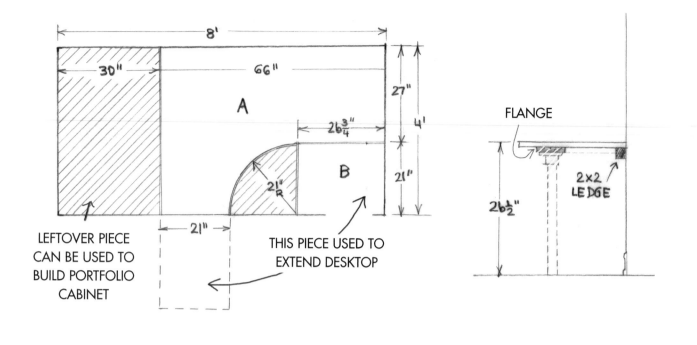

8'

30"    66"

A

27"

4'

26¾"

21"

2½"

B

21"

LEFTOVER PIECE
CAN BE USED TO
BUILD PORTFOLIO
CABINET

THIS PIECE USED TO
EXTEND DESKTOP

FLANGE

2x2
LEDGE

26½"

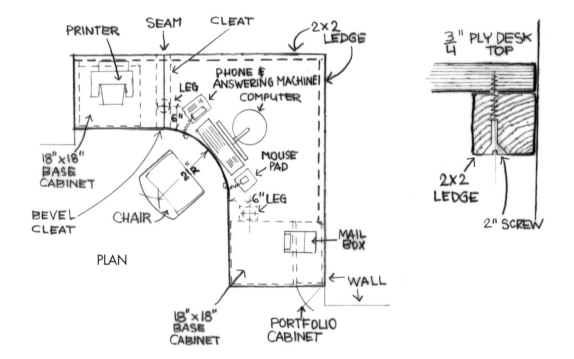

PRINTER    SEAM    CLEAT    2x2 LEDGE

PHONE &
ANSWERING MACHINE

LEG

COMPUTER

6"

MOUSE
PAD

18"x18"
BASE
CABINET

BEVEL
CLEAT

2'R

CHAIR

6" LEG

MAIL
BOX

PLAN

18"x18"
BASE
CABINET

PORTFOLIO
CABINET

← WALL

¾" PLY DESK
TOP

2x2
LEDGE

2" SCREW

Fig. 6.23

Make a list of essential office equipment, measure each piece and draw it onto graph paper using the same scale as the desk plan (1" to the foot). Copy the pieces onto card stock and cut them out. These templates can be moved around over your desk plan to help you determine where to place your office equipment. This gives you a chance to change your desk design if the equipment doesn't fit into the proposed space.

To build the desk, mark the lines to be cut on the back of the plywood so that when you cut the wood using a portable circular saw (and an electric jigsaw for the curve), the saw teeth will not tear out the top surface veneer. Cut the two pieces (A and B) that make up the desktop out of one ¾"-thick 4'x8' sheet of plywood. The two sections are joined together by screwing a 4"-wide cleat, made from plywood, to the underneath seam where the plywood pieces meet. Bevel the front edge of the 4" cleat so that it is not as visible.

Although there are different ways that the table can be supported, we chose to screw a 2" x 2" ledge onto the wall for the back end of the desk to rest on. To secure the desktop to the ledge, drive 2" screws through the underneath side of the 2" x 2" ledge and into the bottom of the plywood desktop.

The front of the desk is supported by two 2"-diameter threaded steel pipes, which can be bought from a plumbing supply outlet and cut to your specifications. To make the leg support under the "seam" of the desk, screw a pipe flange onto the top end of a 2" steel pipe. Attach this leg to the cleat under the desk unit, using four screws. Repeat this process for the second leg support, positioning it as shown in the plans.

# Armoire Workstation

Sometimes there simply isn't any extra room available to convert into an office or workspace (especially for apartment dwellers). One solution is to build a home office disguised as an armoire or freestanding wardrobe (see Fig. 6.24). A mini office center with doors that can be closed to hide works in progress when guests are visiting is a perfect solution. Although you can buy a ready-made armoire office, they can be quite expensive. By building your own you can save hundreds of dollars and design it to suit your specifications.

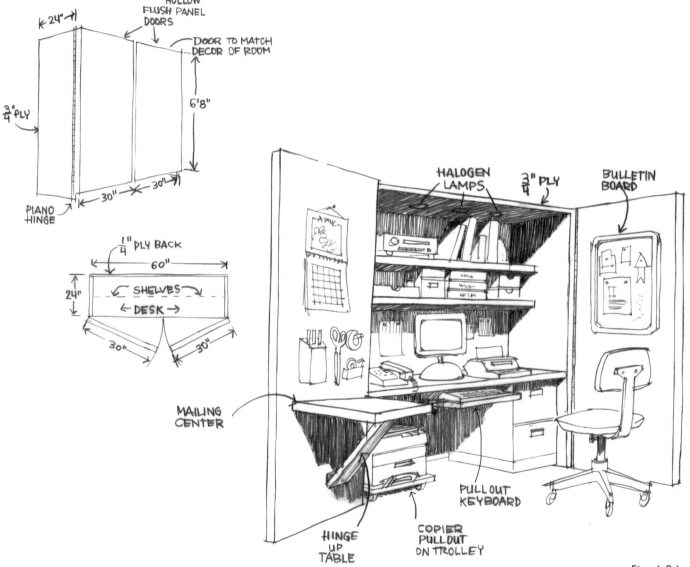

Fig. 6.24

To build the armoire workstation, purchase two hollow-core flush doors, 2' 6" x 6' 8", from your local lumberyard. These lightweight doors come with a mahogany (luan) veneer surface, which can either be painted, stained, oiled or left natural, depending on your décor. At the same time, have your lumberyard mill worker saw the ¾"- and ¼"-thick plywood panels into the sizes shown below. Purchase a 10'-long board, 5/4" x 12", and have them saw it in half to make into shelves. You will also need lumber for a 5'-long 1x4 to act as a backsplash and to reinforce the butt joint in the back wall of the armoire. And don't forget to buy wood glue, a box of 2"-long finishing nails and three pairs of 1" x 2" hinges. Metal shelf standards and a pullout keyboard tray can be ordered from a catalog if not available locally (see Fig. 6.25).

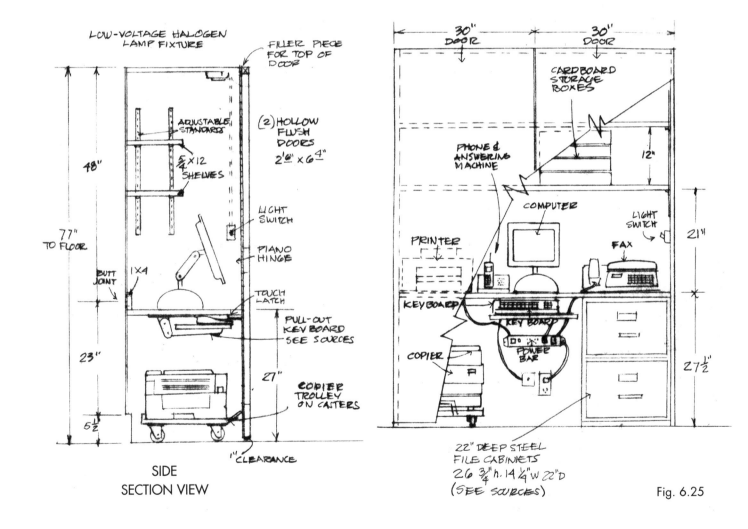

SIDE
SECTION VIEW

Fig. 6.25

# Workspace for Kids

When you have two kids in one room, with not a lot of space, this hobby/work area is a perfect solution. It can easily be made into a workshop or home office after it outlives its original purpose, minimizing the built-in obsolescence factor of children's furniture.

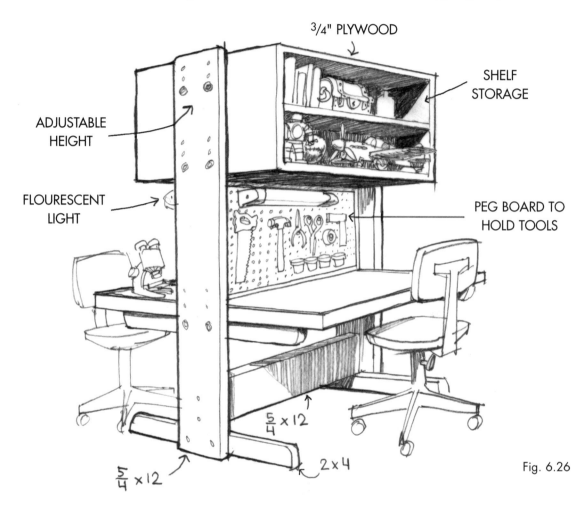

3/4" PLYWOOD

SHELF STORAGE

ADJUSTABLE HEIGHT

FLOURESCENT LIGHT

PEG BOARD TO HOLD TOOLS

$\frac{5}{4} \times 12$

2 x 4

$\frac{5}{4} \times 12$

Fig. 6.26

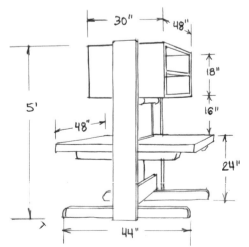

30"

48"

18"

5'

48"

16"

24"

44"

Fig. 6.27

# Mini-Office on Wheels

Organization of storage space is especially important in a home office. Because of the many built-in distractions that go along with working at home, it is often difficult to separate one's personal life from one's professional life. Office files and work projects should be "camouflaged" so, when the workday ends, they blend in with the surrounding environment. This storage stool/ottoman combination is a perfect way to put the lid down on work at the end of the day (see Fig. 6.28). The stool contains a drawer, a small yet accessible file cabinet and a shelf on which to store telephone directories, a dictionary or other reference books. When it is not being used, the foam cushion, which is attached to a hinged top piece, flips up, revealing a flat work surface.

Fig. 6.28

Begin by cutting all the pieces from a 48"-long clear mahogany 1x6 and a piece of ½" plywood, using the cutting plan as your guide (see Fig. 6.29). For the legs, rip four 1½" x 12" pieces, two 1" x 12" pieces and two ½" x 12" pieces. For the side trim, rip two pieces, each measuring 1½" x 14¾"; for the back trim, rip one piece measuring 1½" x 14¼".

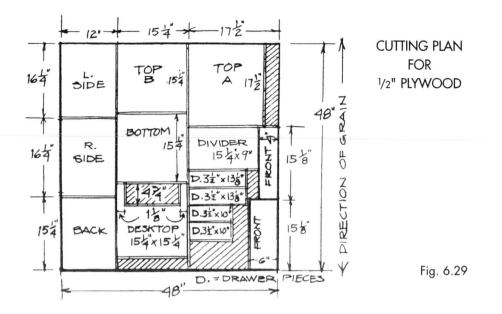

CUTTING PLAN
FOR
1/2" PLYWOOD

Fig. 6.29

## Materials List

| Quantity | Size | Description | Use |
|---|---|---|---|
| 1 sheet | 4' x 4' | 1/2" A-A plywood | front, back, sides, tops, bottom, divider and drawer |
| 1 | 9 1/2" x 13 5/8" | 1/8" birch plywood | drawer bottom |
| 1 | 48" | 1x6 clear Philippine mahogany | leg and trim pieces |
| 1 | 9 1/2" | 1x4 hardwood | ledge |
| 6 | 10" | 1/2" x 3/4" hardware | drawer slide cleats and runners |
| 1 pair | 1" x 2" | brass hinges | bottom shelf |
| 1 | 3" | touch latch | lower cabinet door |
| 1 | 17 1/2" | 1/2" x 1/2" continuous (piano) hinge w/screws | top hinge |
| 1 | 17 1/2" x 17 1/2" | 1 1/2" thick foam | seat |
| 1 | 27" x 27" | fabric | seat |
| 1 pair | 12" | Stanley brass-plated lid supports | top |
| 4 | 1 5/8" diameter | nylon twin-wheel plate casters | bottom |
| 1 box | 1 1/2" | galvanized finishing nails | drawer |
| 6 | 3/4" | #6 flathead screws | runners |
| 8 | 1" | #6 flathead screws | seat |
| 1 bottle | 8 oz. | carpenter's glue | |
| 1 can | 10 oz. | water-based wood putty | |
| 1 sheet | 60-grit | sandpaper | |
| 1 sheet | 120-grit | sandpaper | |
| 1 sheet | 220-grit | sandpaper | |
| 1 quart | | clear water-based acrylic urethane wood finish | |

Glue and clamp each leg together to form four L-shaped legs (see Fig. 6.30). The two front legs are assembled in a different manner than the two back legs. When the glue has dried, sand the legs so they are perfectly smooth, using 60-, 120- and 220-grit sandpaper.

1 x 6 CUTTING PLAN

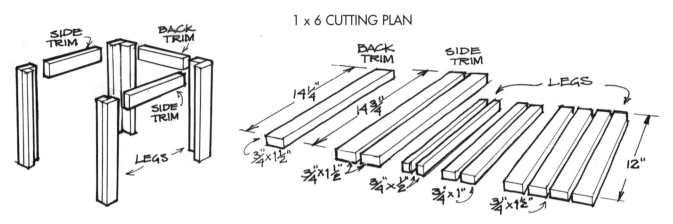

Fig. 6.30

Prepare to glue the two side panels to the two pairs of legs (see Fig. 6.31). Ensure you have the pieces matched properly and that the good side of the plywood faces out before gluing them together. When the glue has dried completely (three to four hours), glue and clamp the back and the desktop pieces to the two side pieces, positioning the desktop 2" below the top edge of the panels. Then glue the bottom and the divider in place. The resulting file compartment will be 4¾" from front to back.

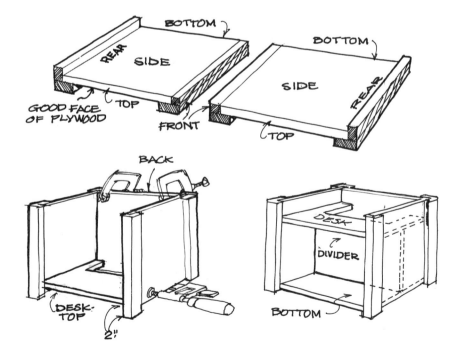

Fig. 6.31

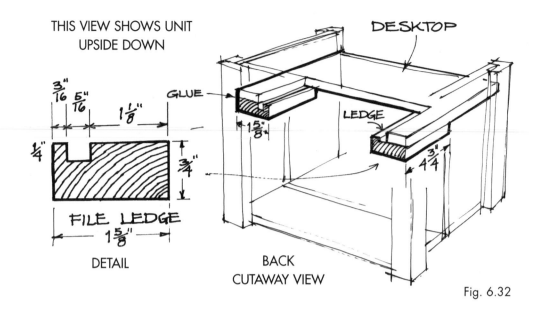

THIS VIEW SHOWS UNIT UPSIDE DOWN

FILE LEDGE

DETAIL

DESKTOP

LEDGE

BACK CUTAWAY VIEW

Fig. 6.32

To build a ledge on which to hang files, rip a 9½"-long piece of 1x4 hardwood so that it measures 1⅝" wide. Then cut it into two pieces, each 4¾" long. Cut a 5/16"-wide dado, ¼" deep, 3/16" from the edge of each piece (see Fig. 6.32). Glue and clamp each piece to the underside of the two projecting arms of the desktop. Glue and clamp the two side trim pieces and the back trim piece in place.

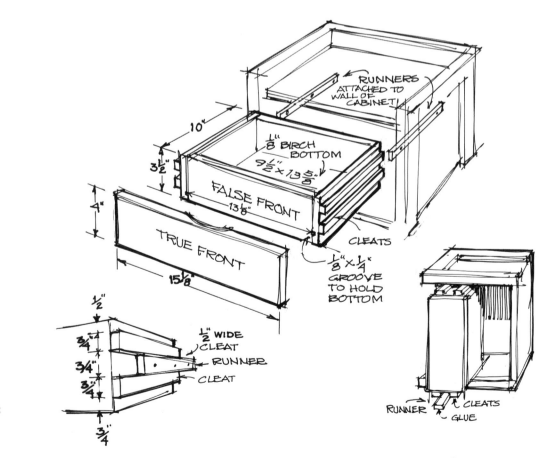

Fig. 6.33

TOP VIEW SECTION

DETAIL TOP VIEWS

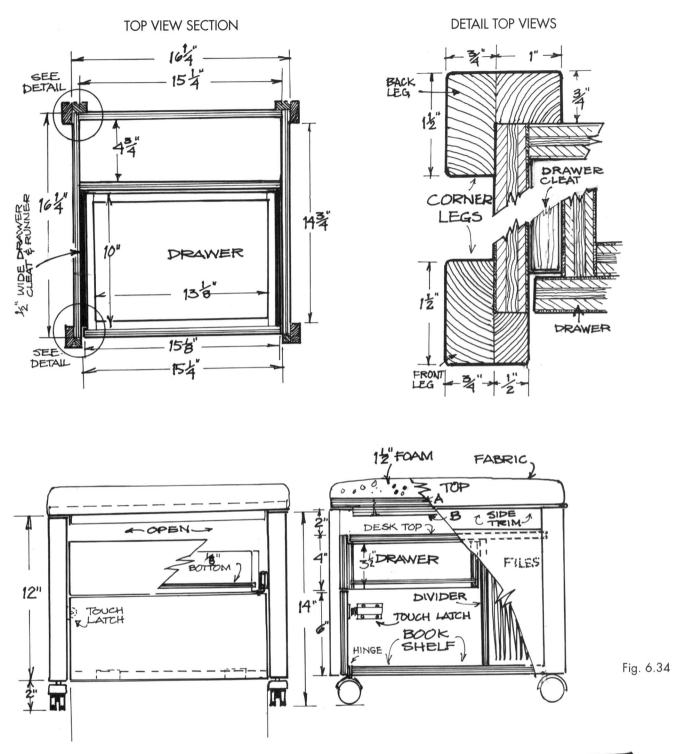

Fig. 6.34

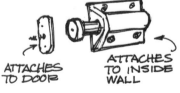

TOUCH LATCH DETAIL

Construct a drawer to fit under the desktop. Begin by cutting a ⅛"-wide, ¼"-deep dado ¼" in from the bottom edge of all four drawer pieces (see Fig. 6.33). Cut a 9½" x 13⅝" piece of birch plywood for the drawer bottom, and insert it into the dado in the sides, false front and back piece. Glue and nail the side pieces to the false front and

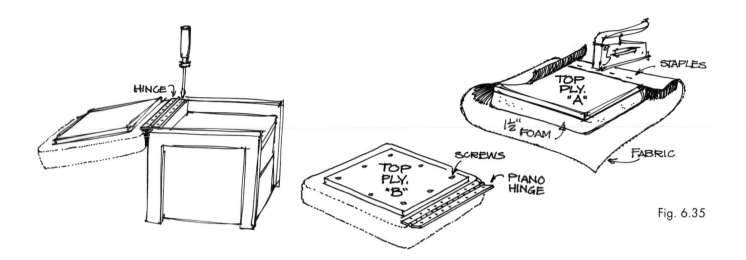

Fig. 6.35

back pieces, using the galvanized finishing nails. Note: The "true" front piece will be added later.

To mount the drawer to the box, rip six pieces of hardwood (poplar, birch, etc.), each ½" x ¾" x 10". Using 220-grit sandpaper, sand the pieces until smooth. Glue and clamp two parallel cleats to each side of the drawer, ¾" apart and ½" down from the top edge of the drawer. Test to make sure that the runner piece slides smoothly between the two cleats. Apply glue to one side of one of the runners and turn the box on its side. Place the runner between the cleats so that the glued side is facing out, and carefully position the drawer in place. Allow the glue on the runner to set up for a few minutes. Without disturbing the position of the runner, carefully pull the drawer all the way out. Clamp and screw the runner to the inside of the box, using ¾" countersunk flathead screws. Follow the same procedure for the other side of the unit.

Once the drawer is installed, glue and clamp the 4" x 15⅛" true front of the drawer onto the false front. This will allow you to make any necessary adjustments so that the front is perfectly aligned.

To make the bottom storage compartment, attach two 1" x 2" brass hinges to the front edge of the bottom shelf and the bottom inside face of the door. To hold the door shut, install a touch latch on the left side of the door and on the inside of the box (see Fig. 6.34).

Cut a 17½" x 17½" piece of 1½"-thick foam and a 27" x 27" piece of fabric. Wrap the fabric around the foam and under the top (A) piece of ½" plywood. Fold in the corners neatly and staple the fabric

to the plywood. Screw the second top (B) to the first (A), using 1"
countersunk #6 flathead screws (see Fig. 6.35).

Cut and attach the continuous (piano) hinge to one of the
bottom edges of the cushion/top. Screw the other side of the hinge to
the top of the back trim. To prevent the top lid from opening up too
far, install a pair of brass-plated lid supports, screwed to the lid and
to the 2"-high sides above the desktop.

Attach the casters equipped with mounting plates and screws.
Screw one caster to the underneath of each corner. No hardware is
necessary for the drawer. Instead of installing a drawer pull, you can
make a finger hold. Use a dowel wrapped with 60-grit sandpaper to
shape the top inside edge of the drawer (see Fig. 6.36).

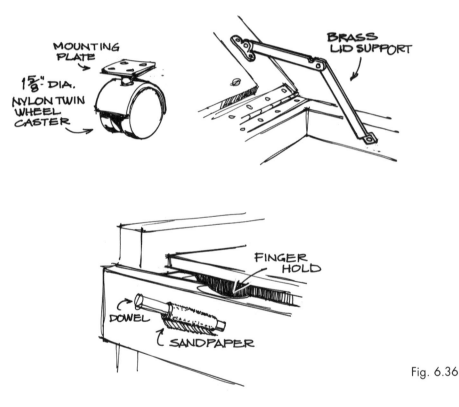

Fig. 6.36

Finally, fill any nail holes with wood putty and sand all the
surfaces with 60-, 120- and 220-grit sandpaper. Finish with three
coats of a clear water-based acrylic urethane wood finish.

# Wall File

This wall file is designed to hold 9¼" x 11¾" letter-size folders, 8½" x 11" writing pads and 4⅛" x 9½" business envelopes. The eight center cubbies can accommodate stationery, envelopes, incoming mail, bills and other papers. The unit is secured to the wall by screwing the back into the wall studs. We accented the clear birch plywood by painting the dividers bright cadmium red before installing them (see Fig. 6.37).

Fig. 6.37

Using the cutting plan as your guide (see Fig. 6.38), begin by cutting out the top, bottom and two end pieces for the case from the ¾" plywood. Next, cut out the two partitions, the middle shelf and the back pieces from ½" plywood.

Before the case of the wall file is assembled, ⅛"-deep slots have to be cut in the top, bottom and shelf pieces to hold the dividers. Measure for the placement of the slots by dividing the length of the unit (48") into thirds (16"). Then divide each third into four equal sections, making a total of 12 pigeonholes, and mark them on the underneath side of the top piece.

| Materials List | | | |
|---|---|---|---|
| **Quantity** | **Size** | **Description** | **Use** |
| 1 | 36" x 48" | ³/₄" birch plywood | case (top, bottom and ends) |
| 1 | 24" x 48" | ¹/₂" birch plywood | partitions, shelf and back |
| 1 | 33 ³/₈" x 38 ¹/₈" | ¹/₈" birch plywood | dividers |
| 2 | 48" strips | ³/₄" half-round molding | trim |
| 2 | 14" strips | ³/₄" half-round molding | trim |
| 2 | 12 ¹/₂" strips | ¹/₂" half-round molding | trim |
| 1 | 15 ¹/₂" strip | ¹/₂" half-round molding | trim |
| 1 box | 1 ¹/₂" | finishing nails | case, partitions and shelf |
| 1 box | 1" | brads | trim |
| 4 | 2 ¹/₂" | #10 roundhead screws with washers | |
| 1 bottle | 8 oz. | carpenter's glue | |
| 1 sheet | 60-grit | sandpaper | |
| 1 sheet | 120-grit | sandpaper | |
| 1 sheet | 220-grit | sandpaper | |
| 1 can | 10 oz. | water-based wood putty | |
| 1 pint | | paint or clear water-based acrylic urethane wood finish | |

After all the divider slots and locations for the partitions have been marked on the top piece, transfer these measurements to the bottom and the middle shelf pieces by laying all three boards down on the floor and drawing the lines across the boards using a T-square. The middle shelf will have to be turned over and marked on the other side as well. Use a circular saw, table saw or radial arm saw with a ¹/₈"-wide blade to cut a ¹/₈" x ¹/₈" dado at each divider line.

Assemble the case by gluing and nailing the ends to the top, bottom and back, using the finishing nails spaced 3" apart. Glue and nail the two partitions and the middle shelf together, positioning the shelf halfway up the partition pieces. Slide this unit into the case at the partition locations previously made and glue and nail it from the top and bottom, placing nails every 3".

Cut the dividers out of the ¹/₈" plywood (see Fig. 6.39) and slide them into their respective slots; they do not need to be glued. Sand the front edge of the dividers with 120- and 220-grit sandpaper. If you choose to accent the plywood dividers or the interior of the wall file with paint or acrylic finish, do so now, sanding lightly between coats. Once the trim is installed, the dividers will not be removable.

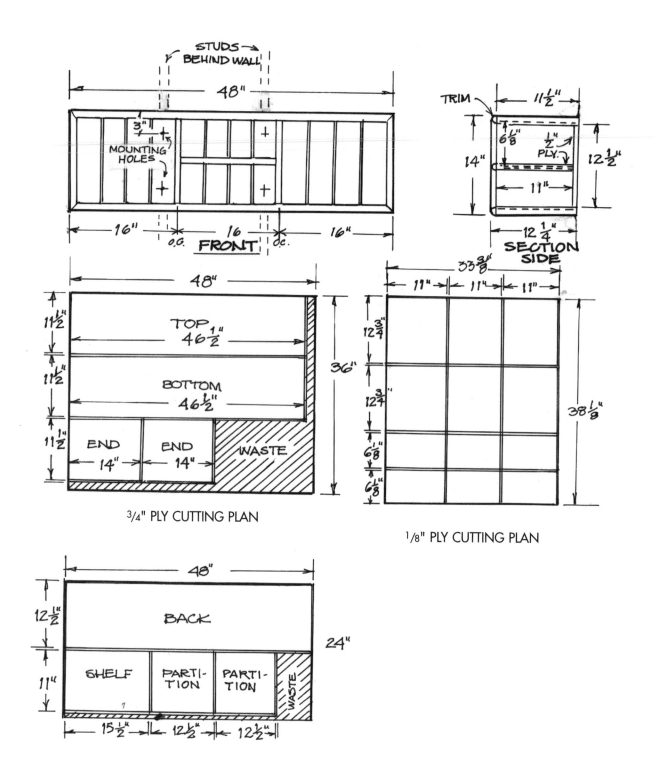

STUDS →
BEHIND WALL

48"

STUDS →

3"

MOUNTING
HOLES

16"

16

16"

o.c.    **FRONT**    o.c.

TRIM

11½"

6⅛"

½"
PLY.

14"

12½"

11"

12¼"

**SECTION
SIDE**

48"

11½"

TOP
46½"

11½"

BOTTOM
46½"

36"

11½"

END
14"

END
14"

WASTE

**¾" PLY CUTTING PLAN**

33⅜"

11"    11"    11"

12¾"

12¾"

6⅛"

6⅛"

38⅛"

**⅛" PLY CUTTING PLAN**

48"

12½"

BACK

24"

11"

SHELF

PARTI-
TION

PARTI-
TION

WASTE

15½"    12½"    12½"

**½" PLY CUTTING PLAN**

Fig. 6.38

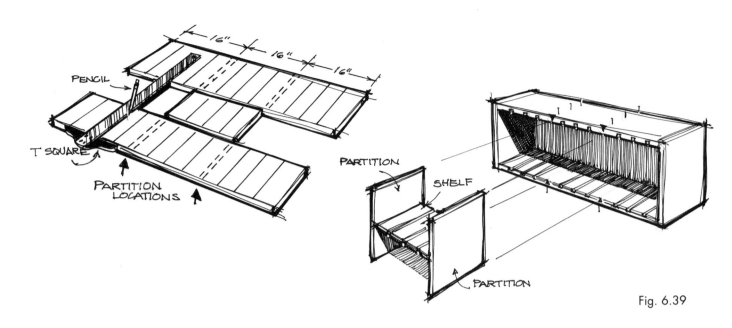

PENCIL

T SQUARE

PARTITION LOCATIONS

PARTITION

SHELF

PARTITION

Fig. 6.39

Trim the front edges of the case, partitions and shelf piece with half-round molding. The purpose of the trim is to hide the ends of the ⅛" dadoes and to hold the dividers in place. Cut two 48"-long strips of ¾" half-round and two 14"-long strips of ¾" half-round. Miter the ends of each piece at a 45° angle, and glue and nail them onto the front edges of the case, using 1" brads. Cut the ½" half-round molding to size and glue and nail it to the front of the two partitions and the center shelf piece. Set the nail heads, fill with wood putty and sand the outside of the completed unit, using 60-, 120- and 220-grit sandpaper.

To finish the outside of the wall file, apply at least three coats of either paint or a clear water-based acrylic urethane finish, sanding lightly between coats with 220-grit sandpaper. We chose the second option, giving our wall file a smooth, finished look that matched our apartment furniture.

To hang the unit on the wall, find and mark the stud locations behind the wall. Drill two 3/16"-diameter holes through the back of the unit, 3" below the top, the same distance apart as the studs. Determine how high you want your wall file to be, and then drill a ⅛"-diameter hole in the wall 3" below this point. Screw the unit to the wall and interior stud, using a 2½" #10 roundhead screw and washer. Place a level on the top of the unit and drill another screw into the right hole. Since this unit will be rather heavy when filled, drill two more holes and insert screws lower down and into the same wall studs.

# Artist's Studio Storage

Artists very often have a problem storing their paintings safely. Canvases can easily be scratched or ripped and should not be resting against each other or exposed to direct sunlight. Accessibility is also important. Rollers underneath storage units can make it easier to move heavy framed paintings around a studio. A more elaborate storage system used by artist John Hulsey holds both paintings and painting supplies. Two lightweight, hinged storage "doors" roll closed to hide the contents of the unit. While in the closed position, the outside of the doors can be covered with tacked-on drawings (see Fig 6.40).

CLOSED-DOOR VIEW

DOORS COVERED WITH 1/2" HOMASOTE FOR PINNING UP SKETCHES

3 HINGES

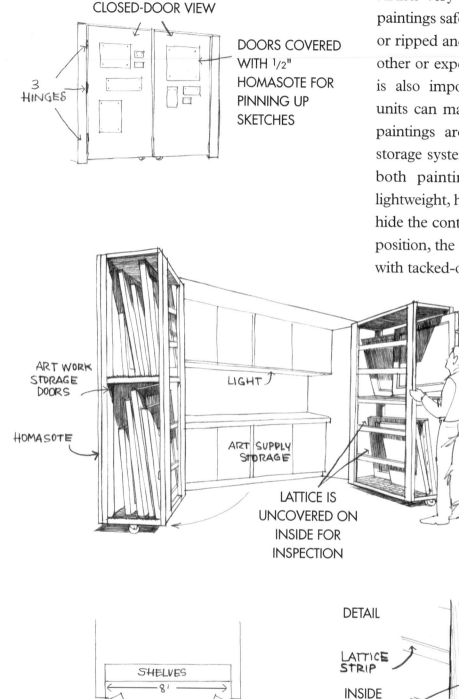

ART WORK STORAGE DOORS

HOMASOTE

LIGHT

ART SUPPLY STORAGE

LATTICE IS UNCOVERED ON INSIDE FOR INSPECTION

SHELVES

8'

HINGE

DETAIL

LATTICE STRIP

INSIDE

1x4

CARPET TO PROTECT PAINTINGS

NOTCH CUT FOR 1x4

1x12

1x4

1/2" 4'x8' HOMASOTE BOARD

OUTSIDE

HEAVY DUTY PLATE CASTER

Fig. 6.40

# Shelves

Fig. 6.41

Open shelves are one of the most useful, practical projects you can build for your workshop. They can be fairly simple to construct as long as you follow a few basic rules:

○ Decide how the shelves will be used and where they will be placed before you buy any lumber. If they will hold books or decorative objects, you will need to buy lumber that is wide enough to accommodate them. You will also want to vary the distance between the shelves, since the items will be of different heights. With this in mind, do a rough sketch of the project. Once you've come up with a design you like, draw a plan to scale (1" = 1') on graph paper, and double-check your measurements (see Fig. 6.41).

- Remember that shelves can sag without adequate support. If you are using ¾" stock (such as 1x12s), make sure that you support the shelves every 40" to prevent them from bending in the middle under a heavy load. Or use ⁵/₄" stock, which is thicker, stronger and more attractive than ¾" stock and can support spans up to 4' without sagging. When selecting your lumber, check it carefully so you don't buy cupped or warped boards.

- Most walls have baseboards. Don't forget to take this into consideration when planning your shelves. You may have to notch out a small section of wood on the bottom of the shelf supports to allow space for this molding.

- Floors are rarely perfectly flat. Check them using a level and a square, and trim the bottom of the shelf uprights if necessary so they will sit squarely on the floor.

- If the shelves are going to be higher than 3', attach them to the wall with 3" #10 drywall screws or drywall anchors so they cannot be pulled over accidentally.

- If you foresee moving shelves around in your workshop, or using them for different purposes, you may want to design shelves that can be disassembled and reattached to fit on another wall.

- The type of wood you use for shelves depends on whether or not you are going to paint them. If you are, #2 common 1x10s or 1x12s are fine. Fill any holes or knots with a water-based wood putty. Sand all the wood and roll on a coat of primer before assembling. Remember that knots in #2 common lumber can bleed through paint, so be sure to use a good shellac-based sealer.

If you are not painting your shelves, the best wood to buy is ⁵/₄x8 or ⁵/₄x10 clear white pine. It is expensive, but it looks beautiful when sanded and covered with a light stain. Two other less expensive alternatives are 2x8s or 2x10s – thicker, rougher lumber with a rustic appearance. It would require too much sanding to make this lumber practical to paint, but it is attractive when stained a dark brown or ebony. This lumber measures 1½" thick and is able to take heavier loads than the ⁵/₄" stock, which only measures about 1".

## Finished Open Shelves

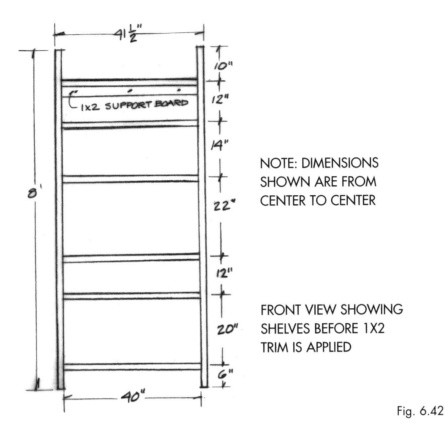

NOTE: DIMENSIONS SHOWN ARE FROM CENTER TO CENTER

FRONT VIEW SHOWING SHELVES BEFORE 1X2 TRIM IS APPLIED

Fig. 6.42

You may want to design and build open shelves that fit your own specifications rather than use the dimensions included here (see Fig. 6.42). As you work on the design, remember to measure your tallest books or objects to be displayed and make sure at least one set of shelves can accommodate them.

We chose 1x10 #2 common pine for this project for two reasons: This size of board fits most books and #2 pine is more economical than clear pine. Since the shelves were to be covered with books, we felt that spending extra money on clear pine was unnecessary. To strengthen the unit and give it a more substantial, built-in look, we trimmed the edges with 1x2 #2 clear poplar (see Fig. 6.43).

Before beginning this project, measure your ceiling height to ensure you will have at least 1" of clearance between the ceiling and the top of the bookcase for installation. If the 8' uprights are too long for your ceiling, cut them to the appropriate height. Stand them up

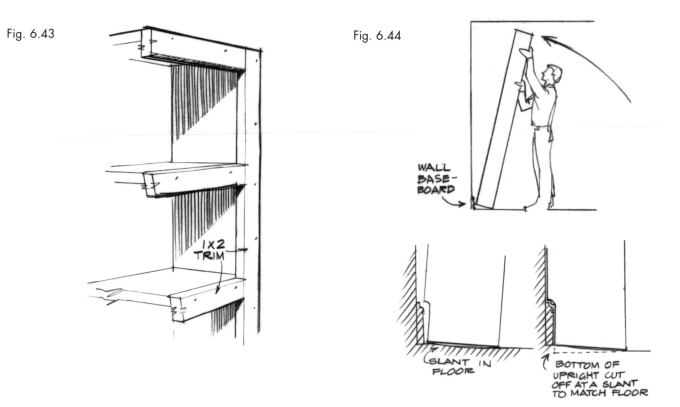

Fig. 6.43

1X2 TRIM

Fig. 6.44

WALL BASE-BOARD

SLANT IN FLOOR

BOTTOM OF UPRIGHT CUT OFF AT A SLANT TO MATCH FLOOR

again and mark a profile of where the baseboard of your wall meets the bottom back of both uprights (see Fig. 6.44).

Next, carefully measure and mark the two 1x10s that will be used for the shelves (see Fig. 6.45). Each shelf should be exactly the same length. Use either a handsaw or a portable circular saw to cut each shelf to a length of 40", as shown in the cutting plan. Then stand them all together to make sure they are equal in length. If you have to remove a fraction of an inch and are using a handsaw, try this trick: Clamp a piece of scrap 1x10 over one end of the shelf board, mark where the cut should be and saw through both boards at once (see Fig. 6.46).

Lay the two uprights flat on the floor, side by side. Determine at what height you want each shelf. Lay a T-square flat across the two uprights and mark a pencil line across both of them where the top of each shelf will be located; continue the line around the four edges of the uprights (see Fig. 6.47). To assemble the shelves, turn one of the uprights over and start four 2" finishing nails, approximately 2" apart and slightly below the line. Lay the bottom shelf and the upright both on edge, brace the opposite end of the shelf against a solid surface, like a wall, and finish hammering in the nails (see Fig. 6.48).

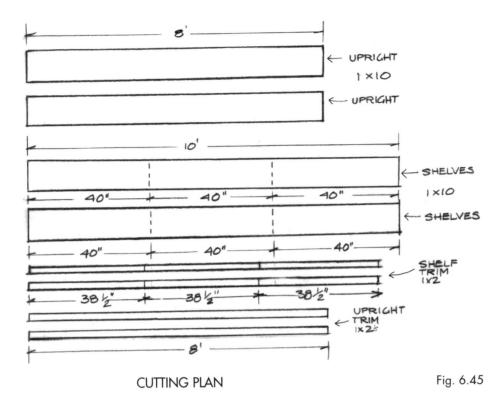

CUTTING PLAN                                    Fig. 6.45

Follow the same procedure for the top shelf and remaining inside shelves. When you have all six shelves attached to one upright, turn the unit over and repeat the same procedure on the other side. To accommodate a wall baseboard, lay the unit on its side and cut out the marked profile of the baseboard using an electric jigsaw.

Fig. 6.46

Stand the unit up and check for plumb with a level and square. You may find that the shelving unit tips slightly forward. This is often the case on a wooden floor that has not been sanded as deeply and smoothly next to the wall. You can rectify this by taking the unit down and trimming the bottom end of the uprights at a slight slant.

As a safety precaution, we suggest screwing the bookcase to the wall at the top to prevent it from falling forward and possibly causing

Fig. 6.47

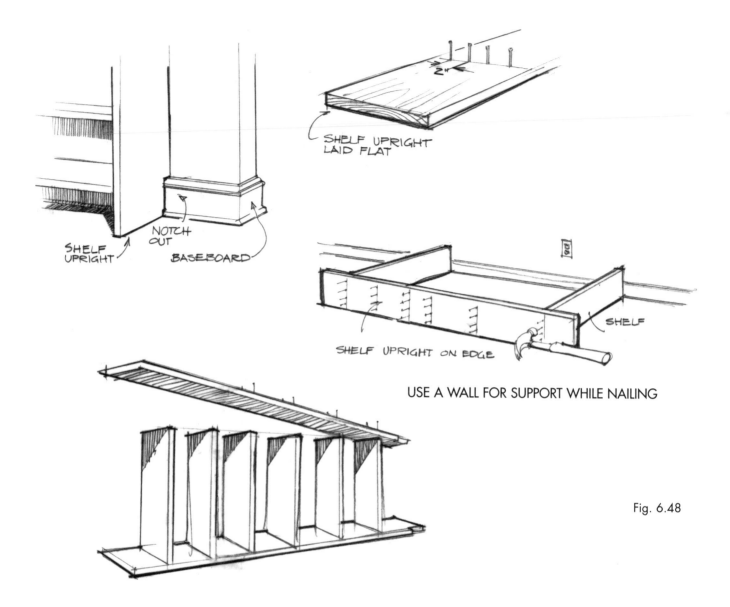

SHELF UPRIGHT LAID FLAT

SHELF UPRIGHT

NOTCH OUT

BASEBOARD

SHELF UPRIGHT ON EDGE

SHELF

USE A WALL FOR SUPPORT WHILE NAILING

Fig. 6.48

injury. To do this, carefully measure and cut a support board out of 1x2 pine. Locate the wall studs as described below, and screw through the support board and wall and into the studs. You can also attach the support board to the wall using wall anchors made for wallboard. Then hammer one 3" finishing nail in at an angle every foot along the top shelf so that the nails penetrate the support board. This will secure the shelf to the wall (see Fig. 6.49).

To give the shelves a more finished look, cut two 1x2s to the same length as the uprights. Using 1½" finishing nails spaced 6" apart, nail the trim to the front edge of both uprights so that one edge overlaps the inside of the unit by ¾" and the other edge is flush with the outside of the upright. Next, cut two 10' lengths of 1x2 into six 38½" lengths, to trim the fronts of the shelves. Place the front trim flush with the top of each shelf, overlapping ¾" at the bottom, and secure it with finishing nails spaced 6" apart (see Fig. 6.43).

Sand the shelves smooth using 100-grit sandpaper, followed by 220-grit sandpaper and then a sanding block. Cover with a coat of primer, then paint the shelves the color of your choice.

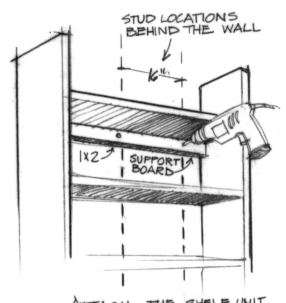

STUD LOCATIONS BEHIND THE WALL

6"

1x2 SUPPORT BOARD

ATTACH THE SHELF UNIT TO THE WALL USING A 1x2 SUPPORT BOARD SCREWED THROUGH THE WALL INTO THE STUDS INSIDE THE WALL.

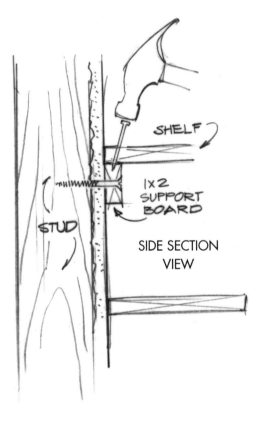

SHELF

1x2 SUPPORT BOARD

STUD

SIDE SECTION VIEW

Fig. 6.49

## *Attaching Wall Shelves*

When attaching wall shelves or cabinets to a wall, there are various techniques used for different types of wall materials.

Most houses today are built with ½"-thick drywall nailed over 2x4 or 2x6 studs, spaced 16" or 24" on center. Since the drywall consists of relatively soft plaster sandwiched between two pieces of paper, it has very little holding power, which means nails and screws can easily pull out.

The best way to prevent this from happening is to locate the studs behind the wall and screw through the unit you're hanging, through the drywall and into the wood studs. To locate wall studs, measure from the nearest corner in 16" or 24" increments (depending on the age of your house). If your house was built before 1930, chances are that the studs are 2x4, spaced 24" apart, or randomly spaced from the center of one stud to the center of another. Most wall studs in houses built after 1930 are 16" on center. More recently (after 1970), some builders switched to 2x6 wall studs, spaced 24" apart. Many people swear by using a simple electronic stud finder that can be bought in a hardware store; however, they are not foolproof. When in doubt, make a test hole by hammering in a finishing nail to see if you have found the stud, before attaching the screws. Caution: Always turn off the electricity in this part of your house at the fuse box or circuit breaker.

Russell Speer built his garage as a woodworking shop using salvaged windows and overhead beams. The shop is heated with radiant heating through a concrete slab. His wife, Rosemary, has her textile studio next door.

Roger Bates' office workspace reflects the Cotswold architecture of his home. (See page 67)

Shari and Art Lukach's Tudor style writer's retreat. Built by the author. (See page 83)

Kate Williams adapted this classic American farmhouse for her product design and painting studio.

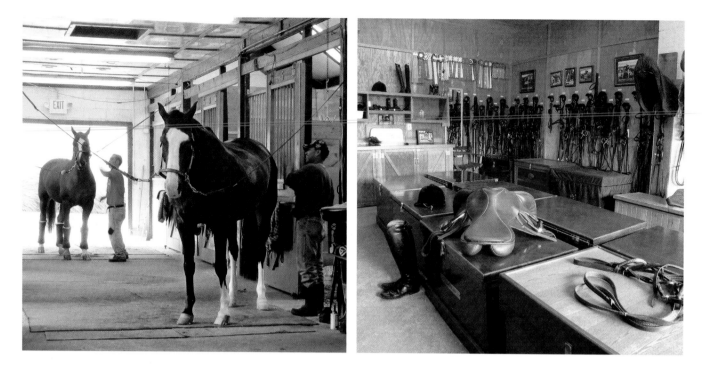

Two Tree Stables and its well organized tack room. (See page 113 in text)

Roy Sebazco dust-proofed his temporary basement workshop by sealing the walls with plastic sheeting and installing a high-powdered dust-collection system before building this prototype racecar.

Builder Robert Schmitter added this garage onto his house for under $3500, including a concrete floor and recycled windows and doors.

Authors, Jeanie and David Stiles, built this L-shaped corner desk for the home office in their apartment. (See page 135)

Lauren Jarrett, painter/illustrator, works in her home studio. The French doors provide natural light and a view of her garden.

Architect, Richard Lear has a combination office and drafting studio in Bridgehampton, N.Y.

Alan Applebaum's home office is built under the eaves of a dormer.

This state of the art woodworking shop in Sagaponack, N.Y. was converted from a 19th century horse stable.

Wood is stored in easily accessible bins.

This beautiful cabinet, made from leftover exotic woods, holds the owner's hand tools.

Two walk-around workbenches provide plenty of space for working on large projects.

Ann & John Hulsey live and work out of their home which features two separate art studios and a design/landscaping studio upstairs. Some of the important features of this house include a hand-made taboret on rollers, plenty of storage for paintings, and large windows to allow in natural light. (See page 108)

(top left) Metal sculptor, Hans Van de Bovenkamp, works in this well-lit studio with glass-paned overhead garage doors. Other outbuildings on the property include a gallery to house sculptures and a drawing studio with double gable roof.

Tex Beha's home office addition, built on top of a single story house, looks out over the water.

Marsha Lipsitz, a ceramic artist, works in a 20' x 20' studio next to her house. Open shelving displays her whimsical sculptures.

Natural light floods Dawn Lesh's pottery studio, built in the same architectural style as her home. A double-insulated "damp room" keeps clay cool. Cabinets and plenty of open shelves display her English functional pottery.

Photos: Sam Mead

(top) Sam Mead added onto his garage to make this small, but efficient, woodworking shop. (See page 100)
(bottom) Artist, Louis Copt, installed a garage door at one end of his painting studio to facilitate bringing large canvases in and out of the space. A corner studio takes advantage of the natural light and view.

Photos: Louis Copt

Painter Marilyn Church uses this well-lit addition to her home as an art studio. It is equipped with a hand-made model platform and sculpting stand.

Connie Fox built this painting studio in her house to accommodate her extra large canvases. Six skylights flood the space with light.

The exterior of this inconspicuous shed hides the high-tech office of architect Dan Rowen and his wife, Coco, a writer and editor. (See page 110)

Another view of Connie Fox's studio showing storage space.

Isador Shiffman has converted his garage into a potter's workshop.

Norman Mercer creates his polymer sculptures in a state-of-the-art workshop attached to his house. Cabinetry and lighting make this space bright and easy to work in.

John Sutton built this barn with the help of his friends, to house his well-equipped woodworking shop. The heavily insulated shop is heated by a wood-burning stove.
(See page 98)

Dean Foster's machine shop in Sagaponack, New York.

Designed by the author for
Pamela Abrahams, Senior
Editor at *Country Living
Magazine*, this garage features
a second story art studio for
pottery and painting.
(See page 105)

Author's woodworking shop built next to his home in East Hampton, NY. (See page 96)

An addition built onto an existing house can make a perfect workspace. (See Chapter 3)

# SEVEN

# WORKSHOP ACCESSORIES

If your building skills are a little rusty these four small but very useful projects are a good place to start. Each one is as useful and practical as it is easy to build and will be a welcome addition to any workshop.

## Toolbox

Our toolbox contains a compartment for loose hardware, has room for a nail box and can even accommodate an 18" handsaw. If your handsaw is longer, simply adjust the dimensions given here to the appropriate length. Another feature of our toolbox is that it uses standard-size lumber, which means it requires very little cutting. This is an easy, quick-to-construct project.

Referring to the cutting plan (see Fig 7.1), begin by cutting the end pieces and then the bottom. Clamp a 4'-long piece of 1x10 #10 pine to a sturdy work surface. Make the two angled cuts for the end pieces by measuring and

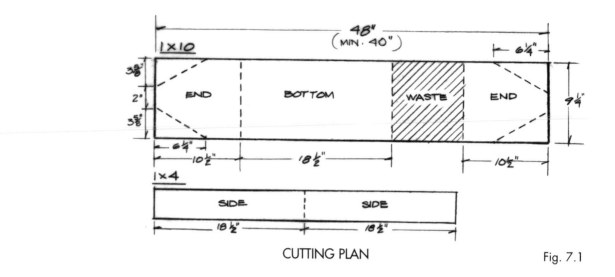

CUTTING PLAN                                    Fig. 7.1

marking 6¼" down from both top corners of the board and then measuring and marking 3⅝" in from the top corners (see Fig. 7.2). Using a straightedge as your guide, draw a pencil line connecting these two points, and saw off the two angled corners with an electric jigsaw or a handsaw. From the end of the board, measure down

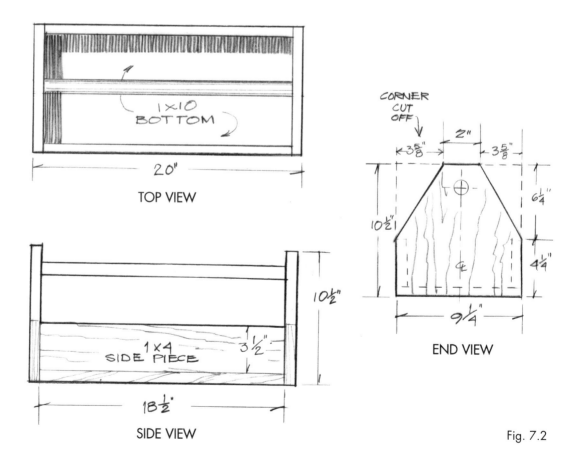

TOP VIEW

SIDE VIEW

END VIEW

Fig. 7.2

10½" and make a mark. Place a combination square flush against the side of the 1x10 and use it to draw a straight line across the board at the 10½" mark. Saw off this end piece. Turn the board around, clamp it to your work surface and follow the same steps to create the second end piece, so that you end up with two identical end pieces (see Fig. 7.3).

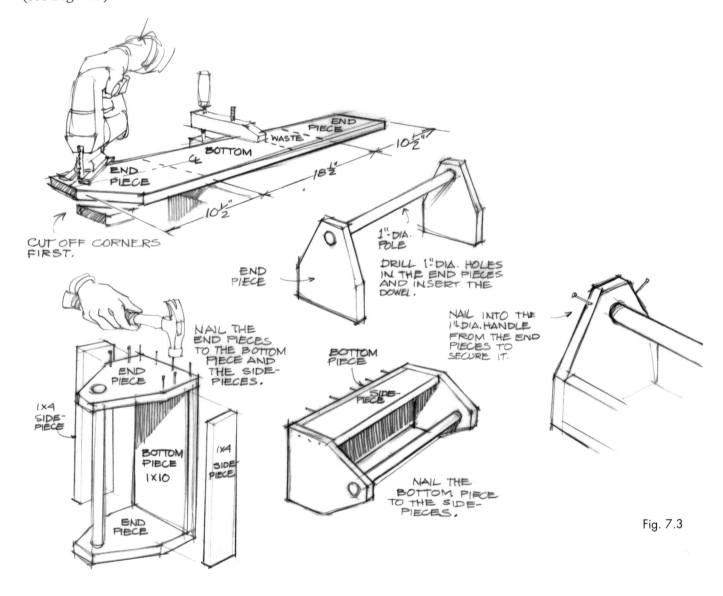

CUT OFF CORNERS FIRST.

END PIECE

WASTE END PIECE

BOTTOM

10½"

18½"

10½"

END PIECE

1"-DIA. POLE

DRILL 1"-DIA. HOLES IN THE END PIECES AND INSERT THE DOWEL.

NAIL INTO THE 1"-DIA. HANDLE FROM THE END PIECES TO SECURE IT.

NAIL THE END PIECES TO THE BOTTOM PIECE AND THE SIDE-PIECES.

END PIECE

1X4 SIDE-PIECE

BOTTOM PIECE 1X10

1X4 SIDE PIECE

END PIECE

BOTTOM PIECE

SIDE-PIECE

NAIL THE BOTTOM PIECE TO THE SIDE-PIECES.

Fig. 7.3

Next, make the bottom of the toolbox. Clamp the remaining piece of 1x10 to the work surface. Measure and mark 18½" down from the end of the board. With a combination square flush against the side, draw a straight line across the board at the 18½" mark. Saw off the bottom piece.

To make the two identical sidepieces, clamp the 1x4 to the work surface. Measure, mark and cut two pieces, each 18½" long. Ensure that the two sides and bottom piece are exactly the same length. Sand all five pieces until they are smooth, using 60-grit sandpaper followed by 120-grit sandpaper wrapped around a sanding block.

Using a combination square, find the center of each of the two end pieces and make a mark 1¼" down from the top of each. At this mark, use a 1" spade bit to drill out a 1"-diameter hole where the dowel handle will be positioned in each end piece.

For the toolbox handle, use a handsaw to cut a 1"-diameter dowel to measure 20" in length. To keep the dowel from rolling while you saw, use two clamps to secure it to your work surface. Twist one end of the dowel through the hole in an end piece, and then do the same with the other end of the dowel and the remaining end piece. Inserting the dowel at this stage makes the ends more stable, making it easier to install the bottom piece. Once the toolbox is assembled, it is much more difficult to get the dowel through the holes in the end pieces.

Next, turn the unit over on one side and wedge the bottom piece between the two end pieces. Nail the end piece to the bottom, using 2" finishing nails placed approximately 2" apart. Turn the unit over and repeat the process for the other end.

To attach the sidepieces to the bottom and end pieces, keep the toolbox on its side and wedge the sidepieces between the two end pieces and on top of the bottom piece. Nail the end pieces to the sidepieces, placing the nails approximately 1" apart. Turn the toolbox over on its side and, bracing it with one hand, nail the bottom piece to the bottom edge of the two sidepieces, spacing the 2" finishing nails approximately 2" apart. Turn the box over on the opposite side, and repeat the process.

To keep the handle in place, nail one 2" finishing nail through the two slanted edges of each of the end pieces and into the 1"-diameter dowel. Fill the holes with wood putty. After the putty has dried, sand the holes with 60-grit sandpaper and a sanding block. Give the entire box a final sanding, using 120-grit sandpaper and a sanding block. Although we finished our toolbox with a simple wood sealer, this rugged piece will survive with no finish at all.

# Tool Rack and Shelves

All carpenters' workshops need racks for tools and shelves for storage. This tool rack is easy to make since it requires only 1x4 and 1x2 lumber. The 1x2 is used as a support for the shelf and a means for screwing the shelf to the wall. You'll need to cut the two pieces of 1x4 for the ends, then lay out your hand tools and draw on the remaining 1x4 where you need to drill holes or make notches to accommodate the various tools. Nail the 1x4 end pieces to the 1x4 shelf top, allowing a ½" lip above the ends of the shelf to prevent items from falling off. Screw the 1x2 support piece to the wall and nail the shelf top to the 1x2 support. Then screw the end pieces into the wall (see Fig. 7.4).

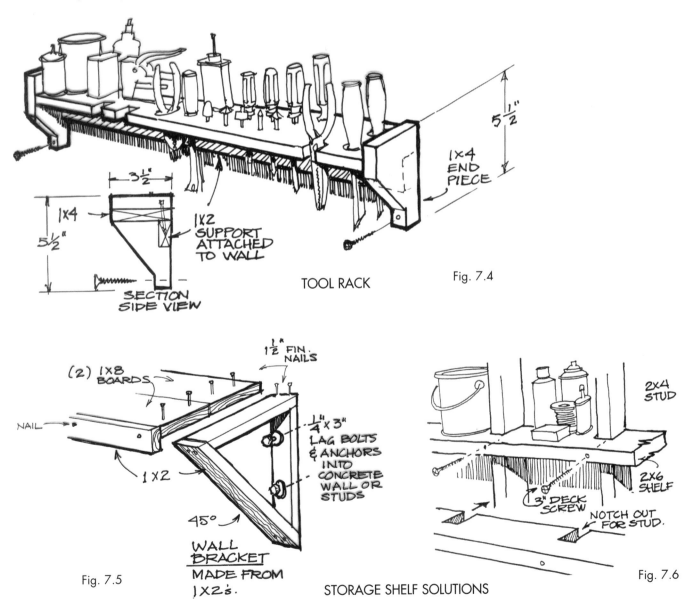

TOOL RACK    Fig. 7.4

WALL BRACKET MADE FROM 1X2's.    Fig. 7.5

STORAGE SHELF SOLUTIONS    Fig. 7.6

# Saw Guide

To make perfect right-angle crosscuts, you can either use a miter box or build your own saw guide. The advantage of a saw guide over a miter box is that you can cut wide boards. Making accurate right-angle crosscuts is important in every aspect of carpentry; therefore, we strongly suggest that you build this simple saw guide. The materials required are inexpensive, it takes less than an hour to construct and it will greatly increase the accuracy of your cuts.

We have added two triangular pieces of wood, which not only make the saw guide easier to use but also enable you to make 45° miter cuts for moldings. Our saw guide is adjustable in case it gets out of alignment, and it takes only minutes to change. Although the saw guide is set up for ¾"-thick wood, it can be modified to accept 1½"-thick wood by adding another 1x3 to the fence and using longer screws.

Only two cuts are needed in the 36"-long 1x10: a 45° diagonal cut and a 90° perpendicular cut. Check the angles of both with a combination square to make sure they are exact, for all future cuts will depend on these. The other two pieces of lumber, the 1x3 "fence" and the 1x2 "hook," should each be cut 26¾" long. The 1x3 should be perfectly straight, as it will be used as the guide for cutting lumber when the project is completed (see Fig. 7.7).

Place the base piece on top of a stable work surface. Lay a bead of carpenter's glue on the top surface of the hook, spreading it evenly

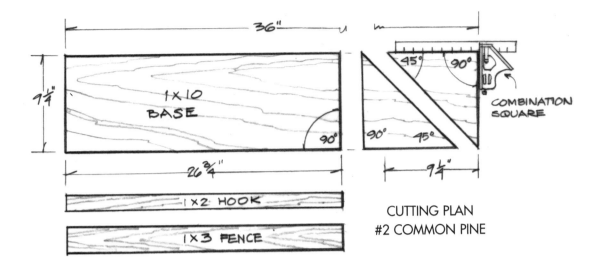

CUTTING PLAN
#2 COMMON PINE

Fig. 7.7

with a flat stick. Using two wood clamps, attach the hook to the underneath front edge of the base piece. Make sure that the front and side edges of the two pieces are flush with each other. The hook is the part that rests against your workbench, counter or table.

When the glue has dried, glue and clamp the fence to the top rear of the base piece. Next, use a combination square and pencil to mark a line from the center of the base piece perpendicular to the fence. Double-check the accuracy of your line with the square (see Fig. 7.8).

Temporarily position the two triangular pieces of wood over the middle of the fence. Align them so that their back edges are flush

> Tip: To make sure the 90° and 45° cuts are exact, ask the lumberyard to cut these for you using a radial or miter saw.

HOW TO BUILD A SAW GUIDE

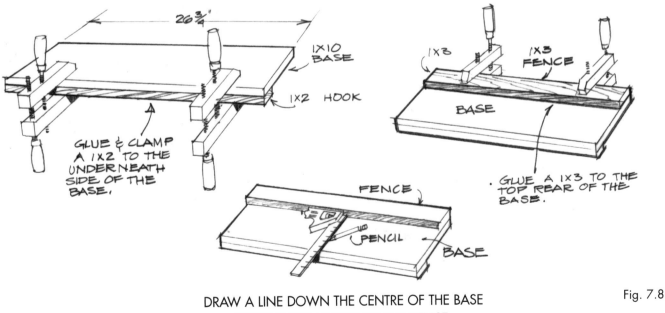

DRAW A LINE DOWN THE CENTRE OF THE BASE
PERPENDICULAR (90°) TO THE FENCE.

Fig. 7.8

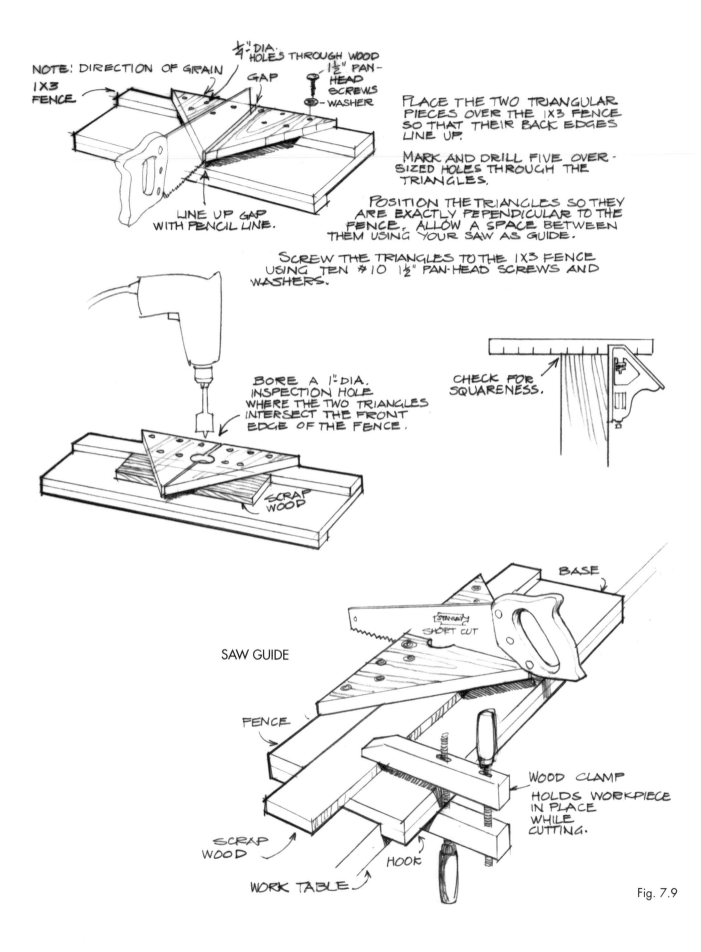

NOTE: DIRECTION OF GRAIN

1X3 FENCE

¼" DIA. HOLES THROUGH WOOD

GAP

1½" PAN-HEAD SCREWS

WASHER

LINE UP GAP WITH PENCIL LINE.

PLACE THE TWO TRIANGULAR PIECES OVER THE 1X3 FENCE SO THAT THEIR BACK EDGES LINE UP.

MARK AND DRILL FIVE OVER-SIZED HOLES THROUGH THE TRIANGLES.

POSITION THE TRIANGLES SO THEY ARE EXACTLY PEPENDICULAR TO THE FENCE. ALLOW A SPACE BETWEEN THEM USING YOUR SAW AS GUIDE.

SCREW THE TRIANGLES TO THE 1X3 FENCE USING TEN #10 1½" PAN-HEAD SCREWS AND WASHERS.

BORE A 1" DIA. INSPECTION HOLE WHERE THE TWO TRIANGLES INTERSECT THE FRONT EDGE OF THE FENCE.

SCRAP WOOD

CHECK FOR SQUARENESS.

BASE

SHORT CUT

STANLEY

SAW GUIDE

FENCE

WOOD CLAMP

HOLDS WORKPIECE IN PLACE WHILE CUTTING.

SCRAP WOOD

HOOK

WORK TABLE

Fig. 7.9

with the back edge of the fence. Ensure that the grain of the wood is running from front to rear, not sideways.

With a pencil, mark five screw locations on each triangle directly over the fence, as shown (see Fig. 7.9). Remove the triangles and, using an electric drill, bore ¼"-diameter (oversized) holes where the marks are, all the way through the triangles. Make sure that the right angles of the two triangular pieces are perpendicular to the fence (use the pencil line as a guide). Allow for a slight gap between the two triangles, exactly the same width as your saw blade. You can even use the saw as a spacer when you are attaching the triangles.

Screw the triangles down onto the fence with 1½" #10 pan-head screws and washers. We recommend attaching the triangles with screws rather than glue so you have the option of adjusting the gap later on simply by loosening the screws and repositioning the triangles.

In order to place each new piece of wood correctly under the triangles, you will need an inspection hole to see where to cut. Use a 1"-diameter spade bit to bore a hole through the triangles at a point where the saw slot intersects the fence. Before drilling this hole, place a piece of scrap wood under the spot where you will be drilling, so the drill bit will not cause tear-out on the underneath surface of the wood when exiting the triangles.

Test the accuracy of the saw guide by sliding and clamping a piece of scrap lumber under the triangles, flush against the fence. Carefully and slowly insert your saw in the saw slot (it should be tight at first) and saw through the scrap lumber. When sawing, the "power" stroke should be the forward stroke, moving away from your body. Keep checking as you saw to make sure that the saw blade is positioned correctly and is not tilting to one side or the other or tipping too far forward or backward (see Fig. 7.9).

At first it will be difficult to know when you have sawed through the scrap wood. Don't be fooled by the top of the saw, which is tapered down toward the tip. After several cuts, you'll be able to feel and hear a difference when the saw has gone through the wood. Don't be afraid to overcut slightly into the base board, as this will happen from time to time. Just don't overcut so much that you cut the whole saw guide board in half!

When you have finished the trial cut, remove the scrap wood and check to see if it is square. Do this by holding a combination square against the end of the wood. If it's not square, loosen the screws and adjust the triangles so they are properly aligned.

Always remove the sawdust from underneath the triangles before inserting the next piece of wood against the fence.

# Drafting Table

You can save hundreds of dollars by building your own drafting table (see Fig 7.10). Use MDO (medium density overlay) plywood, which

EASY-TO-BUILD DRAFTING BOARD

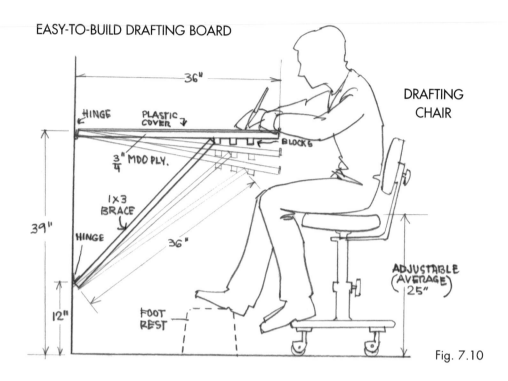

Fig. 7.10

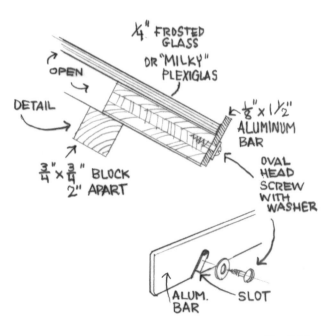

Fig. 7.11

is flat and stable and has a smooth surface. From a half-sheet of MDO, cut a 36" x 48" piece and hinge it to the wall, making sure the hinge screws go into a wall stud. Glue and screw short 1" x 1" blocks about 2" apart down both edges on the underneath side of the MDO board and attach 1x3 braces, hinged to the wall. The hinged braces allow you to adjust the angle of the drawing board. To stop pencils from rolling off the table, screw a ⅛" x 1½" bar of aluminum to the front edge of the plywood. Cut open slots for the screws so that the bar can be raised or lowered (see Fig 7.11).

Most professional drawing boards are covered with 1/16" thick plastic sheeting called SAFO, which comes in various colors, including cream, light green and gray. It can be attached to the table with double-sided tape.

# SKILL REVIEW

## Measurements and Materials

Remember that lumber is sold in nominal dimensions. So, for example, a 2x4 actually measures only 1½" x 3½". This is a result of the final planing, surfacing and anticipated shrinkage of the wood as it dries. This ½" discrepancy changes in wide boards – lumber with a nominal measurement of 8" or more in width measures ¾" less. The difference in the thickness of the boards, however, remains the same. So a 2x8, for example, will measure 1½" x 7¼".

Plywood is generally sold in 4x8 sheets of ⅛", ¼", ½" and ¾" thickness. Bring your tape measure to the lumberyard when you are

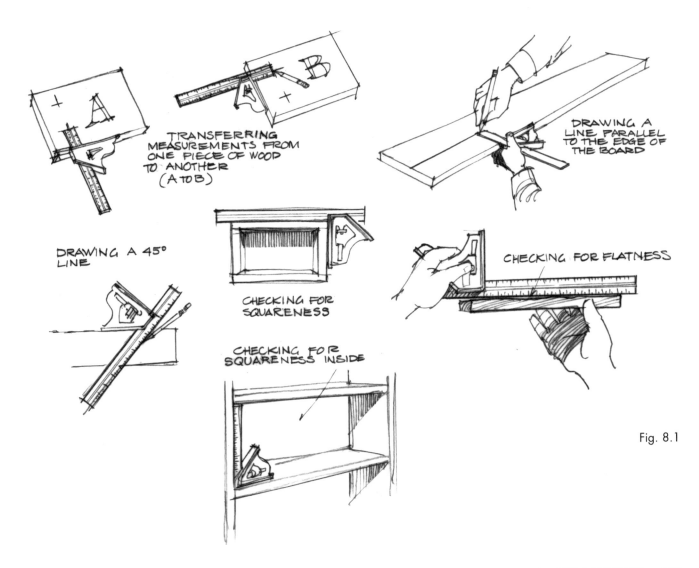

TRANSFERRING MEASUREMENTS FROM ONE PIECE OF WOOD TO ANOTHER (A TO B)

DRAWING A LINE PARALLEL TO THE EDGE OF THE BOARD

DRAWING A 45° LINE

CHECKING FOR SQUARENESS

CHECKING FOR FLATNESS

CHECKING FOR SQUARENESS INSIDE

Fig. 8.1

picking out plywood, because it can be $^1/_{32}$" to $^1/_{16}$" less thick than how it is labeled. Unless this is taken into consideration when building a project, your joints (if cut exactly as specified) will always be a little off.

If you watch professional carpenters at work, you'll notice that every so often they will stop and recheck their project's measurements with a combination square. This is a good habit to get into, since a project will quite often get "out of square" during the building process.

The combination square is one of the most essential tools to have in your toolbox (see Fig. 8.1). It can be used to measure small objects, to mark cuts at 45° (mitered) angles and 90° (right) angles, to measure the depth of a mortised hole and to check that an object is square or flat. It is also useful for drawing parallel lines. You can even use a combination square to take measurements and transfer them to another piece of wood without reading the numbers. Do this by loosening the knurled nut and sliding the rule forward until the end of the rule lines up with the point you are measuring on the first piece of wood. Tighten the nut and move the combination square to the new piece of wood, marking at the end of the rule.

There are other useful squares that you may want to add to your toolbox as you gain more experience (see Fig. 8.2). They include:

**Framing square:** A framing, or carpenter's, square is made from one piece of steel or aluminum with measurements marked along the inside and the outside of its two "legs." The 2" x 24" leg is referred to as the blade and the 1½" x 16" leg is called the tongue. The two legs meet at a 90° angle at the heel. When purchasing a framing square, be sure it is rust-resistant and that the numbers are incised into the surface of the metal. A framing square is longer than a combination square and is more practical when building large projects. It is used to mark straight lines across boards and to check for squareness on projects such as cabinets, doors, workbenches and sheds. Be careful not to step on, drop or bang up this square, since accuracy depends on its exact shape. When laying out projects using 2x4s, it is helpful to remember that the tongue of the square is 1½" wide.

**T-square:** A T-square used to be thought of as a draftsman's tool, but today it comes in 48" lengths and can be used for measuring, marking and cutting drywall and other sheet materials such as plywood. It is made of aluminum.

**Speed square:** A speed square is a durable, multipurpose tool. It can be used for marking right-angle cuts, and its thick edge makes it especially handy as a saw guide when cutting lumber with a portable circular saw. It is quite popular among house carpenters because it won't break or bend if stepped on.

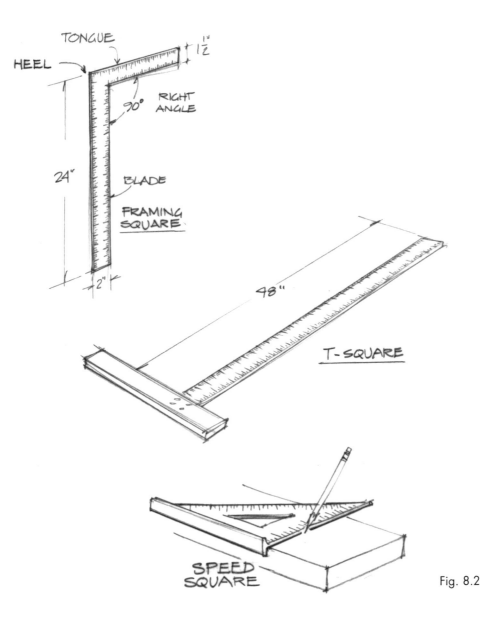

Fig. 8.2

# Cutting and Drilling

## *Handsaws*

Saws come in all shapes and sizes and are used for different purposes. The most common is the traditional crosscut saw. The Egyptians first used a similar saw more than 5,000 years ago. If you have inherited a handsaw or found one at a yard sale, you should take it to your local hardware store or lumberyard and have it sharpened. Nothing dulls the enthusiasm of an aspiring carpenter as much as struggling with a dull saw.

The ripsaw is used only for "rip" cuts, which are made along the length of the board with the grain of the wood. The teeth of the ripsaw are larger than those of the crosscut saw and are shaped so that the front of each tooth is at a 90° angle. The traditional crosscut saw, on the other hand, has small teeth that are slightly slanted back. The ripsaw cuts wood along the grain, while the crosscut saw – as the name implies – cuts wood across the grain (and through plywood). In a pinch, you can use a crosscut saw to cut with the grain, but you can't use a ripsaw to cut across the grain. Therefore, if you are investing in only one saw, a crosscut saw is the better choice (see Fig. 8.3).

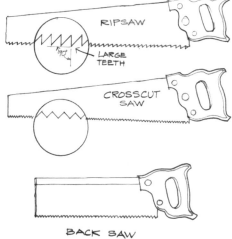

Fig. 8.3

### Sawing with a Handsaw

Before you start cutting, you must first measure and mark a cut line on the board. Place a combination square flush against the edge of the board and, holding the square firmly with one hand, draw a line across the board, using the edge of the square as your guide. One useful trick is to mark your lumber so it is clear which side of the mark is the waste side.

If possible, clamp the board you are cutting to a strong base support; otherwise, brace the board with your knee and your free hand. A chair, stool, low sawhorse or other suitable work surface positioned so that it is between knee and knuckle height makes a comfortable base when sawing by hand. A support that is too high makes sawing difficult, since it places your wrist in an awkward, weak position. If the support is too low, the tip of the saw may hit the ground (see Fig. 8.4).

Position yourself so that your arm is in line with the saw and the cut line. Grasp the saw handle firmly with a straight wrist, resting the saw blade on the cut line. Hold the saw at a 45° angle and start the cut by pulling the saw back toward you, using a very short movement. (Because the saw teeth are facing forward, it is easier to make the beginning cut in the wood by first pulling back on the saw rather than pushing forward.) Make a small cut in the board, check to see if it is on the cut line, and then continue sawing.

As the cut progresses, the saw strokes should become longer, and more force should be given to the forward stroke, away from your body. This is the stroke that actually does the cutting. As you cut through the board, stop occasionally and check to see if you are on the cut line. If not, move the saw back a few inches and bring the cut back onto the line. (Hopefully, any mistakes will be on the waste side of the line.)

If possible, have a helper lightly support the waste end of the wood so it doesn't drop off, causing the end to split. Ensure your assistant doesn't lift up on the wood, as this can cause the saw blade to bind.

If you are rip cutting, you can saw more efficiently and quickly by holding the handsaw at a steeper or more upright angle.

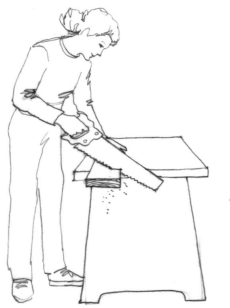

A GOOD SUPPORT HEIGHT FOR WORKING IS BETWEEN KNEE AND KNUCKLE HEIGHT WHEN STANDING UP STRAIGHT.

Fig. 8.4

# Power Saws

Since power tools operate at very high speeds, they can be dangerous if not handled correctly. Before even turning on a power saw, check that the electric cord is out of the way of the saw blade and that the work area is clear of any possible obstructions. Also, make a habit of stopping for a moment from time to time and looking around you to see that everything is safe and in its proper position. Always wear safety goggles or glasses and ear plugs when using these power tools.

## Electric Jigsaw

If you plan on building several projects in this book, we suggest buying an electric jigsaw. Of all the power saws, it is the least expensive, the quietest, the least dangerous and one of the easiest to use. Unlike other power saws, it also has the advantage of being able to cut curves. If buying new, choose an electric jigsaw with variable speeds, which provides you with more options. You will probably want to buy additional blades from the saw manufacturer. It's best to change a blade as soon as it becomes dull and starts to cut slowly.

## Sawing with an electric jigsaw

One of the advantages of an electric jigsaw is its ability to cut both curved and straight lines in wood. Before beginning a cut, position and clamp the wood to a table or sturdy work surface, placing the less desirable side of the wood faceup. The section to be cut off should extend past the edge of the table by at least an inch (see Fig. 8.5).

If you are making a straight cut, make a mark with a pencil at the measurement to be cut and place a combination square flush against the edge of the board at this mark. Holding the square firmly with one hand, draw a line across the board, using the edge of the square as your guide. Remove the square and place the front of the baseplate of the jigsaw on the material to be cut.

Never assume that you can make a straight cut with a jigsaw without using a speed square as a saw guide. After you have lined the saw up with the cut mark, position the speed square so that the lip of the square overlaps the top edge of the board and the remaining leg is flush against the baseplate of the jigsaw. Make sure the saw blade is lined up with, but not touching, the cut line before turning on the saw.

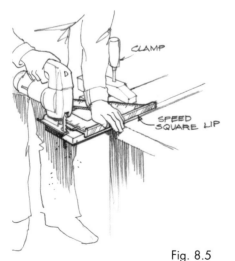

CLAMP

SPEED
SQUARE LIP

Fig. 8.5

Put on your safety goggles, then turn the saw on by gradually squeezing the trigger. Move the saw forward slowly until the blade enters the wood. Ensure you are cutting on the waste side of the wood. Keep a firm grip and press down, resisting the tendency of the saw to hop up. Keep the saw firmly pressed down against the wood during cutting, and keep your shoulders and your eyes in front of the saw. Be aware that the blade will be exposed underneath the wood, so make sure that this area is clear. Never reach underneath your work while the saw is on.

When you have finished cutting, always unplug your saw. Test the accuracy of a straight cut by standing the piece on a level surface. If there are any high spots, remove them using the jigsaw, a file or coarse (40-grit) sandpaper wrapped around a 1x4 sanding block.

> Before you begin cutting, give your saw blade a shot of silicone spray to make the saw glide more easily.

## Portable Circular Saw

Years ago, David built a cabin in the woods using only hand tools, and although he got a great deal of satisfaction and pride from not polluting the woods with the screeching sound of a portable circular

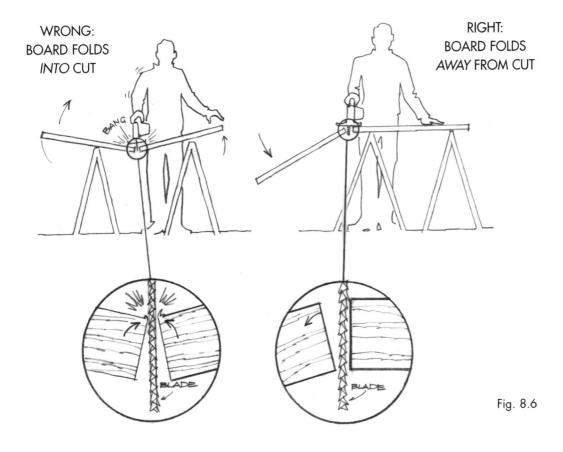

WRONG:
BOARD FOLDS *INTO* CUT

RIGHT:
BOARD FOLDS *AWAY* FROM CUT

BLADE

BLADE

Fig. 8.6

saw, it took several years to finish. With the aid of electricity, however, the same cabin could easily be built in a month.

Our favorite portable circular saw is relatively lightweight and has a 6" blade. If you are right-handed, it is especially helpful that you can see the blade as it cuts the wood, since the blade is mounted on the left side of the saw. The portable circular saw is the tool of choice for such projects as decks and sheds, and it is absolutely essential for house building. The advantage of using a portable circular saw over hand sawing is that ripping through long boards or cutting sheets of plywood takes seconds, rather than minutes.

## Sawing with a portable circular saw

Making crosscuts with a portable circular saw is much faster than with any of the previously mentioned tools, but certain safety precautions should be observed. When crosscutting lumber, ensure that the piece you are cutting falls away from, not toward, the saw blade; otherwise, this can pinch the blade and cause it to kick back dangerously toward you. For instance, never place a piece of lumber over two sawhorses and then cut between them. Instead, position the lumber over the sawhorses so that the portion to be cut off is unsupported and will fall away from the outside edge of the saw blade. If you can, have an assistant catch the cut-off piece of lumber before it falls to the ground (see Fig. 8.6).

Sawing plywood can be difficult if you are using a standard 4x8 sheet. Most lumberyards, however, will cut a full-size sheet to your specifications if you give them your cutting plan and pay a nominal milling fee. You can also do it yourself with a portable circular saw. Clamp the saw guide to the plywood and mark the cut line using a straight board or snap a chalk line. Ensure the plywood sheet is supported so that it will not fall when you are finished with the cut.

## Cutting Plywood

Plywood is made up of several thin layers of wood glued together. Exterior plywood is made with waterproof glue and is commonly available at lumberyards in face grades of A, B and C. For indoor projects, look for a grade that has at least one good side to use for the exposed side of your project. Also, try to avoid sheets with numerous voids or gaps in the edges. When appearance is important, use cabinet-grade plywood, which is faced with an unblemished veneer of birch, oak or maple, to mention a few of the most commonly available.

When cutting up a 4x8 sheet of plywood for smaller projects, we recommend sawing it in half lengthwise before you begin cutting out pieces for your project – provided the measurements permit such a cut, of course.

To rip-cut a sheet of plywood into two 2' x 8' pieces using a circular saw, lay the sheet on three sawhorses or other supports, and slide three scrap boards under it so both of the 2'-wide pieces will be supported when the cut is finished. Measure and mark where the 24" center is on each end. To achieve perfectly straight cuts make a saw guide out of two very straight boards screwed together as shown below and clamp to plywood. This provides a shoulder for the circular saw to run against. While cutting the plywood, hold the saw firmly against the guide as you cut along the line (see Fig. 8.7).

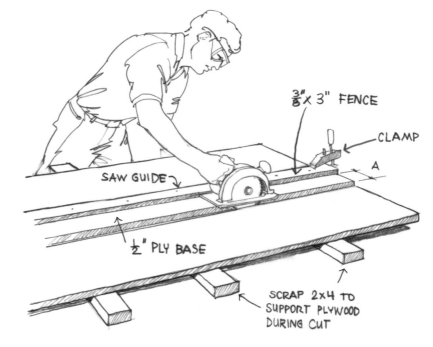

A = DISTANCE FROM OUTSIDE EDGE OF SAW GUIDE TO INSIDE FACE OF SAW BLADE. THIS CAN BE EASILY ACHIEVED BY FIRST ASSEMBLING THE JIG USING A WIDER 1/2" PLYWOOD BASE AND THEN CUTTING OFF THE EXCESS USING THE FENCE AS A GUIDE.

$\frac{3}{8}$" X 3" FENCE

CLAMP

A

SAW GUIDE

$\frac{1}{2}$" PLY BASE

SCRAP 2x4 TO SUPPORT PLYWOOD DURING CUT

Fig. 8.7

## Other Power Saws

Table saws are serious machinery for doing professional-quality work. A table saw is indispensable for the average woodworking shop and is the favorite of most shop carpenters because it is accurate and has such versatility. It can even be fitted with a sanding disk to give your projects a finished, professional look. Use this saw with respect. Although extremely useful, a table saw is a powerful tool that operates at a high speed.

Keep the following tips in mind with every cut (see Fig. 8.8):

○  Wear plastic safety glasses, especially when making rip cuts. When cutting cedar or pressure-treated wood, it is also a good idea to wear a dust mask.

○  Always use a push stick to keep your hands away from the saw blade when feeding pieces of wood through the saw. For ease of viewing, we have left the blade guard off the illustrations in this book, but for safety, always use the guard when operating a table saw.

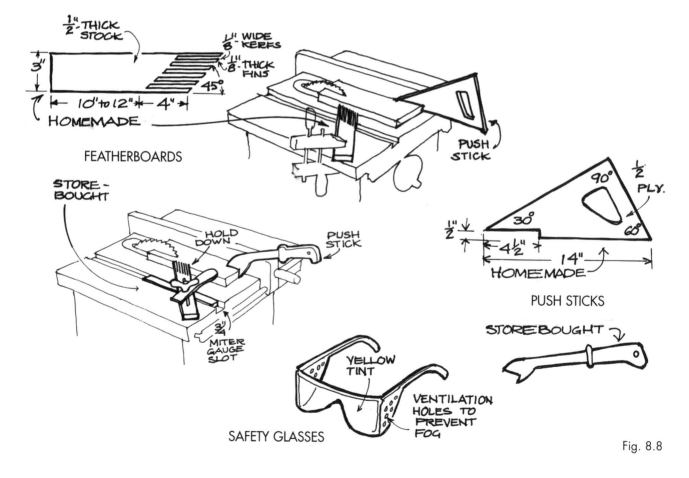

Fig. 8.8

○ Don't attempt to cut small pieces of wood that could fall through or get jammed in the saw blade slot.

○ When ripping, use a "featherboard" accessory (see Sources) to keep the board lightly pressed against the fence. You can make your own featherboard and clamp it to your table saw, or buy one that fits into the ¾"-wide slot normally used for a miter gauge. The store-bought featherboard has an added hold-down feature that prevents kickbacks.

One thing a table saw can't do well is crosscuts. For this job, a sliding compound miter saw or "chop saw" comes in handy. We have both, and keep a ripsaw blade on the table saw and a crosscut blade on the miter saw. Both saws are high-speed, expensive tools and can't be beat for accuracy. Other power saws include the reciprocating saw and the band saw.

## Tear-out

Tear-out is the term given to the tiny splinters left on the edge of plywood when cutting across the grain. They can give you a handful of splinters if you're not careful. Whether you are using a handsaw or a table saw, you won't see the tear-out until you turn the sheet of plywood over, since the splintered edges appear only on the exit side.

Tear-out can be minimized by using a finer-toothed handsaw (13 teeth to the inch) or by holding the saw at a shallow angle to your work. The best way to prevent tear-out, however, is to use a utility knife to score two parallel cuts on either side of the saw exit line, just deep enough to sever the wood fibers of the first ply of the plywood. If you are using a jigsaw or a portable circular saw, make the score cuts on the top side of the plywood, since the good side of the wood faces down and the saw blade teeth will be exiting through the top surface. If you are using a handsaw, table saw or radial arm saw, score on the bottom side of the wood, since the good side of the wood faces up.

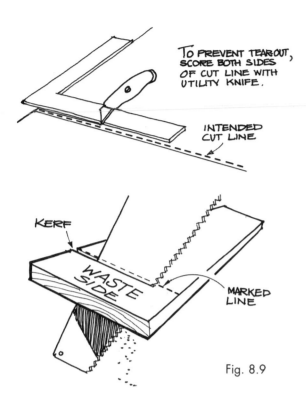

## Kerf Cuts

A kerf is the thickness of the cut that is made when a saw passes through the wood. The sawdust left underneath your work represents the wood that is removed when you make a cut. There is a carpenter's expression "leave the line," which means to make sure that the kerf of the saw is always on the waste side of the marked cutting line; otherwise, you will end up with a finished piece of wood that is shorter or narrower than you want it (see Fig. 8.9).

Fig. 8.9

## Rabbet versus Butt Joints

Use rabbet joints whenever possible (see Fig. 8.10). We have found that taking the time to include this extra step may actually save time in the assembly, gluing and clamping of the piece. It will also lend strength to the joint. However, if you don't have a table saw, a simple butt joint can be made using basic hand tools. Practice making a few rabbet cuts on pieces of scrap wood before you try them on a project.

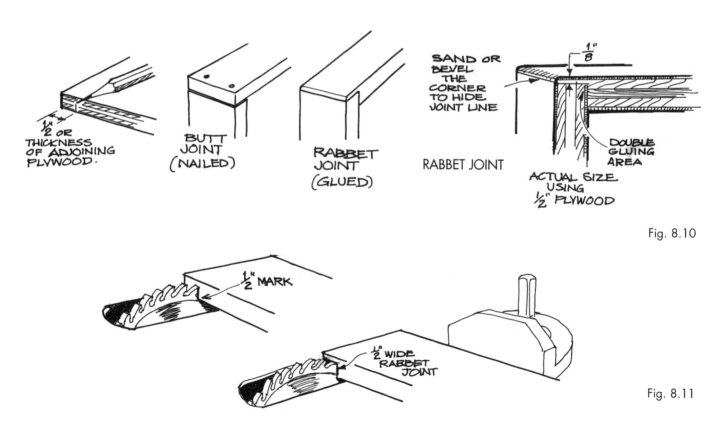

Fig. 8.10

Fig. 8.11

To set up your table saw for cutting rabbet joints, set your fence away from the blade the same thickness as the wood you are using. For ½" plywood, for example, you would set your fence at ½", leaving a ¼" lip. Back off the wood slightly before turning on the saw. Holding the wood snug against the saw fence, push the wood through the blade. The first cut is the critical one. Remove the board, pull back the miter gauge and reposition it for another pass. Try to cut away about 3/32" of wood on each pass, until all the wood in the rabbet groove is removed, leaving you with a lip of about ⅛" (see Fig. 8.11).

Setting up the saw for a rabbet joint takes only a couple of minutes and not only gives you a much stronger joint with almost twice as much gluing area, but also results in a more professional-looking project. While you have the saw set up, it makes sense to rabbet all the other joints as well. Once the project is completed, slightly round off the corner of the joint, using a sheet of 120-grit sandpaper, followed by 220-grit sandpaper on a block (see Fig. 8.12).

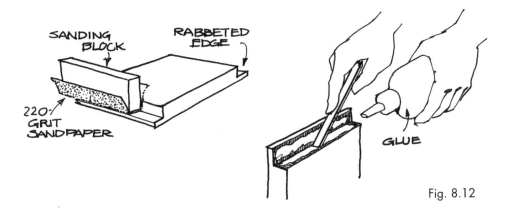

Fig. 8.12

You can also use a dado blade, a router or a jointer to make a rabbet joint, but all of these take much longer to set up. Using a table saw will give you a fairly coarse cut as compared to a router, but any rough surfaces can be easily smoothed with a file or sanding block.

Since a rabbet joint is stronger than a butt joint, it is generally not necessary to use nails to hold the pieces together as long as you glue them and clamp them while the glue is drying. This relieves you of the arduous task of countersinking the nails and filling the nail holes with wood putty. You also avoid the risk of hammering a nail out of alignment and having it protrude out the side of the wood, or of having the hammer slip and dent the wood.

# Electric Drills

It is impossible to know when the first drill was invented; however, we do know that primitive man used tools to burn holes through wood. On a visit to the Egyptian Room at the Metropolitan Museum of Art in New York, we spotted something that looked very familiar. On the floor was a rough-hewn sled built 4,000 years ago, used for hauling huge stone coffins. The sled was made of heavy timbers carefully joined with wooden pegs. What caught our eyes was the familiar cross mark that the ancient carpenter had made on the wood to indicate where the hole should be "drilled." David had drawn a similar cross mark that morning, for the same reason, on some architectural drawings. A crude form of metal drill existed even back then. However, the ancient Egyptians must have spent several hours making one hole, while today we can do the same thing in seconds using an electric drill.

Today's tools have become so sophisticated that any brace-and-bit or hand-operated drill you may have inherited could eventually become a collector's item! These "antique" boring tools have been replaced by what is perhaps the most useful tool that one can own: a variable-speed reversible (VSR) electric drill. This versatile tool can be used for a variety of tasks. When fitted with a screwdriver bit, for example, it can eliminate the frustration of trying to screw into hardwoods like oak or maple. It used to take hours to build things using hand tools and slotted screws. Today, with Phillips-head or square-drive screws and a VSR drill, screws can be driven into wood in minutes – and removed just as easily should you need to reposition them.

In addition to drilling holes and driving screws, electric drills can be fitted with several other attachments, such as a sanding disk for rotary sanding, a rotary drum for sanding inside tight curves, a wire brush for removing rust, a buffer for polishing the car or a countersink for sinking screws. There are even attachments for stirring paint and trimming shrubs. Recent models come with a keyless chuck, which makes it easier to change bits.

Cordless battery-operated drills are another option, but be sure to buy one that is strong enough – at least 9 volts. To test for this, put on a leather glove and hold the chuck while you turn on the drill. A strong drill should be difficult, if not impossible, to keep from turning.

When drilling large holes, especially through plywood, the surface of the wood where the drill exits is likely to split. To avoid this, drill only far enough through the first side so that you can see a hole made by the point of the drill on the back. Turn the board over, and using the small hole as a guide for the drill, finish drilling the hole completely through.

In the earliest stages of development, cordless drills were a disappointment because their batteries could not hold a charge for long. But improvements have made it possible to use these drills for up to an hour. It is a nuisance, of course, when the drill runs completely out of power, but this will rarely happen if you remember to remove the battery from the drill and place the battery in the charger after each use. If you use your drill a lot, it's useful to keep a backup battery charged.

## Chisels

A wood chisel is often used for making joints or shaping wood. A set of three chisels, ¼", ½" and ¾", should take care of all your needs and last you a lifetime. Contrary to what you might expect, we have

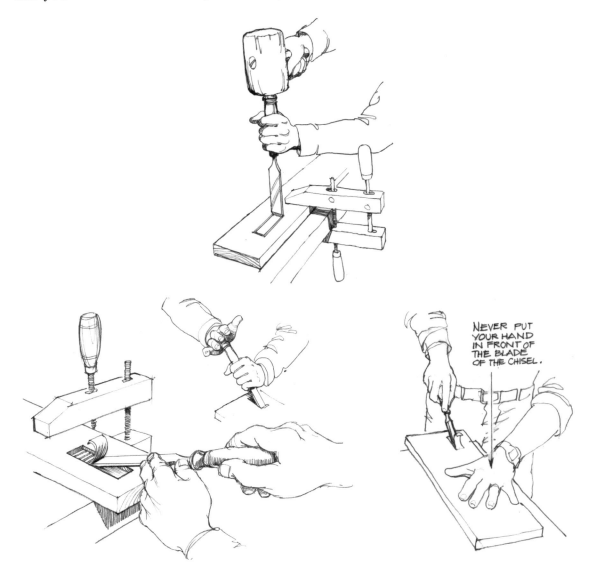

NEVER PUT YOUR HAND IN FRONT OF THE BLADE OF THE CHISEL.

Fig. 8.13

found that using a chisel that is too big is slower than using a small one. The wider the chisel blade, the more difficult it is for it to penetrate the wood. If you plan on buying only one chisel, we recommend choosing one with a ¼" blade.

One of the basic rules David remembers from shop class was "never hit wood with metal." If you are using a wood-handled chisel, never hit it with a metal hammer – use a wooden mallet instead. A high-impact plastic-handled chisel, however, can be hit with either a wooden mallet or a metal hammer.

Much chiseling is done without a mallet or hammer, either by hitting the chisel with the palm of your hand or by using the weight of your body, as when you are "paring" (removing waste material in thin layers). Use wood clamps to hold the piece of wood that you are chiseling securely to a worktable, and never put your hand in front of the chisel (see Fig. 8.13).

One of the most typical uses for a chisel is cutting out a groove, or mortise, for hardware, such as a door hinge or a cabinet door pull. To do this, use a pencil to mark the shape of the groove. Holding the chisel in a vertical position with the beveled side facing into the groove, tap the chisel with a mallet to make cuts approximately ⅛" deep around the outline of the groove. Next, holding the chisel in the same vertical position, make a series of parallel cuts, ⅛" apart and ⅛" deep, inside the groove. Chip out the excess wood in the groove either by holding the chisel almost parallel to the wood and lightly tapping the end of the handle with the palm of your hand or by holding the handle with both hands and moving the bevel carefully through the groove. For a deeper groove, repeat the same process (see Fig. 8.3).

## Files and Rasps

Although you may not need one often, there are times when you can't do without a good file or rasp. These tools are generally used when there is not enough wood to remove with a saw, but too much to remove using only sandpaper. When the edge of a board doesn't line up correctly with another board, for instance, it can be shaved down using a rasp or file.

The basic difference between a rasp and a file is that a rasp has larger, more aggressive teeth and is used more for shaping wood. A file, with its smaller and finer teeth, is for smoothing wood.

Files and rasps are fairly inexpensive. If you prefer to start out with only one shaping tool, we recommend a four-way rasp/file, which has both coarse and fine teeth, with file and rasp teeth on both sides. Files and rasps generally come without handles; however, wooden handles are sold separately and can be fitted to your individual tool. As you become a more proficient carpenter, a set of six rifflers makes an excellent investment, as these tools are perfect for getting into small corners.

To use a file or rasp, securely clamp the piece to be filed to a work surface. Grasp the tool with both hands, one on the handle and the other on the point, guiding the tool. Use downward pressure to force the teeth of the tool into the wood. Too little pressure causes the tool to catch on the wood grain, resulting in a rougher surface. Always file across the work at an angle to avoid leaving ragged, overly rough surfaces. And remember, files and rasps are made to cut on the "push" stroke only. Lift the tool and bring it back into position before beginning the next stroke (see Fig. 8.14).

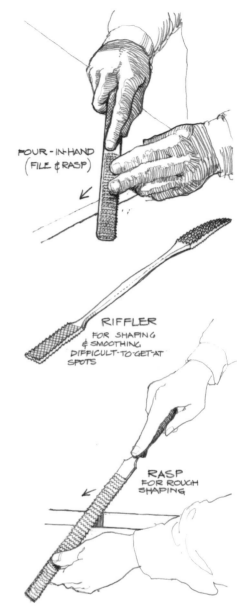

FOUR-IN-HAND (FILE & RASP)

RIFFLER FOR SHAPING & SMOOTHING DIFFICULT-TO-GET-AT SPOTS

RASP FOR ROUGH SHAPING

Fig. 8.14

# Fastening with Screws and Nails

For every construction project you tackle, you will have to decide what type of fastener – nails, screws, bolts or glue – should be used to join the building materials together. The most common fastener is a nail, which, of course, requires a hammer to drive it into the wood.

## *Hammers*

When buying a hammer, there are some essential points to keep in mind: price, use, weight and handle composition. A good all-purpose hammer costs under $20. Cheap hammers are a bad investment, not only because they often result in bent nails, but also because the hammer head is more likely to chip, sending fragments of metal flying.

The most common, practical hammer for woodworking projects is the claw hammer, which comes in weights ranging from 7 ounces to 20 ounces. A 7-ounce hammer is useful when hammering small nails or brads. It is also a good hammer for a child to use. The 13-ounce size is a solid-weighted hammer that will do most jobs without being overly heavy.

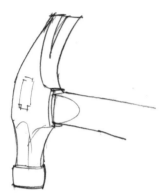

Choosing between a metal or a wooden hammer handle is really a personal decision. If you can, borrow both types from friends and get some hands-on practice before buying one or the other. We have never broken a metal-handled hammer, but several of our wooden-handled hammers have bit the dust. Some old-timers, however, swear by their wooden-handled hammers.

The two most common types of claw hammers are the curved claw hammer and the 16- to 20-ounce straight claw (framing) hammer. The straight claw hammer is used for heavy, rough work; the curved claw hammer is best suited for general carpentry. The curved claws can remove nails easier than the straight claw hammer. The claws on both hammers cannot draw a nail out of a board unless the nail head is sticking out at least ¼"; therefore, it's a good idea to stop short of hammering nails all the way in until you are confident that everything fits together perfectly.

Most people start out using a hammer by gripping it halfway up the handle, close to the head (similar to choking up on the bat in baseball), instinctively feeling that this gives them more control.

## BASIC NAILS

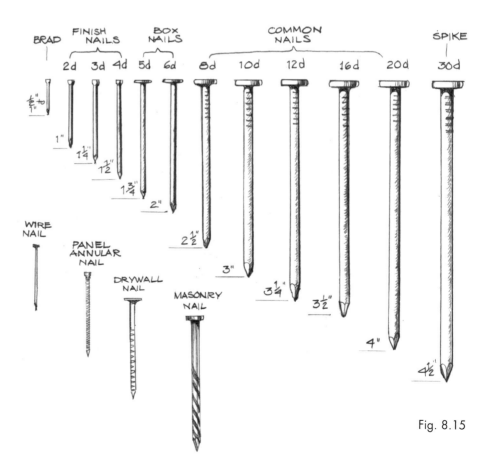

Fig. 8.15

Choking up on the hammer does give you more control, which is useful when hammering small nails, but because there is less force in each blow, it requires more energy to finish hammering each nail. Holding the hammer near the end of the handle leads to more efficient hammering.

# Nails

Nails are the quickest and most economical way to join two pieces of wood. They are usually sold in 1-pound and 5-pound boxes but can be more economically bought loose from bins at the lumberyard. Nails are often sold using the antiquated "penny" system, abbreviated as "d," which indicates the nail's length (see Fig. 8.15). This and the "board foot" system of pricing lumber are slowly disappearing from use.

## Hammering Nails

Nails can resist shear force; however, they can also easily and unexpectedly pull loose when nailed into the softer end grain of wood (see Fig. 8.16). When hammering nails into the end grain, use a longer nail than you normally would, to ensure that the nail is securely embedded in the wood.

If you are nailing short, fine brad nails, such as those used on the back of a picture frame, you may find that your fingers are dangerously close to the head of the nail. To avoid hitting your fingers with the hammer, hold the nail with a pair of needle-nose pliers (see Fig. 8.17).

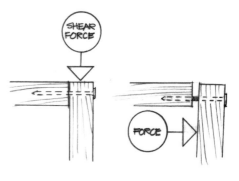

Fig. 8.16

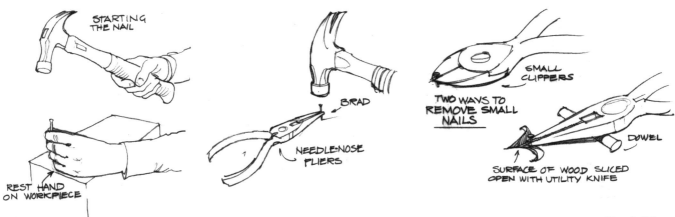

Fig. 8.17

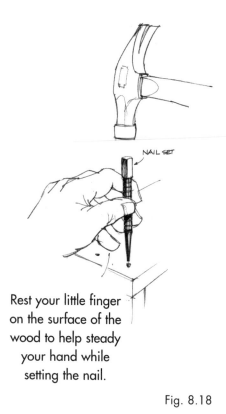

NAIL SET

Rest your little finger on the surface of the wood to help steady your hand while setting the nail.

Fig. 8.18

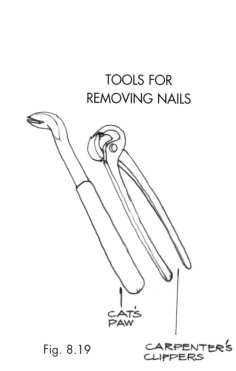

TOOLS FOR REMOVING NAILS

Fig. 8.19

CAT'S PAW

CARPENTER'S CLIPPERS

Ideally, nails and screws should go completely through the first piece of wood and two-thirds of the way through the second piece of material you are nailing into. Before you begin nailing, make sure the wood is centered over a very solid surface; otherwise, the force of each blow will be reduced, making it more difficult to drive the nails. If you are working on a table, center the wood over one of the supporting table legs. Try to direct your blows so that the lower center face of the hammerhead strikes the nail and the handle of the hammer is parallel with the work piece. There is more weight behind each blow this way, and you are less likely to miss the nail.

When you think the nail is about to come through the underside of the first board, stop for a moment and look underneath to ensure that the two pieces you are joining are still lined up perfectly. As it is easy for the boards to shift slightly after the first blow of the hammer, it is important to check this early on; otherwise, you may pay dearly later. Once the boards are aligned perfectly, hold them together firmly with your other hand or clamp them together, then give the nail a decisive blow, locking the two boards together in the correct position.

The last blow of the hammer is the most difficult, since it should be done with enough force to send the nail into the wood without denting the surface of the wood with the hammerhead. This stroke takes practice to perfect. Once you have mastered it, it will become second nature to you and will improve the look of your carpentry (see Fig. 8.18).

## Removing Nails

Removing nails is a science in itself, often requiring patience and forethought. If the nail is a small one, such as a 1" brad, it can be removed with a pair of small clippers by levering the nail up a bit at a time. If you need to remove a nail and its head is sunk in the wood, you may have to perform some minor "surgery," cutting the wood out around the nailhead so you can get a grip on it. If you are careful, you can split, but not remove, the wood around the nailhead and lift the offending nail out using needle-nose pliers placed on a small dowel for leverage (see Fig. 8.17).

To remove medium-sized nails, a pair of carpenter's clippers can be used without doing too much damage to the wood. If you are removing a particularly long nail with a claw hammer, you may find it impossible to do unless you place a small block of wood under the hammerhead to provide more leverage. Also, when removing nails from softwoods such as pine, cedar or redwood, place a scrap of flat wood under the hammerhead to avoid leaving a dent.

To remove large nails (3" and up), a special tool called a "cat's paw" is hammered into the wood under the nailhead and used to lift the nailhead out (see Fig. 8.19).

If you don't have clippers or a cat's paw, use the claws on your hammer. However, you must first lift the nailheads up so that you can get a grip on them. Do this by hammering a scrap piece of wood against one of the two nailed boards until they begin to separate. Tap the pointed end of the nails (on the bottom side of the board) so the nailheads protrude out the other side of the board far enough to get a grip on them (see Fig. 8.20).

Even the best carpenters are known to bend nails at times. If this happens to you, remove the nail and start over with a new one rather than try to straighten the old one. It doesn't pay to reuse a bent nail, since nails cost as little as three for a penny.

Sometimes a nail will hit a knot in the wood. Once you feel resistance, stop hammering immediately, as removing a nail deeply embedded in a knot can be difficult. When you do encounter a knot, you have two choices: Either remove the nail and drill a pilot hole through the knot, or remove the nail and reposition it in a different spot.

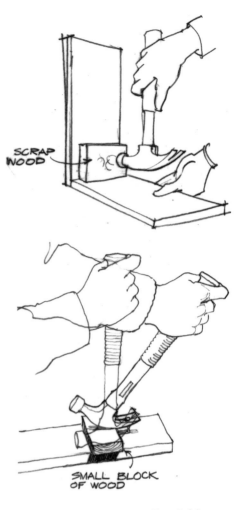

SCRAP WOOD

SMALL BLOCK OF WOOD

Fig. 8.20

## Screws and Bolts

Most of the projects in this book are assembled using either nails or screws. For holding power, screws are far stronger than nails because the screw threads bite into the wood surrounding the screw hole. Another advantage to using screws instead of nails is that they can be removed easily if things don't fit together perfectly. Screws come in different lengths, ranging from ¼" to 4", as well as in different thicknesses or sizes, ranging from #0 to #24 gauge, which translates as 1/16" to ⅜". The most commonly used screws for woodworking are #4, #6, #8, #10 and #12 gauge (see Fig. 8.21).

In general, the thicker the screw, the more substantial the holding power. A good rule of thumb is to use #4 screws when screwing into wood that is ½" thick, #6 or #8 screws for wood ¾" thick and #10 or #12 screws for 1½" wood. Wood that is thicker than 1½" is generally joined together using lag screws or bolts.

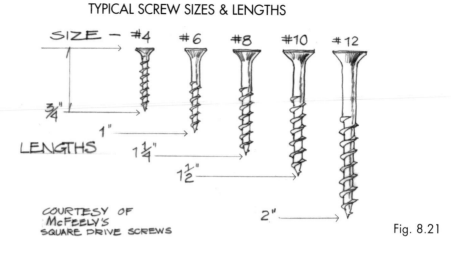

Fig. 8.21

The screw size to use also depends on the task. For instance, #4s are used primarily for very lightly stressed assemblies, such as crafts, small boxes, dollhouses or hinges; #6s have similar light-duty applications but can also be used for more robust stress levels, such as toys, children's furniture and drawer slides; #8s are the most common all-purpose screws and are often used for cabinets, furniture, doors, benches and other light construction; #10s are used for general construction and outdoor projects such as decks, boatbuilding, lawn furniture and more heavy-duty furniture; and #12s are used as heavy-duty construction fasteners for hanging heavy solid-core doors on sheds or barns, as well as for rough framing.

Whenever possible, use a screw that is two to three times as long as the thickness of the wood you are screwing into. Screws or nails going into the end grain of another piece of wood should be even longer, since end-grain wood has less holding power than the flat or edge grain. When fastening woods of varying thickness, screw through the thinner and into the thicker piece of wood.

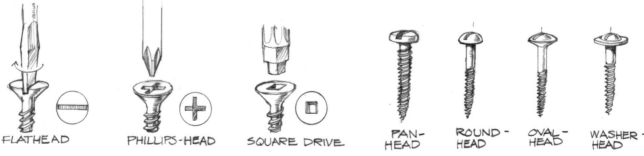

Fig. 8.22

## Making Pilot Holes

Pilot holes are drilled into wood for two reasons. The first is to facilitate the drilling of the screw. The second and less obvious reason is more important: Drilling pilot holes before using screws creates tighter, stronger connections between two pieces of wood.

To understand this, think of the screw as a clamp. When screwing two boards together, the threads on the bottom part of the screw pull the bottom board tightly against the top board. Because a pilot hole is slightly larger in diameter than the threaded part of the screw, it allows the screw to slip easily through the first piece of wood and bite into the second piece of wood, clamping the two pieces firmly together (see Fig. 8.23). If pilot holes are not used, the screw threads can actually work against you. When driving several screws into a piece of wood, for example, you may find that if the first screw is not driven and held tightly, it prevents the rest of the screws from pulling the two pieces of wood together.

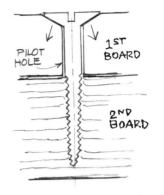

Fig. 8.23

## Countersinking and Counterboring

If you do not want screw heads to be above the surface of the wood you have two choices. You can either countersink the screws so they are flush with the surface of the wood, or you can counterbore the screws below the surface and fill the recessed area with wood putty

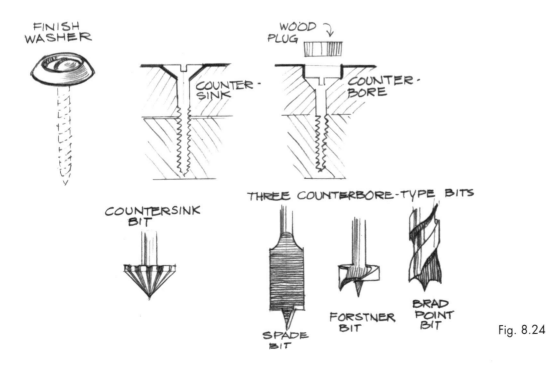

Fig. 8.24

or a wooden plug. Even a regular Phillips screwdriver can be used to slightly sink the head of a screw; however, this can create a splintery hole that is not as neat as you might wish. It is much more professional looking to use a countersink or a counterbore bit and to finish off the job properly. Both bits fit into an electric drill and are quick and easy to use (see Fig. 8.24).

# Clamping and Gluing

One of the most worthwhile and often overlooked tools for woodworking is the clamp. It's difficult to glue two pieces of wood together perfectly without using clamps. Clamping the wood that you are working with also enables you to have both hands free. Professional carpenters may have as many as 50 clamps in their shop. There are numerous types and shapes, the most common of which include the hand-screwed wood clamp, pipe clamp, bar clamp, C-clamp and spring clamp (see Fig. 8.25).

CLAMPS

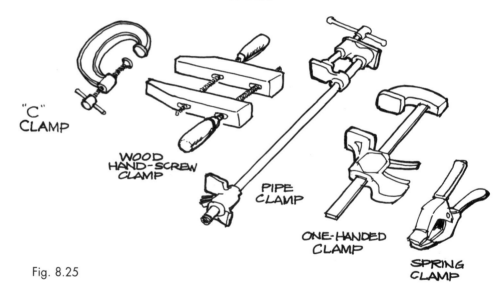

Fig. 8.25

Joints that have been glued and clamped look more professional; they don't have unsightly gaps that require being filled with wood putty.

Over the past few years, glues have been improved and are now much stronger and more durable. For woodworking, yellow carpenter's, or wood, glue is generally used. Many yellow glues, however, are not water-resistant. If your project is for outdoor use or will be subject to moisture, ensure you chose a water-resistant glue.

Before gluing and clamping pieces of wood together, always be sure to have water and a clean rag or sponge nearby. Watch for any glue that drips, seeps out of a joint or runs down the side of the wood, and wipe it up immediately. Glue dries quickly and leaves a stain on wood that often shows up only when you are finishing the job, especially when staining.

For a rabbet joint, apply the glue in a very thin bead along each surface of the joint and the end grain of the adjoining piece of wood. Allow the glue to soak into the end grain for a minute, and if the resulting finish appears dull, apply another very thin coat. Use a small chip of wood or Popsicle stick with the end cut off square to spread the glue, being careful not to let the glue reach the edge of the wood. Check all the joints for perfect alignment and be careful not to put any stress on the joints once the glue begins drying. For maximum strength, allow the glue to dry overnight.

When building smaller projects like drawers or cabinets, clamps are useful for holding your work together while the glue is drying. A variety of clamps are available. For objects 3" to 4" in size, we use rubber bands cut from old bicycle inner tubes; for those 6" to 8" in size, we recommend using two wood hand-screwed clamps; and for larger pieces, over 1' long, we use ½" pipe clamps. Two other types of useful clamps are spring clamps and one-handed clamps, good for clamping objects 9" to 16" long.

After clamping the pieces together, remember to check all sides to make sure that they are aligned and fit together properly.

Don't expect glue to fill gaps or spaces in uneven wood. Instead, use wood filler or sand the wood evenly. Glue will seep into the end grain of wood very quickly. If the wood does not look wet after applying a first coat of glue, give it a second coat to ensure a good bond.

**Caution:** Do not let glue freeze, as this causes it to become gummy and lose its strength. Never apply any type of yellow glue if the temperature is below 55°F (12°C).

> When gluing and clamping pieces of wood together, place a piece of waxed paper between the clamp jaw and the wood to prevent any glue from sticking to the jaws of the clamp. Also, adjust the jaws so they are holding the wood firmly but not too tightly.

# Finishing

## *Edging*

Depending on the kind of plywood you use, you may want to cover up the edges to give the project a more finished look. With a high grade of plywood, you may choose to leave the edges exposed to show off the plies of wood. On the other hand, the edges of a more economical or less perfect grade of plywood may contain blemishes, voids and other irregularities. If the plywood is to be stained or painted, you can seal the edges with wood filler, spackle, epoxy or even auto body filler (Bondo) and sand it smooth. Another alternative is to cover the edges with an edge banding. This is a thin veneer of wood or plastic that comes in a roll and is either self-adhering or heat-sealed to the edge of the plywood.

We prefer to make our own edging and glue it on using carpenter's glue. To do this, take a leftover piece of wood from the project you have built and rip-cut it to the same dimension as the plywood edge you are covering. From this piece of wood, rip-cut $1/16$" thick strips (see Fig. 8.26), then cut the strips to the appropriate lengths. Apply a bead of carpenter's glue to the back side of each strip and attach it to the plywood edge, using pushpins every 3" to hold it in place. Once the glue has dried, remove the pins and sand the edges smooth. The holes left by the pins will fill with sawdust and be almost indistinguishable.

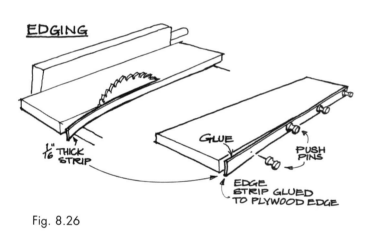

Fig. 8.26

## *Sanding*

Although sanding can be one of the most boring parts of carpentry, it is a crucial last step. This is the time to correct any minor mistakes or imperfections. Nothing creates a more professional, finished look than a perfectly smooth, sanded surface.

Sandpaper comes in 9" x 11" sheets or belts and is available in several grits ranging from coarse to medium to fine, calibrated in numbers. Generally speaking, 36-grit refers to very coarse, 40- to 50-grit refers to coarse, 60- to 100-grit refers to medium, 120- to 220-grit refers to fine, and 240-grit and higher refers to extra-fine. (The larger the number, the smaller the grit size.) The sandpaper grit grade is listed on the back of each piece of sandpaper. Coarse sandpaper is used more for shaping, and fine sandpaper for smoothing wood surfaces.

When sanding, begin with coarse sandpaper, such as 40-grit, in order to remove uneven surfaces and to clean up any joints that don't line up perfectly. Change to medium grade, such as 60-grit, to further level and smooth the wood surface. Finish using fine sandpaper such as 120- or 220-grit, until the surface of the wood is as soft and smooth as satin.

Always use a sanding block when sanding flat surfaces to prevent irregular shallow valleys in the wood that will show up when a glossy finish is applied.

The best and cheapest sanding tool is a sanding block made from a scrap piece of 1x4 or 1x3 with a half-sheet of sandpaper wrapped around it. To neatly cut a sheet of sandpaper in half, place it rough side down on a flat table, lay a steel straightedge or ruler on top and rip the sandpaper against the straightedge. Fold the sandpaper over the block of wood and hold the paper in place with your hand as you sand, using long, even strokes moving along the grain of the wood.

End grain can be sanded in any direction. When sanding uneven or contoured surfaces, such as moldings, use a foam sanding pad or sanding block for best results. To sand in tight corners, use a full sheet of sandpaper folded into eighths. To sand the inside of holes, curl sandpaper into a tight roll or make a sanding stick.

It's important to have good lighting when you are sanding so you can see what kind of job you are doing. Check your progress repeatedly, being careful not to sand off too much of the wood, especially when rounding off edges and corners. Trust your sense of touch to determine how smooth the work is.

Sharp corners and edges often look and "feel" better if they are rounded off slightly. Even if you own the latest and most expensive sanding machinery, the smoothest finish is achieved by giving your project a final hand sanding.

For light sanding between coats of varnish, urethane or paint, use 220-grit sandpaper. Cushion the face of the sandpaper by placing a piece of cloth or soft cardboard between the sandpaper and the sanding block.

## Power Sanders

To be perfectly honest, sanding can get boring, especially if you have large surfaces to cover. Power sanders can help speed up the sanding process (see Fig. 8.27).

**Electric palm sander:** This is a great sander for most of the projects in this book, and a good one can be bought for under $50. The advantages of an electric palm sander are that it sands flat, without any chance of gouging the surface of the wood, it is lightweight, relatively quiet and easy to operate and it uses only a quarter of a 9" x 11" sheet of sandpaper. The only disadvantage, if you can call it that, is that a palm sander does not remove a lot of material in a short time.

**Random orbit sander:** For a tool that can cover a larger area, the next step up is a random orbit sander. Most of these sanders come with replaceable self-adhering sandpaper with holes in it, enabling the sanding dust to be sucked up into a canister that can be removed and emptied. The face of the random orbit sander spins in a circular, orbital motion. This type of sander is a vast improvement over the standard circular 4" disk pads that run off an electric drill.

**Belt sander:** This heavy-duty sander is useful if you need to remove a lot of material from long boards. It is an aggressive machine and can run away from you if you don't keep a firm grip on it. However, nothing beats this sander for removing material in a hurry, especially if you use it with a coarse sanding belt.

Fig. 8.27

# Finishes

After rough-sanding your project with 60-grit sandpaper, use a nail set to hammer the finishing nails below the surface. Never substitute a blunt nail for a nail set, as it seldom works and can skid off the nail you are sinking, resulting in additional holes or dents in the wood. Hold the nail set directly over the nail, and sink it with one or two sharp blows of the hammer (see Fig. 8.18). The nail set leaves a ¼" hole, which should be filled with wood putty. After filling the nail holes, wait 15 minutes, and then sand the surface smooth using 120-grit sandpaper.

Although wood can be painted, you can show off your skills by simply applying a coat of protective oil. This transparent penetrating waterproofer creates a moisture barrier on the surface of the wood. Before you start, make sure that the wood's surface is completely clean and dry so the oil can penetrate the wood evenly and thoroughly. Test a small amount on a piece of scrap wood. Then, in a well-ventilated workspace, apply the oil liberally with a brush. After 15 minutes, go over the surface again with a brush or cloth to eliminate any puddles.

**CAUTION:** Before applying any finishes to wood, carefully read the directions and warnings on the label. Many finishes are combustible and have toxic vapors. Always wear protective rubber gloves when applying finishes.

Tung oil, which resists moisture and mildew and leaves wood with a natural-looking, durable finish, is another finishing choice. It's available in both high and low gloss. Apply a small amount using a soft, clean cotton cloth and rub it thoroughly into the wood. Allow the wood to dry completely, and then buff it lightly with a piece of fine steel wool. Wipe the surface clean with a soft cloth and apply a second coat.

Another alternative, which results in a natural-looking finish that shows off a smooth sanding job, is to apply a couple of coats of wax to the surface of the wood. Apply a small amount with a clean cloth, rubbing the wax in with the grain of the wood. After wiping off any excess wax, buff the surface until it has a natural glow. Repeat the process one or two more times, until the wood has a rich luster.

Ching, Francis. *Building Construction Illustrated.* 1975. Van Nostrand Reinhold.

Paul, Donna. *The Home Office Book.* 1996. Artisan.

Stiles, David and Jeanie. *Cabins A Guide to Building Your Own Nature Retreat.* 2001. Firefly Books.

Stiles, David and Jeanie. *Garden Retreats: A Build-It-Yourself Guide.* 1999. Storey Books.

Stiles, David and Jeanie. *Fun Projects for You and the Kids.* 2002. Lyons Press.

Stiles, David and Jeanie. *Playhouses You Can Build, Indoor and Backyard Design.* 1998. Firefly Books.

Stiles, David and Jeanie. *Rustic Retreats: A Build-It-Yourself Guide.* 1998. Storey Books.

Stiles, David and Jeanie. *Sheds A Do-It-Yourself Guide for Backyard Builders.* 1998. Firefly Books.

Stiles, David and Jeanie. *Storage Projects You Can Build.* 1996. Houghton Mifflin.

Stiles, David and Jeanie. *Treehouses, Huts and Forts.* 2002. Lyons Press.

Stiles, David and Jeanie. *Tree Houses You Can Actually Build.* 1998. Houghton Mifflin.

Nagyszalanczy, Sandor. *Setting Up Shop.* Taunton Press. 2001.

_____. *Design Guide for Frost-Protected Shallow Foundations.* National Association of Home Builders, Research Center. 400 Prince George's Blvd., Upper Marlboro, MD. 20774. 800-638-8556.

## CONSTRUCTION MATERIALS

### Cement Board
Durock
United States Gypsum
125 South Franklin St.
Chicago, IL 60606

### Ridge Vents
Cobra
800-688-6654

## DESIGN & ART SUPPLIES

### Blick Studio
www.dickblick.com
800-828-4548
Easels, brushes and paints.

### Cheap Joe's Art Stuff
cheapjoe@aol.com
800-227-2788
For art supplies, creative inspiration and peace of mind.

### Daniel Smith
www.danielsmith.net
800-426-6740
Art supplies, graphic materials and easels, including The Backpacker's Easel.

### New York Central Art Supply
www.nycentralart.com
800-950-6111
212-477-0400

### Pearl Paint
www.pearlpaint.com
800-221-6845
All-inclusive art supply store

### Quill
800-789-1331
Office supply source, including 22"-deep steel file cabinets.

### Sam Flax
www.samflaxny.com
800-628-9512
Contemporary office furniture, art supplies, desk accessories, storage and organization materials.

### Utrecht Art Supplies
www.utrechtart.com
800-223-9132

## DUST COLLECTORS

### Oneida Air Systems, Inc.
www.oneida-air.com
800-732-4065
Dust collectors for woodworking shops.

### Penn State Industries
www.pennstateind.com
800-377-7297
9900 Global Road
Philadelphia, PA 19115
A good dust-collecting and woodturning source for carpentry shops. They also carry portable and table saws and lathes.

## HARDWARE and LUMBER

### McFeelys Square Drive Screws
www.mcfeelys.com
800-443-7937
3720 Cohen Place
Lynchburg, VA 24501
Woodworking materials, including square drive screws.

### Pressure-Treated Plywood (ACQ)
www.treatedwood.com
800-421-8661
200 East Woodlawn Rd.
Charlotte, NC 28217

### Whitechapel Ltd.
www.whitechapel-ltd.com
800-468-5534
P.O. Box 11719
1135 Mapleway
Jackson, WY 83002
A terrific catalog of European and American architectural fittings and hardware.

## HOME OFFICE FURNITURE

### Design Within Reach
www.dwr.com
800-944-2233
A great catalog with classic modern furniture for home and office/studio.

### IKEA
www.ikea.com
A good source for home office furniture.

### Rockler Companies Inc.
800-279-4441
A wide range of keyboard slides.

### Gibraltar
616-748-4857
323 East Roosevelt Ave.
Zeeland, MI 49464
Table legs for office furniture.

## POTTERY SUPPLIES

### Bailey Pottery
www.baileypottery.com
800-431-6067
Ceramic supplies and pottery equipment.

## TACK ROOM EQUIPMENT
www.statelinetack.com
888-839-9640
Stable and tack room supplies including solid brass brackets, bridle hooks and tack trunks.

www.buytack.com/stable
800-451-4600
Supplies for horses and stables.

## TOOLS

### Garrett Wade
www.garrettwade.com
800-221-2942
Tools, supplies and accessories for workshops, including top-quality axes and a handmade heavy-duty Swedish splitting maul and wedge.

### Harbor Freight Tools
www.harborfreight.com
800-423-2567
Good prices for power tools and hand woodworking tools.

**Hitachi Koki USA, Ltd.**

www.hitachipowertools.com

800-706-7337

A terrific source for power tools,
including sliding compound miter saws.

**Sears Craftsman Club**

www.sears.com

800-682-8691

Craftsman power tools, including the
contractor's table saw.

**Woodcraft Supply Corp.**

www.woodcraft.com

800-225-1153

Hand and power tools for your workshop.

**Woodworker's Supply**

www.woodworkers.com

800-645-9292

Woodworking hand tools.


## WINDOWS

**Marvin Windows**

www.marvinwindows.net

800-564-4206

Barn sash windows: 24" x 36" and
22" x 33" (bare wood).

**Recycled Products**

800-765-1489

319-465-6124

18294 Amber Rd.

Monticello, IA 52310

Frames made from recycled plastic milk and
water bottles, barn sashes in various sizes,
approximately $35–$45.

# *Note to Readers*

Since many of our readers invariably change our plans to fit their particular needs, we have purposely omitted exact specifications and dimensions. We assume that the reader will seek qualified, licensed architects or engineers to make more detailed plans for submission to their local building and health departments, as required.

NOTE: Every effort has been made to design all the projects in this book to be safe and easy to build; however, it is impossible to predict every situation and the ability of each carpenter who builds them. Therefore, it is advised that the reader seek advice from a competent, on-site expert.

DISCLAIMER: David and Jeanie Stiles make no express or implied warranties, including warranties of performance, merchantability and fitness for a particular purpose, regarding this information. Your use of this information is at your own risk. You assume full responsibility and risk of loss resulting from the use of this information. The authors will not be responsible for any direct special, indirect, incidental, consequential or punitive damages or any other damages whatsoever.

Please visit our website at www.stilesdesigns.com and send us pictures of your workshop.

www.stilesdesigns.com